DEVIANT MATTER

SEXUAL CULTURES

General Editors: Ann Pellegrini, Tavia Nyong'o, and Joshua Chambers-Letson
Founding Editors: José Esteban Muñoz and Ann Pellegrini

Titles in the series include:

Times Square Red, Times Square Blue
Samuel R. Delany

Private Affairs: Critical Ventures in the Culture of Social Relations
Phillip Brian Harper

Tropics of Desire: Interventions from Queer Latino America
José A. Quiroga

Our Monica, Ourselves: The Clinton Affair and the National Interest
Edited by Lauren Berlant and Lisa A. Duggan

Black Gay Man: Essays
Robert F. Reid-Pharr

Queer Globalizations: Citizenship and the Afterlife of Colonialism
Edited by Arnaldo Cruz-Malavé and Martin F. Manalansan IV

Queer Latinidad: Identity Practices, Discursive Spaces
Juana María Rodríguez

Love the Sin: Sexual Regulation and the Limits of Religious Tolerance
Janet R. Jakobsen and Ann Pellegrini

Boricua Pop: Puerto Ricans and the Latinization of American Culture
Frances Négron-Muntaner

Manning the Race: Reforming Black Men in the Jim Crow Era
Marlon B. Ross

In a Queer Time and Place: Transgender Bodies, Subcultural Lives
J. Jack Halberstam

Why I Hate Abercrombie and Fitch: Essays on Race and Sexuality
Dwight A. McBride

God Hates Fags: The Rhetorics of Religious Violence
Michael Cobb

Once You Go Black: Choice, Desire, and the Black American Intellectual
Robert F. Reid-Pharr

The Latino Body: Crisis Identities in American Literary and Cultural Memory
Lázaro Lima

Arranging Grief: Sacred Time and the Body in Nineteenth-Century America
Dana Luciano

Cruising Utopia: The Then and There of Queer Futurity
José Esteban Muñoz

Another Country: Queer Anti-Urbanism
Scott Herring

Extravagant Abjection: Blackness, Power, and Sexuality in the African American Literary Imagination
Darieck Scott

Relocations: Queer Suburban Imaginaries
Karen Tongson

Beyond the Nation: Diasporic Filipino Literature and Queer Reading
Martin Joseph Ponce

Single: Arguments for the Uncoupled
Michael Cobb

Brown Boys and Rice Queens: Spellbinding Performance in the Asias
Eng-Beng Lim

Transforming Citizenships: Transgender Articulations of the Law
Isaac West

The Delectable Negro: Human Consumption and Homoeroticism within US Slave Culture
Vincent Woodard, Edited by Justin A. Joyce and Dwight A. McBride

Sexual Futures, Queer Gestures, and Other Latina Longings
Juana María Rodríguez

Sensational Flesh: Race, Power, and Masochism
Amber Jamilla Musser

The Exquisite Corpse of Asian America: Biopolitics, Biosociality, and Posthuman Ecologies
Rachel C. Lee

Not Gay: Sex between Straight White Men
Jane Ward

A Taste for Brown Bodies: Gay Modernity and Cosmopolitan Desire
Hiram Pérez

Embodied Avatars: Genealogies of Black Feminist Art and Performance
Uri McMillan

The Color of Kink: Black Women, BDSM, and Pornography
Ariane Cruz

Archives of Flesh: African America, Spain, and Post-Humanist Critique
Robert F. Reid-Pharr

Black Performance on the Outskirts of the Left: A History of the Impossible
Malik Gaines

A Body, Undone: Living On After Great Pain
Christina Crosby

Wedlocked: The Perils of Marriage Equality
Katherine Franke

The Life and Death of Latisha King: A Critical Phenomenology of Transphobia
Gayle Salamon

Queer Nuns: Religion, Activism, and Serious Parody
Melissa M. Wilcox

After the Party: A Manifesto for Queer of Color Life
Joshua Chambers-Letson

Sensual Excess: Queer Femininity and Brown Jouissance
Amber Jamilla Musser

Afro-Fabulations: The Queer Drama of Black Life
Tavia Nyong'o

Queer Times, Black Futures
Kara Keeling

Queer Faith: Reading Promiscuity and Race in the Secular Love Tradition
Melissa E. Sanchez

Frottage: Frictions of Intimacy Across the Black Diaspora
Keguro Macharia

Archiving an Epidemic: Art, AIDS, and the Queer Chicanx Avant-Garde
Robb Hernández

Becoming Human: Matter and Meaning in an Antiblack World
Zakiyyah Iman Jackson

Keeping It Unreal: Black Queer Fantasy and Superhero Comics
Darieck Scott

The Tragedy of Heterosexuality
Jane Ward

Sexuality Beyond Consent: Risk, Race, Traumatophilia
Avgi Saketopoulou

The Sex Obsession: Perversity and Possibility in American Politics
Janet R. Jakobsen

Queer Childhoods: Institutional Futures of Indigeneity, Race, and Disability
Mary Zaborskis

Bottoms Up: Queer Mexicanness and Latinx Performance
Xiomara Verenice Cervantes-Gómez

Deviant Matter: Ferment, Intoxicants, Jelly, Rot
Kyla Wazana Tompkins

For a complete list of books in the series, see www.nyupress.org

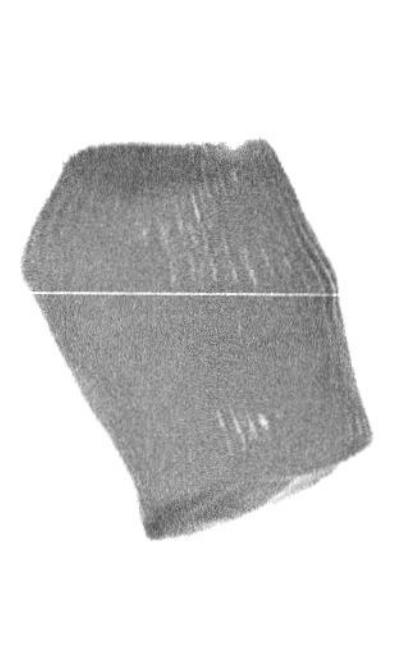

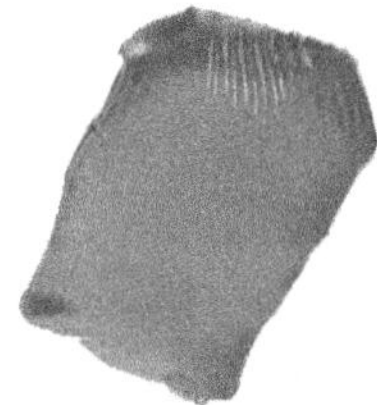

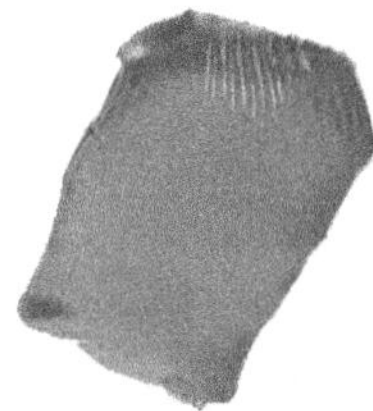

DEVIANT MATTER

Ferment, Intoxicants, Jelly, Rot

KYLA WAZANA TOMPKINS

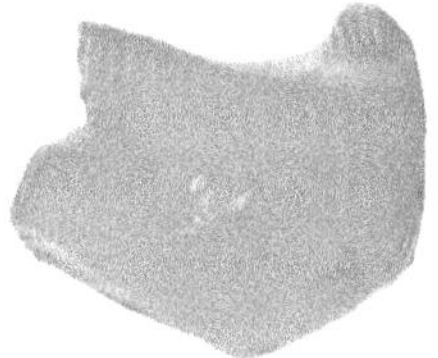

NEW YORK UNIVERSITY PRESS
NEW YORK

NEW YORK UNIVERSITY PRESS
New York
www.nyupress.org

Please contact the Library of Congress for Cataloging-in-Publication data.
ISBN: 9781479819201 (hardback)
ISBN: 9781479819225 (paperback)
ISBN: 9781479819218 (library ebook)
ISBN: 9781479819232 (consumer ebook)

This book is printed on acid-free paper, and its binding materials are chosen for strength and durability. We strive to use environmentally responsible suppliers and materials to the greatest extent possible in publishing our books.

Manufactured in the United States of America

10 9 8 7 6 5 4 3 2 1

Also available as an ebook

CONTENTS

INTRODUCTION

Sometime in the fall of 1998, during my first month of life in the United States and at Stanford University as a graduate student, my friend Amelia and I were invited to a potluck hosted by some fellow students. We had at that time been taking a Food and Literature class with a well-known early-modern Italianist professor in which my obsession with jelly had become a running class joke. We looked for jelly everywhere in history that semester; someone even brought a perfect tomato aspic to class.

To prepare for the potluck dinner, Amelia and I spent hours constructing a layered jelly sculpture in a tall glass bowl: melting colored gelatin into hot water and pouring different layers onto each other. Naturally we didn't leave ourselves enough time for each layer to solidify on its own, so the whole bowl became a muddy brown mess, as the colors bled into each other where they touched. Even worse, because we had decided it was a good idea to separate each uncooled jelly layer with candy supermarket-birthday-cake toppers, all of them numbers for toddler birthdays like *2!* and *3!*, there were these storm-like tendrils of grayed food coloring that leaked between each layer of jelly as the candy numbers melted down and leached their food dyes into warm liquid jelly.

As one might be able to tell already, by bringing a failed jelly sculpture to a dinner party, Amelia and I were acting out rather badly. And though I couldn't quite articulate it then, I can see now that we were acting out into an affective schism that we felt separated us from the deep civility and lush propriety of our new institution and our newly chosen profession: me, a first-generation graduate student and immigrant working on race and food and clearly committed to interdisciplinary irreverence, and Amelia, who was then planning to write about food and the marketplace in Jewish and Italian literature, the two of us obviously feeling that we were failing at the performance of ease and entitlement that we thought we were supposed to bring to the first year of graduate school.

That schism only widened when it came time to serve dessert, and as we upended the bowl to release the jelly sculpture, the whole thing flooped out with a kind of loud, sucking, farting noise made by our trying to loosen the material from the kinetic suction energy with which the layers of gummy food had adhered to one another and the bowl. The sound echoed through the apartment, causing everyone to pause in shock and disgust; Amelia and I dissolved into hysterical, heaving laughter. As I recall, nobody ate our masterpiece but us. It sat, glorious in its failure, shivering on the table at the sound of surrounding conversation until the very end of the party.

Jelly, the commercials tell us, jiggles. What "jiggle" means, really, is that gelatin renders waves of energy visible to the eye in real time, allowing scientists to measure, and the rest of us to witness, otherwise invisible energy through its effects as responsive, relational, material change. Gelatin makes visible what is generally invisible to the eye, like sound waves or other seismic and vibrational activity. Gelatin absorbs and makes visual and kinetic what is sometimes not describable or utterable—what is felt—but is nonetheless present in its vicinity; it makes what might otherwise be preconscious visible. At the same time, gelatin acts out what approaches and touches it, absorbing what (in the terms of non-Newtonian physics) "stresses" it and then bouncing back. Just as the disaster dessert from my memory echoed the sound of conversation around it in tiny trembling melty jiggles, it also disrupted the party by making unsavory—distasteful—sounds that unnerved and embarrassed us all. While I'm not sure we were expecting the jelly to upend that dinner party, I know that Amelia and I lost the plot when it did, if only because we recognized that the jelly was saying something out loud that we either could not say or did not know how to say. By making that wet sucking sound, by refusing to stay still like a respectably dead food object, our lively jelly sculpture expressed something we didn't yet dare articulate about our own sense of displacement and discomfort among the civil discourse of seedling academics, in the huge, wealthy private school that had chosen to let us in. And it also expressed for us something (which to be fair was not *entirely* adult) about how we already wanted to imagine living in a sensory ecology otherwise to where we were.

* * *

I start this book with this story, now over twenty years old, because it crystallizes my interest in a set of materials—not limited to gelatinous and viscous matter but also including ferments, rotting and putrefied matter, and also intoxicating materials—that I have come to understand as related to each other both historically and aesthetically. Although the title of this book leans on the nounness of the word "matter," in this book I refer to ferment, intoxicants, jelly, and rot not only as kinds of matter but also as *materialities*. I am interested not so much in their thingness or quiddity or in their exteriority to human language or knowledge as I am interested in their recurrence across time and across multiple cultural media as sensual qualities that also describe the sensory organization—what Amit Rai calls the "ecology of sensation"—that attaches to minoritarian life.[1] This move from "matter" to "materiality" signifies a shift from an interest in the thingness of a thing to its qualitative expressiveness, to the sensual niceties of how an object acts upon a world constituted of other objects and also upon everything and everyone who lives in between the two polarities of subject and object, which is to say, most of us. Here I depart from the strictest dictionary sense of "matter" as "physical objects, vaguely characterized," as one *Oxford English Dictionary* definition might have it, to analyze what the *OED* refers to as "materiality," meaning "material or physical aspect or character; outward appearance or externality."[2] The journey from matter to materiality depends on the addition of the suffix ("-ity"), which the *OED* charmingly describes as historically used for "playful or pedantic nonce-words of English formation."[3] The nonceness of "materiality," its situational and temporal quality—a word is a nonce-word if it is made into a word only for its moment of use, and it often signifies to a world of sound outside of language—also overlaps with the contemporary idea of a criminalized sexual deviant: in particular someone jailed for crimes against children.[4] Perhaps etymologically related to the term "nancy-boy" (an effeminate male), the idea of erotic and gendered deviance, we will come to see, haunts the materialities I examine in this book.

My title, *Deviant Matter*, serves as a figure for thinking about materiality, art, politics, and affect across multiple scales, ranging from the microbial to the intimate and everyday to the juridical. In this book, ferment, intoxicants, jelly, and rot are lively materials that are marked by movement: they catalyze feeling; they provoke disciplinary responses aimed at containment, management, or extraction; they are defined by transformation; and they act in uncannily agential ways that undermine human-centered subject-object hierarchies and the social systems that spin outward from them. For instance, on an intimate level, the materials that I am studying move their consumers: they affect them, producing feelings and sensations that are then linked to a system of social value. These sensations come to be understood as productive, exciting, disgusting, intoxicating, or even hallucinatory. The sense of kinetic movement, of liveness, on the part of the material affects and sensations I study—yeast ferments, gelatin jiggles, drugs and alcohol have a mysterious psychic alchemy, and animal products actively mold and rot—is another expression of movement: these are lively substances that at times seem to, or even do, have a will of their own. Shifting through multiple states and phase changes, falling apart and reforming again, they energize and choreograph both themselves and human behavior.

This deep dive into ferment, intoxication, rot, and jelly is a speculative experiment in finding new ways to produce histories of the past and of the present at the scale of the sensory—which is to say simultaneously aesthetic and affective—everyday. In order to do so, *Deviant Matter* moves back and forth between these subject-like objects, each teeming with various kinds of nonhuman energy, and multiple human subjects, in particular those humans who have had the taxonomizing energy of objectification and dehumanization leveled at them by similar or related regimes of aesthetic and hygienic disciplinarity: queer folk, poor whites, Black and brown communities. I do so in order to ask what we can learn from the affective and aesthetic affiliation between seemingly disparate categories of beings and things. *Deviant Matter* is about objects and subjects: the places where they touch and the overlaps between them. But when I say that I am interested in materiality, in fermentation, intoxicants, jelly, and rot, what I mean is that I am also interested in the turbulent affects and motile atmospheres that are produced by the symbolic and material proximities between these various and different bodies.

At the center of this book is food, but while food plays a starring role, I am not interested in how or why food *is* food in and of itself. Rather, I place ferment, intoxicants, jelly, and rot inside and alongside the larger continuum of objects that scholars and artists refer to when they call something aesthetic, including but not limited to art. These deviant materialities linger in or produce sensory orders—aesthetic fields or environments—that either reveal the field of politics' deep investment in the management of aesthetics *as* a field of aesthetics or, alternately, reveal how and where deviant materialities disturb the field of politics itself. They reflect or unsettle objects and worlds that are highly aestheticized but that pretend not to be, such as science, politics, and various governance and administrative discourses. Reliant for power and validity on their affiliation with rationality, impartiality, and apparent objectivity, these discourses might seem precisely the opposite of the aesthetic, their supposed plainness and systematicity a corollary of their possession of the institutional value of truthfulness and rationality and thus to claims of, to paraphrase Jacques Rancière's words, legibility within the field of politics as valid citizens of politics itself.[5]

* * *

Ferment, intoxicants, jelly, and rot have their own material histories that are also scientific and cultural histories. Ferment is a biochemical process whose naming indexes an anglophone history of describing a heated-up and possibly insurgent crowd feeling, perhaps even an early theory of crowd affect. Physical intoxication is itself often produced by fermentation and sometimes accompanied by liquid effervescence—the term that Émile Durkheim used to describe the phenomenology of collectivity in the context of religious feeling.[6] Intoxication is an affective state, and its etymology contains within it, as Mel Chen has so superbly explored, an understanding that toxic materials can invade the body, either via the environment or through consumption, and so become contiguous with the body's biochemistry, thus troubling subject/object divides that undergird both racialization and disability hierarchies.[7] As Chen masterfully shows, intoxication also refers either to affective disinhibition or to ways of living a cognitive life otherwise to or at odds with the taxonomic supremacy of certain forms of rational attentiveness that are rewarded by ableism and other forms of prejudice against differently abled peoples.

Jelly—or, more texturally, gelatinousness—describes the qualities of a set of materials, but it also holds a history as food made from reusing the animal waste left over from butchers and slaughterhouses, a food that, as I will discuss in the final chapter, some nations sought to put to the service of feeding the poor. Gelatin also belongs to a larger family of materials thought of as exhibiting rheological or non-Newtonian properties: their molecular structure allows them to move (or be experienced in the mouth) in ways that can seem uncannily human and therefore abject because they are strangely reactive and thus neither subject nor object. The gelatinous can be uncannily sticky or tacky, uncomfortably viscous, or agentially lively. Gelatinousness and its affiliated viscosities—muds, colloids, emulsions, among them—describe what it feels like to push through a heavy space and time, and yet they can also denote being fully present to that historical density, not only erotically and sensually but in accord with other, surrounding, touching, bodies.

And rot is, finally, as the fermentation guru Sandor Katz tells us, fermentation that we do not want to like.[8] Rot is decompositional, a texture (as anyone who lived through the Trump years knows) affiliated with living next to and with broken infrastructure. And yet in its decompositional possibilities, rot is also a process and materiality in which life and death coexist, a sign of the social catchments in which the failures and violences of the state produce harm but also fertilize the possibility of living otherwise to the sensual impoverishments of taxonomic normativity and state rationality. Rot both decomposes life and ferments future growth in a material coevality of life with death. And then too, as trash and waste and poison overtake the globe, rot (or as Donna Haraway would have it, compost) comes to describe the totality of living in ecological collapse.[9]

Ferment, intoxicants, jelly, and rot are materialities because they recur as figures that describe the alternately dense, prickly, sticky, oozing, pleasurable, effervescent, confusing, decaying qualities that everyday life can take on as one presses against it. These materialities are sensory, but they are often discordantly sensory: the sensations they produce come from their unexpected movements, their strange sounds, their discordant physicality, their bad smells, their uncanny feel in the mouth. As material and affective categories, they confuse the senses, in part because they fail to obey the dictates of their own objecthood: they poison, confuse, and inebriate; they jiggle and slither; they multiply and decay; they give birth out of death. They also fall, at times, on the lower end of the scale of material and aesthetic value, at least within the sensory cosmologies of the West. They are minor aesthetic categories, if I may borrow a phrase from Sianne Ngai: in refusing to uphold (and thus even critiquing) classical orderings of the senses—such as the supremacy of the visual or the distancing and hierarchical taxonomies of aesthetic judgment—their deviance largely adheres to objects and experiences and therefore the waywardness of populations that escape disciplinary and therefore archival capture.[10]

Ferment, intoxicants, jelly, and rot are what I call "deviant matter" because they have often come to be, in the microbiological and post-Pasteurian world, affiliated with foodways, modes of living, spaces, and sensory regimes (palates, for instance) that unsettle the hygienic, disciplinary ordering of the world. They seem to continuously affix to those humans who have come to be designated as less-than-human: the fat, the poor, the queer, the Black, the immigrant, and the brown. Similarly, they are deviant because in refusing the taxonomizing imperatives of classic aesthetics, they often demand multisensory attention: they are flavors that also unfold as touch; they are visualities that seem tactile; and they are objects that move on their own. But finally, ferment, intoxicants, jelly, and rot are also materialities that can describe atmospheres: they are affective and aesthetic formations that undo the boundaries of the liberal-human self, confusing inside and outside, making the singular multiple.

To understand how deviant matter transgresses these boundaries, we must first recognize how those boundaries came to be—because they are neither natural nor ahistorical. Toward this end, I want to pause here and work through a somewhat neglected passage of Michel Foucault's January 18, 1978, lecture, translated in *Security, Territory, Population: Lectures at the Collège de France, 1977–1978*.[11] In that lecture, Foucault develops his theory of the emergence of the notions of security and population as discourses of control, initially rehearsed in relation to the phenomenon of food scarcity and the shift to laissez-faire economics. In this shift, he explains, the government is newly willing to allow grain prices to rise—even when that will cause some subjects to starve to death—in order to avoid the large-scale hunger riots that had historically occurred when the state controlled the grain trade. The key shift that Foucault marks here, somewhat subtended in Foucault criticism, is that under this new regime,

> we succeed in curbing scarcity by a sort of "laisser-faire," a certain "freedom of movement (*laisser-passer*)," a sort "[*laisser*]-*aller*," in the sense of "letting things take their course." It means allowing prices to rise where their tendency is to rise. We allow the phenomenon of dearness-scarcity to be produced and develop on such and such a market, on a whole series of markets, and this phenomenon, this reality which we have allowed to develop, will itself entail precisely its own self-curbing and self-regulation. So there will no longer be any scarcity in general, on condition that for a whole series of people, in a whole series of markets, there was some scarcity, some dearness, some difficulty in buying wheat, and consequently some hunger, and it may well be that some people die of hunger after all. *But by letting these people die of hunger one will be able to make scarcity a chimera and prevent it occurring in this massive form of the scourge typical of the previous systems.* Thus, the scarcity-event is split. The scarcity-scourge disappears, but scarcity that causes the death of individuals not only does not disappear, it must not disappear.[12]

This long quote theorizes hunger, and therefore both energy and materiality, as they intersect at the biopolitical junction that is the human body, inserting human bodily potential into the project of market liberalization at the level of population. The talks collected in *Security, Territory, Population* themselves constitute a larger project in which Foucault theorizes the close ties between population as a political concept, a new politics of truth, the reorganization of the state apparatus alongside a liberal economic model, and indeed, the discipline of economics itself. Indexing a large body of historical scholarship in Europe that considers the riot, in particular bread riots, as historical phenomena, Foucault brings hunger to the fore as a social factor through which large-scale violence or protest on the part of the populace needs to be managed, which is to say securitized in the interests of state stability. *Laissez-faire* in Foucault's terms is also *laissez-mourir* (allow to die): the birth of population as a notion tied to the veredictory value of the market is the birth of a necropolitics of hunger in the metropole, of wedding the maldistribution of vulnerability-to-premature-death to regimes of cost-effectiveness (understood as "Economics") within the European nation-state.[13]

Borrowing from Ruth Wilson Gilmore's definition of racism as "vulnerability to premature death" and keeping in mind Achille Mbembe's now-canonical revision of biopolitics as a death-producing project, I want to join with postcolonial and African American scholars to trouble Foucault's historical timeline, by pointing to the deep origins of biopolitical economics in enslavement, colonialism, and settler colonialism, in which arenas Western liberal economic orders, imported to the colonial metropole in the eighteenth century within the new Malthusian logic of industrialism, were originally rehearsed and perfected.[14] This anecdote from Foucault places hunger at the center of the project of biopolitical population management: lack of access to food obviously determines differential life chances, and through it, states and colonial enterprises exercise their right both to kill and to let die. In Foucault's terms, states and colonial projects install economic logics that produce a notion of "national security" by deflecting or containing the possibility of mass political uprising. For Foucault, the phenomenon of population emerges as he thinks through the way the state responds to mass movement by deploying hunger as a weapon of death. More particularly, by rerouting the causes of starvation from the management of state grain stores to the vicissitudes of the market, Foucault argues, the state invests in the idea that spontaneous mass political movements can be effectively deflected and managed through liberal capitalist discourse: the logic of liberal capital both murders *and* secures. Putting it another way, dissident populace energy is reordered into population logics when the state renders chimeric even the possibility of understanding hunger as state-produced: instead, starvation becomes a problem of the market—which is, after all, not the state's responsibility but a truth-producing regime in its own right. If you are hungry, it is your own fault. The state deploys this material and discursive shell game, reordering the logic of harm under capital, against the specter of the bread riot, the grain-demanding uprising, and the hungry crowd.

What is also striking about Foucault's narrative of securitization is the idea that hunger—which within a merely thermodynamic understanding of the body should actually lead to a *lack* of energy—actually produces a particular kind of affective energy, anger, that propels the body to exceed what it should be capable of. A crowd is the feeling-energy of multiple bodies turned into matter-potential. A bread riot, in other words, is a mass of bodies fed on a different kind of food: it is a mass of individuals dissolved into one, bonded by shared affective orientation, turned into affect-itself.[15] Political crowds, in this sense, could be understood as matter itself, just as affect is matter itself, but it is affect that cannot be so easily extracted or directed toward profit.

Thus, it should come as no surprise that particular forms of matter whose energetic capabilities seem to exceed or undo thermodynamic models of energetic behavior—in the sense of producing more energy than is put into a system or behaving in ways that defy linear causality or mathematically simple relations—come to figure the unexpected capacities of crowd energy. Certainly the movement of these materialities—the ways that they either provoke unexpected responses and embodiments or respond in strangely agential ways or, in the case of ferment and rot, seem to hover in the strange world between effervescent collective feeling, energetic reproductive life, death and decomposition, and ultimately disinhibition or deformation—aligns with the political threat of an insurgent crowd. For these reasons, ferment, intoxication, jelly, and rot recur as figures for the crowd and its uncanny undoing of the boundedness of the atomic liberal self, its teeming energy, its unpredictable, simultaneously agential and agentless willfulness. Given their affiliation with a new microbiological or even microbiopolitical order following the rise of Pasteurian science, each of these kinds of matter comes to figure as a mode of feeling or a mode of thinking as a group or from within a group.

One of my key interventions in *Deviant Matter*, then, is to historicize the microbiopolitics of matter in the United States by posing the legal, scientific, disciplinary, and aesthetic technologies that try to securitize populations against the incipient agency of lively matter itself. In so doing, I discuss how a history of the senses becomes more available to scholarly conversation when we bring a historical examination of the biopolitical regulation and presence of matter in art, science, and law into conversation with an expanded theory of aesthetics. In this sense, *Deviant Matter* is a theoretical and methodological intervention that is distinctly speculative and experimental, pulling together fields of inquiry and archives that are juxtapositional and counterdisciplinary: in theorizing matter, affect, and aesthetics together, I seek to deepen our understanding of aesthetics by finding aesthetic phenomena in places where they are not supposed to be—in the archives of scientific and governmental writing that manages populations by taxonomizing (for instance, as criminals) the very categories through which we understand matter today (say, as intoxicants, narcotics, or medicine; as preserved, fermented, or rotted food; as useful matter or waste). And then, in turn, I seek to deepen a theoretical conversation between minoritarian life and aesthetic theory by listening to the cultural lives of dissident and deviant forms of matter as they find their way into works of political art.

Here I join with scholars such as Neetu Khanna and Elizabeth Wilson in exploring the intimate affiliation between affect and aesthetics that circulates around those feelings we experience as "viscerality." In earlier work, I argued that "hidden within and connected by the folds and twists and turns of our flesh, the gut has everything to do with what is felt. . . . To aim for the visceral is to come at feeling, at sex, at sensation, at theory itself, from a queer place"; the gut, I wrote, "has a mind of its own."[16] In Khanna's formulation, "visceral logics . . . explore the dynamic inter-action between psychic and somatic activities for where these energetics go astray."[17] She continues, "Scenes of viscerality expose how disruptive and non-normative forms of gender and sexuality propel decolonization precisely because this is *where these affective energies go awry*."[18] In *Deviant Matter*, viscerality returns as a subtended theme that pulls together affect and aesthetics as modes of material responsiveness that unsettle civil forms of feeling. Visceral responses return humanistic analysis to the undisciplined materiality of the flesh and body.

Given the centrality of food and food-like materials to this book, it seems important to acknowledge that gut knowledges return us to the status of the stomach as, in Elizabeth Wilson's words, "a second brain."[19] In *Deviant Matter*, however, I seek to extend beyond individual feeling—a limit of the "gut feeling" formulation, I would argue—to phenomena that consistently index mass and crowd feeling. Thus, when I say that these are political aesthetics that are haunted by the political energy of the crowd, I join with other scholars of biopolitics in early America and the nineteenth century, such as Kyla Schuller and Greta LaFleur, in turning away from the elaboration of governmentality at the level of the individual and toward the social production of figures for crowd-level energy and affect. These sensory schema and economic logics mark what Foucault named as the shift from populace to population, a state project of what he called "securitization."[20] Here I draw inspiration from the anthropologist Heather Paxson's insight that "the way we talk about microbes is an applied science of governing microbes, but it is also inevitably a way of governing people."[21] Paxson's term "microbiopolitics" is central to this project because it connects Foucault's idea of biopolitics as the management of life at the level of the population to the governance of human and nonhuman life at the level of the microbial and bacteriological. The editors of a special issue on fermentation in *Current Anthropology* write, "if biopolitics is the governance of human life by appeal to the biosciences, then *microbiopower* is the governance of human-microbial life by appeal to microbiology."[22] The turn to microbial life, however, is also paradoxically a shift to population-level discourse, because the fomenting, fermenting, and self-multiplying microbial world symbolically unseats the individual and shimmers with the figurative threat of the crowd.

Further, as the example from Foucault elaborates, such crowd potential is always met under liberal capital by the disciplinary and management forces that he terms "security." "Securitization" is defined by Neil Ahuja as "transformations in a subject, system, or state that are conceived as reducing the risk of harm or danger emerging from some specific social or environmental context."[23] I would argue additionally that we can understand securitization as being largely about redirecting human energy and resources away from unrest—that fermenting crowd—and into systems of extractability. Such systems of extractability might refer to the measurable laboring energy of populations living under capitalism, whether that labor is variously extracted through enslavement or incarceration, or it might refer to the constrained choices we have come to understand as "work" or "reproduction" under liberal capitalism. As we will see in later chapters, extraction might also refer to the resources such as food that will produce laboring energy in the population. But at the other level, biopolitical securitization is also about managing *feeling*—in particular the forms of feeling that take place at the level of the simmering tensions of unhappy crowds or suppressed populations that have just been given too much to bear. And yet, as Patricia Clough and Jasbir Puar have shown us in their work on virality, it must be understood that from the perspective of securitization, these two seemingly different things—"matter," a tangible quantifiable resource, and "affect," an intangible feeling that connects bodies to each other—can be understood as the same thing, even in the nineteenth century. Writing about the early twentieth century, Clough et al. write,

> Instead of looking to the body-as-organism to actualize labor-power, we are proposing that a dynamic, indeterminate matter is presently being configured in capitalism with corresponding techniques of administration and measurement aimed at a level below, above, or perhaps beyond that of the bounded body-as-organism. Therefore, while we are also concerned with the "dynamic powers" to which Virno refers, we conceive them not as a matter of general intellect, a disembodied matter, but as a generalized matter beyond the laborer's body, a matter of affect-itself. We are proposing that there is an abstracting of affect to *affect-itself*, which disregards the boundedness of the human body, thus troubling the conceptualization of the body as the body-as-organism.[24]

What I hope that this book demonstrates is that what Clough argues is a phenomenon of the early twenty-first century is easily legible as a theory of population energy in the nineteenth century, perhaps because the idea of virality itself emerges as an earlier iteration, as fermentation. In this earlier formulation, feeling-affect and energy-matter were already collapsed into each other.

* * *

Deviant Matter is also my attempt to expand my own understanding of the discourse of aesthetics as it is consistently weaponized against the life worlds of minoritized peoples to explain what it feels like to be so utterly wrong: to be abject, different, not right, in the spaces that will punish you for being so. In the service of this project, I draw heavily on the Caribbeanist Sylvia Wynter's now-canonical essay "Rethinking 'Aesthetics': Notes towards a Deciphering Practice." In that article, Wynter seeks to expand the study of aesthetics into a far wider field of sociopolitical inquiry than simply the study of beauty. For Wynter, an aesthetic constitutes the entirety of the organization of sensory information. Not simply a category of artistic or creative expression, for Wynter, the "aesthetic" traditionally considered is a mode, a way, or a manner that is also formally congruent—isomorphic or homologous to—what came to be known "the human being." As I read it, "being" in this sentence is a verb in the sense that theorists sometimes use the term "becoming." Wynter's human is "being" in the sense that aesthetics is modal: a processual doing in time, in space, in a field of sensory possibility, a modality taking effect, causing effects, doing its effects. A human is a life form that does/being human in the mode in which doing/being human is a project made socially legible—and sensorily present—in time and in space. For Wynter, aesthetics is not only about the taxonomizing orders of people and things that were produced via the intersection of settler colonialism with racial capitalism and chattel slavery but also about a corollary and even homologous ordering of the senses that was in and of itself a colonial and colonizing project.

The point about time is not cosmetic to my engagement with the senses because the organization of labor time has everything to do with how human energy—and thus, as Wynter shows in other work, the genre of humanness itself—is sensed by its practitioners. By example, long before scholars of biopolitics complicated the Foucauldian genealogy of state power by linking it to Europe's colonial and imperial projects, Sidney Mintz made the critical argument that the labor organization of the metropolis was worked out and rehearsed via the forced work-rhythms of enslaved colonial labor. In those work-rhythms, "discipline was probably its first essential feature. . . . The system was time-conscious. This time-consciousness was dictated by the nature of the sugar cane and its processing requirements, but it permeated all phases of plantation life and accorded well with the emphasis on time that was later to become a central feature of capitalist industry."[25] The time-consciousness that Mintz refers to here links in part to what Anna Tsing has argued is the copresence of mold and fungi with other flora and fauna in the plantation ecosystem: left to sit too long without processing (say, by allowing enslaved peoples to rest, a use of time we might think of as almost completely anathema to the necropolitical and extractive imperatives of the sugar plantation), and sugarcane juice would begin to ferment, rendering sugar processing impossible, rotten even, because of how environmental bacteria use up carbohydrate energy to produce carbon dioxide.[26] In using up sugar, fermentation processes would also have rendered the sugar source sour and thus unprofitable—but also perhaps intoxicating and therefore productive of intoxicated *un*productivity. Returning to the aesthetic in the context of the plantation, one sensory world—taste—was born in which sourness came to be seen as sweetness gone bad and rendered unprofitable.[27] The value of sweetness, then, is congruent with and emerged from the time discipline invented in the service of the cruelest labor- and life-extraction schemes ever known to human history. As Wynter shows us, the enslavement project, alongside settler colonialism and the genocide of native peoples, also produced the human as a "form of life" that was extractable from the nonhuman environment, such as mold and fungi, and from peoples whose lack of access to taste (or, in Bourdieu's terms, distinction) relegated them to the margins of humanness.[28]

Sweetness was also the flavor of time discipline deployed in the service of producing cheap energy and caloric fuel in the metropole: "just as work schedules were quickening," Mintz writes, "sucrose was one of the people's opiates, and its consumption was a symbolic demonstration that the system that produced it was successful."[29] Connecting Mintz's insight explicitly to the aesthetic, Wynter defines traditional aesthetics as "secur[ing] the social cohesion of the specific human order of which it is a function."[30] Within this frame, the reward-system attached to belonging to dominant aesthetic orientations and genres of being, such as "humanness," can be understood not only as social but also as a conditioned biochemical brain response:

> Each order of discourse must, therefore, function in a literal sense as the Marxian "opium of the people," whose "truth" is to be defined by the exactitude with which the value-connotations that their signifying practices place on the representation of symbolic "life" . . . are positively marked ones that are then able to activate the internal reward system (IRS), thereby triggering its opiate-induced euphoria coefficient. . . . Bourdieu's correlation of the discourse of the aesthetic with the social relation of dominance and subordination at the socio-political level of class is also replicated at the global socio-cultural level of race.[31]

What I appreciate so much in Wynter's work here is her proleptic inclusion of neuroplasticity—here in the human "form of life"—within the realm of aesthetic analysis.[32] For Wynter, aesthetics and its attendant ideologies become, in the language of evolutionary biology, part of the milieu that produces humanness as a category made and refined—sweetened—in and through the extractive history of racial capital. Following Wynter, aesthetics is not only to be understood as simply the elevating relation between human subject and nonhuman (art) object, although it is that: it is also an atmospheric and environmental sensory regime that works across the scale, from the molecular to the sociopolitical, to produce, reward, and maintain class and race as genres in and of themselves.

Wynter's wedding of aesthetics—the source of "opiate-induced euphoria coefficient[s]"—to politics also does not reduce simply to state aesthetic projects, such as monuments, or grand historical objects, like the US Constitution, although it might include those objects too. And yet we know that politics deploys aesthetics at those grand scales: as authors such as Eric Slauter show, states deploy aesthetic regimes to produce affective effects, and there is a well-developed body of work upholding the idea that at the extremes of spectacular fascism, aesthetic analysis might find congruences between the conscious self-presentation of state ideology and its underlying goals.[33] Susan Sontag's withering read of Leni Riefenstahl's post-Nazi art is an archetype of such writing, seeing politics in the starkly divided binarisms of fascism's high drama:

> Fascist aesthetics . . . flow from (and justify) a preoccupation with situations of control, submissive behavior, extravagant effort, and the endurance of pain; they endorse two seemingly opposite states, egomania and servitude. The relations of domination and enslavement take the form of a characteristic pageantry: the massing of groups of people; the turning of people into things; the multiplication or replication of things; and the grouping of people/things around an all-powerful, hypnotic leader-figure or force. The fascist dramaturgy centers on the orgiastic transactions between mighty forces and their puppets, uniformly garbed and shown in ever swelling numbers. Its choreography alternates between ceaseless motion and a congealed, static, "virile" posing. Fascist art glorifies surrender, it exalts mindlessness, it glamorizes death.[34]

But the work of political aesthetics is hardly confined to works labeled as fascist or produced under fascist governments. As trans theory and prison abolitionists teach us, many subjects do not experience state violence in and through monumentality or explicit targeting. Rather, vulnerable citizens and (to deprioritize the state and its borders) vulnerable noncitizens live state violence via the daily grind of encounters with the heavy momentum of administration, of bureaucracies and their actors (even when, as in the particular moment of the writing of these words, the slow creep of everyday politics sometimes seems to be inexorably swinging toward fascism). This is the realm of regulation: of checkpoints, of lines, of intractable endless forms; of measurement, statistics, and policing.[35]

This grueling slog is what Dean Spade calls "administrative violence": biopower as a statistical and population-based administrative project. To understand "the creation of norms that distribute vulnerability and security," Spade quotes Mitchell Dean to argue that scholars must study

> the routines of bureaucracy; the technologies of notation, recording, compiling, presenting and transporting of information, the theories, programmes, knowledge and expertise that compose a field to be governed and invest it with purposes and objectives; the ways of seeing and representing embedded in practices of government; and the different agencies with various capacities that the practices of government require, elicit, form and reform. To examine regimes of government is to conduct analysis in the plural: there is already a plurality of regimes of practices in a given territory, each composed from a multiplicity of in principle unlimited and heterogeneous elements bound together by a variety of relations and capable of polymorphous connections with one another.[36]

Spade takes up the same passage in his work on administrative violence and critical trans politics, noting that to engage these routines and technologies is to witness how "administrative systems have emerged out of and been focused on creation and management of racial and gender categories to establish the nation itself through gendered-racialize property regimes." Such "population-level interventions, including administrative systems and norms," he writes, "preserve and cultivate the lives of some and expose others to premature death."[37]

Here I turn again to Rancière. In particular, Rancière's definition of the "distribution of the sensible" suggests who is and is not subject to the kinds of aesthetics, the kinds of regulation, that Wynter, Spade, and Dean identify. I quote here at length Rancière's definition:

> [Distribution of the sensible is] a generally implicit law that defines the forms of partaking [in politics] by first defining the modes of perception in which they are inscribed. The partition of the sensible is the dividing-up of the world (de *monde*) and of people (du *monde*). . . . This partition should be understood in the double sense of the word: on the one hand, as that which separates and excludes; on the other, as that which allows participation. A partition of the sensible refers to the manner in which a relation between a shared common (un commun partagé) and the distribution of exclusive parts is determined in sensory experience. This latter form of distribution, which, by its sensory self-evidence, anticipates the distribution of part and shares (parties), itself presupposes a distribution of what is visible and what not, of what can be heard and what cannot.[38]

My interest, then, is to put Rancière's theory of the partition of the sensible to the work of understanding how the distribution of political value—and thus relevance and access to the sphere of politics itself—is predicated on the imbrication of governance with aesthetic valuation. Bringing Wynter into conversation with Spade and Rancière means thinking with, as I hope to do in these chapters, how aesthetics is a governing force that orders the worlds into those who are meant to live, to access the good life, and those who are either murdered or allowed to diminish, be hurt, and die. Yet, as I am arguing here, what Wynter's writing allows us to say is that the work of that aesthetic project, which functions to delineate the human from the nonhuman at the level of the ordering of the senses, also functions in those administrative spaces seemingly devoid of artfulness, of beauty, or of creativity. In fact, as I hope to show, the seeming absence of aesthetics in the spaces where rational governance claims to live is itself a strategy of aesthetic violence. One word for that violence might be "police."

Returning to think with insurgency and control, Rancière describes the disciplinary responses to incipient crowd energy as "police power," which for Rancière is a loose holder for historical categories of law.[39] In classical legal theory, police power refers directly to a state's right to regulate and to make all "necessary" laws. In the United States' particular federalist model, however, "police power" can particularly refer to the states' rights, established by the Tenth Amendment to the Constitution, to exercise rights and powers "not delegated to the United States"—

which is to say, a state's right. In this particular historical model, states are granted the power to establish and enforce laws protecting "the welfare, safety, *and health* of the public." It is at this juncture between health, safety, and welfare (particularly following the rise of microbiology and other sciences), the figure of matter that is deviant emerges. As I argue in chapter 1 of this book, hygienic movements are a particular manifestation of state power closely aligned with what has been otherwise defined as "police power" that in their investment in guarding the hygienic boundaries of a community are particularly empowered to uphold racial inequality. Turning on figures that are simultaneously figural, metaphorical, and material, police power is used by the state to guard against infection and pollution, and it is exercised in the name of managing literal and imagined threats to community security.

* * *

As I began to develop earlier, one of *Deviant Matter*'s larger challenges is to follow behind Wynter in the building of a fuller analytic toolkit to explore Marx's proposal that "the forming of the five senses is a labour of the entire history of the world down to the present."[40] Toward that end, I am interested in the life of matter itself, as a way of thinking *against* the normative logics of the biopolitical state (as I elaborate shortly, specifically in its hygienic iteration). To do this thinking *against* the state, I read *with* materiality—joining a long line of thinkers in affect studies, particularly those who have sought to find new languages and theoretical paradigms for accounting for the sensual and sensory energetic flows between bodies.[41] Additionally, I seek to build on the work of scholars in new materialist and ecocritical thought whose engagement with the active and actant presence of both matter and nonhuman animals has come to be known as the new materialism. But finally, I seek to pull together the insights and work of Black studies, queer of color critique, Marxist cultural studies, performance studies, biopolitical theory, and human geography to return to both the new materialism and affect studies with, as historians of the subaltern have often described it, a view from below. With these forerunners, I listen to materiality as both ontology and epistemology, as a phenomenon that theorizes and performatively unfurls at the (temporal, sensual) scale of everyday life.[42] Attending closely to the effects and sensory presence of these materialities, I meet with the rotten stickiness and decaying give of putrefied material; I listen to the effortless effervescence of ferment and thus also foment; I move analytically with the bounce and return of gelatin and other viscous materials; and finally I think with the disinhibited and disoriented affects of intoxicants.

In line with work in queer and feminist science studies that seeks to, as Karen Barad writes, be *in* the science, not merely above or outside of it, my argument in this book is that matter and materiality *theorize*: my work in *Deviant Matter*, then, is to come as close to *thinking with* matter as I can. Barad describes this ethical commitment to being *with* as "touch," which she also parses as "its physicality, its virtuality, its affectivity, its e-motion-ality."[43] For instance, in her meditation on touch and quantum physics, Barad uses what she describes as the radical alterity of the electron—its simultaneous mattering and nonmattering as particle and as void, its charged negativity, which does not repel but rather produces infinite improvisational and relational possibility—to theorize a queer and radical alterity to selfhood: "In an important sense, in a breathtakingly intimate sense, touching, sensing, is what matter does, or rather, what matter is: matter is condensations of response-ability. Touching is a matter of response. Each of 'us' is constituted in response-ability. Each of 'us' is constituted as responsible for the other, as the other."[44] Because she explains all forms of touch as the repulsion of electromagnetic energies, for Barad, matter is fundamentally defined as sense: *it is sense itself*, as the fact of electron repulsion dictates the shape of the sensory encounter with matter. However, because negative charges ultimately produce repulsion, the sense that is touch is also a paradox: even when one touches one's own body, one is not actually touching so much as experiencing negatively charged repulsion as the quality of touch itself. I return to the question of touch later in this introduction, but here I wish to point out that Barad's argument is in many ways a perfect description of affect in the classically Spinozan vein, in which affect is defined both as the potential to change from one state to another and as change itself.[45] But in both a Levinasian and Derridean vein, Barad's sense of touch is also an expression of the alterity of the self to the self, which is the same alterity of the self to others. Thinking with the ontologies of quantum physics, Barad opens onto alternative epistemologies and ethics of encounter: an onto-ethical-epistemology. That philosophical work also reveals an indeterminacy between subjects and objects that undoes the very stability of form itself: "Ontological indeterminacy, a radical openness, an infinity of possibilities, is at the core of mattering. How strange that indeterminacy, in its infinite openness, is the condition for the possibility of all structures in their dynamically reconfiguring in/stabilities. Matter in its iterative materialization is a dynamic play of in/determinacy. Matter is never a settled matter. It is always already radically open. Closure cannot be secured when the conditions of im/possibilities and lived indeterminacies are integral, not supplementary, to what matter is."[46] Barad's account is an anti-Aristotelian account of form, refuting a hylomorphic account of organic form as teleologically oriented toward fixity. I have elsewhere connected this processual and antiformalist idea to the crudity or "rawness" and incivility of matter.[47]

In seeking to model my own work alongside Barad's, I want to linger for a moment over this idea of the indeterminacy of matter and form to think about what these two terms can and cannot do for each other, particularly in relation to those scholars of materialism who, like myself, seek to integrate the insights of queer of color theory with research into questions of aesthetics and politics. Ferment, intoxicants, jelly, and rot appeal to me as windows into questions of form because, like the nonwhite queer who is so often the "bad" racial or sexual subject, the movement of these materialities across multiple aesthetic fields signifies toward a sensory discordance or wrongness in rooms and fields in which everyone and everything else seems to be right. Less "forms" than recurrent figures of temporary stability, ferment, intoxication, rot, and jelly are processes and states that blur and melt into each other, that are understood less as shapes than as patterns of change that fix and then unfix. Deviant matter multiplies difference, but that difference is not the flat ontology of "diversity" because in effect that difference also accumulates.

By honoring the indeterminacy, or perhaps the theoretical juiciness, of matter, this study also seeks to disturb the separation of ontology from epistemology, subject from object. However, in regard to the mattering of difference, I move in a different direction. While utterly convinced by Barad's investigations into indeterminacy and difference as well as Georges Bataille's rejection of form in favor of the confusion of the senses unleashed by movement itself, in this project, I aim to listen to matter's materiality as its nonhumanness is historically reflected in its various affiliations with those subjects, often designated under the banner of modernity's racial orders as less than or simply nonhuman, deformed, or deviant. As such, I understand deviance to encompass the aesthetic-political expressions that govern the many modes of living and creating that lie outside or direct themselves against aesthetic and political normativity. This definition puts my own critique of formalism into conversation with the critique of "respectability politics" that has emerged from Black feminist and queer history, disability studies, and political theory.[48]

Deviance in this book exists as what Rancière defines as the outer limits of politicity, a limit governed by aesthetics itself: "Aesthetics can be understood in a Kantian sense—re-examined perhaps by Foucault—as the system of *a priori* forms determining what presents itself to sense experience. It is a delimitation of spaces and times, of the visible and the invisible, of speech and noise, that simultaneously determines the place and the stakes of politics as a form of experience. Politics revolves around what is seen and what can be said about it, around who has the ability to see and the talent to speak, around the properties of spaces and the possibilities of time."[49] Against the form, then, I pose the deform, the undone, that which exists at the limits of aesthetics itself. The line from these schools of thought to the fertile ground that is queer of color critique is clear, particularly when we foreground the centrality of racialized sexualities to the history of queer deviance itself. And indeed, the crude and the déclassé have been queer and minoritized aesthetic weapons since white camp first stole from Black culture to cut its baby teeth in twentieth-century queer life.

Earlier, I asserted that ferment, intoxicants, jelly, and rot are materialities that are also atmospheres. Here I want to begin to close this chapter by thinking with Audre Lorde, the poet and political theorist, whose engagement with the senses shows one path into a queer of color, Black, lesbian, and feminist reordering of the world. In a section toward the end of her landmark essay "The Uses of the Erotic," Lorde illustrates her reimagining of the erotic as a sensory and atmospheric quality of the everyday life:

> During World War II, we bought sealed plastic packets of white, uncolored margarine, with a tiny, intense pellet of yellow coloring perched like a topaz just inside the clear skin of the bag. We would leave the margarine out for a while to soften, and then we would pinch the little pellet to break it inside the bag releasing the rich yellowness into the soft pale mass of margarine. Then taking it carefully between our fingers, we would knead it gently back and forth, over and over, until the color had spread throughout the whole pound bag of margarine, thoroughly coloring it.
>
> I find the erotic such a kernel within myself. When released from its intense and constrained pellet, it flows through and colors my life with a kind of energy that heightens and sensitizes and strengthens all my experience.[50]

A reintegration of bodily pleasure and creativity with everyday life and labor, Lorde's expansive theorization of what it might mean to live beyond and outside the extractive and joy-killing organization of sex, art, love, work, and basically everything else under capitalism takes a decidedly materialist, politically multiregistered, turn here. First, Lorde's socialism reworks Marx's idea that the senses are formed through the historical processes structured by capital through a speculative reimagining of what everyday life might feel like—*if* the worker was not alienated from herself and the fruits of her labor, *if* her body was not alienated from itself as well. But this anecdote is also materialist in the sense that Lorde takes up a decidedly chemical and artificial type of matter to express what she might have expressed in far more organic terms.

Why does Lorde use food coloring and margarine to explain her theory of the erotic? How can we account for Lorde's willingness to think about the pleasures of a food replacement often associated with poverty, artifice, and the unnatural, particularly in relation to the speculative sensory economy that she calls "the erotic." Why this debased material? On the one hand, she begins the passage by invoking World War II, a time of rationing and provisioning: to color the drab bag of emulsive nondairy spread is to take what might be undesirable in a hard time and infuse it with softness, radiance, and meaning. The tiny pellet of yellow coloring, which Lorde describes as "intense" and "like a topaz," fully changes a mass of oleaginous matter that exceeds even its own weight and size (a "whole pound"): such is the strength of the color that it changes the mass of whiteness ("a soft pale mass") to a "rich yellowness." In these alterations, the senses merge into one another: touch becomes vision and vice versa.

But just as the touch of multiple hands expands the yellow of the color pellet, so that richness becomes the model for a mode of sensory envelopment that reimagines work and pleasure. The erotic for Lorde is not simply sex, as she and commentators since have expansively taken up: it is a heightened sensory atmosphere made richer by Lorde's attention to her experience of its quotidian sensual textures: "it flows through and colors my life."[51] To release this "kernel of energy" into one's life takes labor, however, and it is Lorde's genius that her metaphor allows her to envision this work within the language of everyday gestures remembered in relation to everyday objects: Lorde's (and one assumes her family's) kneading of the margarine "over and over" lets the reader know that margarine is thick and dense matter, but it is exactly the difficulty of pushing color through the bag that allows its newly brightened materiality—its rich yellowness—to become a way of describing a "heightened and sensitized" experience of work, living, creating, and engaging with others. The labor of enlivening the sensory economies of everyday life is quotidian, gestural, and repetitive—it is a whole pound bag, after all—but it is labor rewarded with joy, presence, and sensory fullness. As she writes, "it is not only a question of what we do; it is a question of how acutely and fully we can feel in the doing."[52] Lorde's erotic is also a temporal formation, one that works to create a deepened sense of the present.

Lorde's words offer more than an example of what it means to think about the matter of the everyday *in and through materiality*, and in *Deviant Matter*, I pay particular homage to the speculative horizontality between objects and subjects that Lorde models in the piece. "The Uses of the Erotic" is a theory of touch and communion that, in practice if not in external declaration, allows for a human and nonhuman assemblage of actors to encounter each other—and for the human body to encounter itself—beyond the heterosexual and dyadic "european-american" tradition:

> The erotic functions for me in several ways, and the first is in providing the power which comes from sharing deeply any pursuit with an-

> other person, . . . the way my body stretches to music and opens into response . . . so every level upon which I sense also opens to the erotically satisfying experience, whether it is dancing, building a bookcase, writing a poem, examining an idea. . . . There is a difference between painting a back fence and writing a poem, but only one of quantity. And there is, for me, no difference between writing a good poem and moving into sunlight against the body of a woman I love.[53]

Lorde's description of the erotic is simultaneously an affective phenomenon shared between subjects and a sensory—and therefore aesthetic—reordering that imagines a world in which the differences in aesthetic hierarchies are "only in quantity." Her words lead me to the central argument of my project: that the sensory and textural quality of affective atmospheres are simultaneously material, historical, aesthetic, and political, and we must think them so with an eye to the deep imbrication of Black, brown, and queer life with the history of matter.

Here—finally—I turn to Cathy Cohen's theorization of deviance when she argues that attentiveness to the social arrangements and choices created by working-class African Americans might yield resources for thinking through future political formations: "through a focus on 'deviant' practice we are witness to the power of those at the bottom, whose everyday life decisions challenge, or at least counter, the basic normative assumptions of a society intent on protecting structural and social inequalities under the guise of some normal and natural order to life."[54] Deviance, in other words, with all of its resonances as departure or movement away from the norm, is the locus classicus of queer and otherwise minoritarian life.

Cohen's suggestion that the study of Black life critically and respectfully turn to those "individuals [who] daily act in opposition to dominant norms" can be seen as proleptic of the work of performance studies scholars as that field's interest in everyday life has evolved from its roots in theater, dance, anthropology, and, most recently, cultural geography. The turn to deviance in Cohen's work is political, of course, in that it pulls from the insights of queer theory to counter and course-correct the politics of respectability that she argues, following Evelyn Higginbotham, structures some fields of Black social and political thought, but it also offers a corrective and solidarity-oriented analytic to the anti-

Blackness and misogynoir of the Reagan era's attack on Black mothers.[55] But for the purposes of this book, I read Cohen's essay "Deviance as Resistance," first and foremost, as a methodological proposal, one that seeks to make visible the deep structures of normative judgment in the social sciences. Her method also turns the emphasis on resistance away from explicitly named political countermovements and charismatic leadership—thus reifying a limited idea of agency—and instead scales analysis down to the level of everyday gestures of refusal in order to "investigate their potential for the production of counter normative behaviors and oppositional politics."[56] In short, I read Cohen's essay as an injunction to find political theory in the collected archive of everyday gesture and feeling.

I do not wish to gloss over Cohen's argument that "most acts labeled deviant or even defiant of power are not attempts to sway fundamentally the distribution of power in the country. . . . These acts, decisions, or behaviors are more often attempts to create greater autonomy over one's life, to pursue desire, or to make the best of very limited life options."[57] But I am attentive to the complexity of her own findings when she concludes this landmark essay with the proposal that "it is possible that eventually the cumulative impact of individual deviant choices may indeed have an effect on power relations, . . . creating spaces or counter publics, where not only oppositional ideas and discourse happen but lived opposition, or at least autonomy is chosen daily. . . . Through the repetition of deviant practices by multiple individuals, new identities, communities, politics may be created."[58] That is, while deviance does not constitute agentic resistance itself, deviant acts *accumulate*. Everyday deviance produces a counternormative politics that imagines and acts otherwise to the constrained and negative choices of a death-producing world.[59]

Listening deeply to Cohen's work, particularly this latter proposal that repetition, accumulation, and multiplicity are key to creating what she terms "potential," we can see how much this foundational work of political theory anticipates the writing that would emerge two decades later under the banner of biopolitical and affect theory, in particular in that field's work on capacity and emergence in relation to the crowd, or multitude.[60] As Kenneth Rogers outlines so beautifully in his essay on "crowdsourcing," many earlier theories depended on a cynicism toward the crowd, based in the idea that the crowd's animal energies suppressed individual rationality. Rogers writes, "The association of diminished ego boundaries with categories of race, gender, and class hierarchies is a thinly disguised expression of fear about the political threat to established power posed by unrestrained extension of democracy to common people via universal suffrage, populism, class solidarity, and racial equality."[61] Far more laudatory, and I suspect more foundational to our current moment, are the Marxist historians and those of the Annales school, like Fernand Braudel, who investigated and valued the force of such crowd phenomena as hunger and scarcity riots.[62]

To my mind, however, Cohen's theorization of deviance entirely bypasses the question of the crowd as undifferentiated mass to provide a far more sophisticated and nuanced take on the time-space of collectivity. She instead imagines the energy of disparate synchronous and asynchronous gestures, choices, acts, and desires as they cumulatively gather momentum and force. This politics of doing, being, becoming, and feeling is a politics of nationhood not entirely separated from Benedict Anderson's idea of imagined community—but one for a people for whom living in the United States has always been, in Fred Moten's words, an experience of statelessness.[63] Sinking more deeply into Cohen's work and returning to Lorde's theorization of the erotic, we might call this a collectivity of feeling, of the worlding work of living on, together.

* * *

Deviant Matter is composed of two parts. Chapter 1 traces the emergence of a particular iteration of Rancière's police power in the hygienic state first theorized by Latour and in this book typified by the work of the US Department of Agriculture, from the nineteenth century to today. The seemingly agential nature of these forms of matter also inspires a disciplinary response from the state, a response that I argue is aligned with new regimes of biopolitical, microbiopolitical, and agricultural energy management. To account for these opposing but interlinked narrative strands, the book takes place in two thematic movements: in chapter 1, I discuss the aesthetic and political heritage of the Department of Agriculture with a mind to the rise of science and social science as analytic tools of the state. Beginning with the founding of the Department of Agriculture in 1862, I use the print culture of this enormous bureaucratic body to build, in a sense, a biographical study of matter in the late nineteenth and early twentieth centuries. As I show, during and after the Civil War, the Department of Agriculture embarked on a large-scale taxonomization project that sought to explain and to order the world of matter across multiple scales: at the state level, at the national level, and (as agricultural chemistry and microbiology took stronger hold in the nation and in the state) at the microscopic level of the cell, the calorie, and the microbe. The growth of this enormous state infrastructure, I argue, was accompanied by the rise of science as an integral tool of state practice, which in turn, as ideas of rationality and objectivity that accompanied science took hold, as the primary affective mode of state governance. Thus, I begin the book by looking at the political aesthetics of regulatory bureaucracy, in particular the bulletins of the Bureau of Chemistry of the Department of Agriculture. As I show, the reorganization of the material and affective life of the nation from the level of the bacterial and microscopic on up can be understood as a heightened project of securitization, of managing and containing the energetic capacity of deviant segments of the population.

This theoretical frame—the idea that we can make biopolitical arguments that trace affective and aesthetic homologies across scales and across media—lays the foundation for the argument I pursue in the second and larger section of the book, chapters 2 through 5. In these chapters, I show that against civility and rationality, dissident and deviant forms of lively matter, such as ferment, intoxication, gelatinousness, and rot, became figures for thinking through the incipient and counterdisciplinary energy of the subaltern communities—white working class, Black, Asian, and queer—that the state has sought to manage and contain.

More playful and speculative, the last four chapters of *Deviant Matter* take up the eponymous categories of ferment, jelly, intoxicants, and rot through an array of texts that range from literature to contemporary video, comics to agricultural bulletins, conceptual art to dietary advice. At times, these texts seem to come together randomly; they certainly make for some strange juxtapositions. In *Deviant Matter*, I am interested in what happens when an object travels through and across time and refracts through multiple genres of cultural texts. This is not a flat ontology, however: it is not an argument that every kind of object can or should be read the same way, no matter its medium. Rather, it is an argument that history, time, and the worlds that objects and subjects traverse are far more promiscuous and strange and interesting than disciplinarity and traditional methodological practices want or allow them, or us, to be. *Deviant Matter* is in part an argument for interdisciplinary method as a form of rigor that tests its own theories thoroughly, that tests them thoroughly with and in and through difference and contradiction.[64] Further, mine is an argument that disciplinarity is a fiction that allows the scholar to believe that an archive is ever complete in the first place.

Promiscuous method is also a theory of touch, in Karen Barad's sense of the word, and it returns me to the materialities that organize the structure of this book. Barad writes, "Theorizing, a form of experimenting, is about being in touch. What keeps theories alive and lively is being responsible and responsive to the world's patternings and murmurings. Doing theory requires being open to the world's aliveness, allowing oneself to be lured by curiosity, surprise, and wonder. Theories are not mere metaphysical pronouncements on the world from some presumed position of exteriority. Theories are living and breathing reconfigurings of the world. The world theorizes as well as experiments with itself. Figuring, reconfiguring."[65] Barad's points us to an idea of theory that begins with touch as a figure for staying present and open to surprise encounters with unexpected materials, and her list alerts us to the importance of juxtaposing objects—to taxonomizing the untaxonomizable—as a way to think in ever more lively ways toward ever more lively and larger horizons.

Entirely predictably (promiscuously), these materialities collapse into each other and escape the bounds of the chapters I have (inevitably, taxonomically) assigned to them—as fermentation produces intoxication or, as in the view of nineteenth-century microbiologists, ferment blurs into rot. Similarly, in some of these chapters, gelatinous textures describe rotting material or, alternately, the joyful give and play of group of bodies adhering to each other in shared movement, their isolated embodiments decaying into shared and even intoxicating sensory presence. These are affective, material, and aesthetic groupings that weave and dodge through an eclectic historical archive but persistently return to a set of four recurrent tropes: In the first, they are almost inevitably connected to the registering of—sensing but not necessarily representing—the massed bodies of politically subaltern peoples in and through forms whose own textural qualities are rendered politically salient through their manifestation as movement under stress or pressure.[66] Second, the apprehension of these categories serves as the mark of the presence of *dissensus* within Rancière's distribution of the sensible.[67] As I show, the gelatinous, for instance, is apprehended via such disorderly sensory registers as haptic encounters with sonic or vibrational kinematic motion made material, flavorful textural touch or mouthfeel, or the aural presence of onomatopoeic textuality.

The third trope that haunts ferment, jelly, intoxicants, and rot is the question of a quality of crowd or mass energy, the potential for mass political insurgency that is postulated to be inherent to the bodies of those subjects understood as proximate to these materialities; in this way, for instance, ferment can be understood as virtuality or possibility. Fourth and finally, these categories emerge as the limit of aesthetic tolerance, as and with a disgust provoked by proximity to or the touching of a material or sensation that, in its capacity for movement, registers as a seemingly disordered sensuality. Ferment, jelly, intoxicants, and rot are thus materialities, but they are also minor categories of political aesthetics not only because, in Sianne Ngai's words, they fail to consistently attract the attention of disciplinary formations but also because, in their dissident sensory organization, they exist as the underbelly, or the political remains, of aesthetics itself.[68] But as I show, all of these textural qualities, whether they adhere to a single material, a subject, or a space—and sometimes precisely because they do not—tend to signify toward something being off, strange, deviant.

1

HYGIENE

As a scholar and theorist of biopower who has sought to situate the workings of biopower within the very particular detailed political and historical framework of the United States, I have often pointed to and referenced its disciplinary interlocutors and its nonstate coconspirators. At some point, however, I realized that I had never really touched the state: I might make claims about its impact, but I rarely picked up the legislative archive or the archives of other institutions that worked to define the normative political flavor of the United States. Certainly before this project, I had never asked of those archives the same questions I asked of film or art or visual print culture or literature. My first tangible encounter with the state, the archive into which this book delves is perhaps a strange one: the first approximately forty-five years of circulars, bulletins, and yearbooks of the US Department of Agriculture (USDA), its extension and experiment stations, and then finally and in particular a small working group inside the department, initially called the Bureau of Chemistry. In this archive, an odd one for someone trained in the humanities, my long-standing interest in historicizing biopower drives my readings: I engage biopower here as a force that not only seeks to shape desires and produces subject-effects in populations but also works to order the world into hierarchies of animate and inanimate matter that affiliate and map onto racial hierarchies—and into related hierarchies of the human and nonhuman.[1]

The archive reveals its secrets, however. In it, we find that hygiene is a diffuse political strategy that emerged as a new disciplinary force in politics, following the rise of Pasteurian microbiology and agricultural chemistry as state science projects.[2] Following Latour's early work on hygiene in France, I trace the US context here, putting that work into deeper conversation with the highly racialized, racist, and settler-colonial nature of US politics. As I show, hygiene infused the US state and its associated political actors by bringing the idea of infectious, fermenting, proliferating, and putrefying microscopic nonhuman cellular life—and therefore *energy itself*—into its view as a simultaneously cellular *and* population-level force that had to be managed, directed, and contained. Progressive-era management defined itself against this force, as containment, cleanliness, rationality, and measured objectivity. Within this framework, which built on the recent adaptation of thermodynamic physics into the politics and philosophy of work, population energy came to be understood as a form of matter, and matter was recategorized in terms of its ability to produce or express population energy. Hygiene, I argue, is an atmosphere, an affective-cum-aesthetic strategy that sneakily penetrated political discourse across the scale from the microscopic management of human and nonhuman life up to the level of federal print culture and its actors. Simultaneously, it shaped the administrative workings of an associative state that includes scientists, scholars, universities, medical organizations, and others. By looking at hygiene in the context of the Department of Agriculture and in the workings of the bureau charged with taxonomizing the chemical, microbiological, and this affective life of the nation, I demonstrate how securitization as a biopolitical project involves the management of not simply material resources but also population energy, precisely because in the eyes of microbiology and its affiliated sciences, *the two are the same.*

Before turning to the archive of the USDA, I want to nuance the particular flavor of police power that is the hygienic state. Taking off from Dean Spade's and others' engagement with the banality (and therefore seriousness) of administrative violence, the remainder of this chapter examines the sorts of affective and aesthetic modes that the logistical life of the state positively produces. Scholars of intellectual history trace the emergence of rationality and objectivity as epistemic shifts in the history of science that specifically defined themselves against aesthetics. Engaging a Foucauldian lens, Lorraine Daston and Peter Galison, for instance, describe the separation of science from art in the nineteenth century:

> In notable contrast to earlier views held from the Renaissance through the Enlightenment about the close analogies between artistic and scientific work, the public personas of artist and scientist polarized during this period. . . . In 1866, the Paris Academie des Sciences praised the geologist Aimé Civil's panoramic photographs of the Alps for "faithful representa-

> tions of the accidents" of the earth's surface, which would be "deplorable" in art but which "must be [the goal] towards which the reproduction of scientific objects tends." The scientific self of the mid-nineteenth century was perceived by contemporaries as diametrically opposed to the artistic self, just as scientific images were routinely contrasted to artistic ones.[3]

This "scientific self," according to Daston and Galison, evinced a "self-denying passivity, which might be described as a will to willessness. The only way for the active self to attain the desired receptivity to nature was to turn its domineering will inward—to practice self-discipline, self-restraint, self-abnegation, self-annihilation, and a multitude of other techniques of self-imposed selflessness. . . . By a process of algebraic cancellation, the negating of subjectivity by the subject became objectivity."[4] Commitment to what Daston and Galison call "mechanical objectivity" in mid- to late nineteenth-century science accompanied the growth of norms of comportment that were explicitly opposed to aesthetic production and aligned with what we might loosely call the minimization of the self.[5] This scientific self (supposedly) approached the world without interference from such bothersome phenomena as subjectivity, particularity, or selfhood to produce scientific knowledge.[6] The frames of state power that leaned heavily on science (and the forms of science that drew heavily on state power, such as agricultural sciences) drew on these affective norms, producing, in their conscious opposition to the aesthetic, forms of expression defined by a paradoxically antiaesthetic aesthetics.

As I discussed in the introduction, Mitchell Dean begins to name this bureaucratic style, in a deeply writerly and readerly way, as "technologies of notation, recording, compiling, presenting and transporting of information."[7] My argument here is that from within the everyday life of logistics and governance, the state's technologies of notation encompass an aesthetic project that disguises itself as not-aesthetic, that norms its own modes of feeling to propose that rationality is not an affective pose. In a critique of political aesthetics grounded in queer of color critique, Manalansan identifies the activity grounding this technology of notation as a tool of hygienic civility: "Measurement, as a set of techniques and methods, is embedded in the ideals of Western objective science and a clear-eyed (tidy) bourgeois view of the world. Hygiene, census, and anthropometric measurements were regimens of control and power. . . .

Measures and the various units of measuration still play a major part of imposing a hegemonic worldview that domesticates wild things and clears away the debris of superstition, sexual deviance, and ideological insurgency."[8] Measurement, as Manalansan uses it, also most closely resembles the language used in the law to wed the idea of objectivity to the proper performance of judgmental affect, that is, *reasonableness*.[9] This suturing of the concrete idea of the fact and the seemingly objective to the very intangibility of a hegemonic affective register is part of what guarantees that measurement, as it is undertaken by the sciences and the social sciences, and reasonableness, as it is enacted by the state itself, are able to perform their particular violences: the seemingly picayune daily functioning of administration creates, in the aggregate, an aura or spirit that dominates or infects the daily life of a bordered space (a nation, perhaps a state, perhaps even just a single institution).

The dryness of the form, the impassivity of "take a number," the gradual accumulation of state objects and processes, and their aesthetic imperatives, produces something like an affective atmosphere, in which hygienic policing and population energy management are both normative and an avenue through which certain disciplinary violences are rendered normal. An aesthetic that claims to be not an aesthetic and an affect that denies that it is an affect, hygiene crucially engages both affect and aesthetics to exert covert biopolitical power; hygiene is, in short, one word for the affective and aesthetic register through which the state comes to be experienced *as* a state. It is mild, moderate, and true, distanced from intense feeling and therefore seductively persuasive of its own innocence. It is clean: emptied of character and subjectivity, objective.

Dean's and Manalansan's respective readings of the everydayness of normative state aesthetics align with contemporary discussions of state power as diffuse and decentralized, as cohering largely around logistical practices and infrastructures that are refined by repetition, often over a period of centuries. Answering the question of whether the state is a unitary object that may be referred to in the singular for the purposes of analysis, Patrick Joyce and Chandra Mukerji write,

> The state is extensive, diffuse, and experimental because it is always being pushed to change by political circumstances. State logistical power is

> both impersonal and material, and thus, it is particularly hard to articulate and thereby to criticize. The power of the state is mostly experienced outside discourse and *below the level of conscious awareness, in the habitus, and the shared practices of life created by logistical governance.* The state's material effects lend strongly to its naturalization, the perception of it as a single, overarching "thing." The inarticulacy of its sociomaterial power makes state practices serve as a context or a landscape in which political action takes place. Thus it is easy to reduce the state to its sites: post offices, law courts, legislatures, highway systems, etc.[10]

Joyce and Mukerji's essay points to the idea that the state is less a unitary body than the *feeling* that it is a unitary body, a shared orientation shaped by logistical practices distributed across the state's multiple governance sites. As they unite, one key experience of the state is depersonalization—but not in the sense that a bureaucrat may be referred to as "faceless." Rather, "The materiality of the state depersonalizes power far more than bureaucratization. Even faceless bureaucrats are more personable than computers, canals, roads, and sewers. And it makes little sense to blow up a sewer because you hate the government if you live where that sewer operates. So, the state becomes complicitous in everyday life *through things*. The power of habits turns into the powers of the state."[11] Joyce and Mukerji's invocation of habit, habitus, and context as a "landscape" that operates "below the level of conscious awareness" echoes Manalansan's invocation of measurement, civility, and hygiene as "spirit, aura, mythology."[12] All of these authors reach for languages to describe how a state can produce or perform a feeling, create (in the terms of affect theory) an "atmosphere."

A state, Joyce and Mukerji theorize, is not a "thing" but a "feeling" that is produced in objects and practice, in the doing and redoing of everyday life. In this analysis, the *things* produced by the state—or, even more specifically, the *things* produced along the regulatory or normative lines legislated by the state—themselves serve as effective signposts of the state's predilection for depersonalization and abstraction precisely because they are objects. In this way, these objects aesthetically stand in for what in other methodological contexts might be referred to as ideology but in fact exceeds ideology to become the aesthetic condition of state politicity that, in Joyce and Mukerji's words, proves "particularly hard to articulate and thereby to criticize" precisely because they are everywhere and nowhere.[13] This everywhereness, the atmospheric nature of infrastructure, is the condition for the primary challenge of trying to articulate and analyze the aesthetics of the state: the language of power in liberal democracy tends to assume that power rests in the hands of its agents, but in fact it is environmental, banal, a precondition of movement through the spaces and structures of a defined nation-space. Power becomes impossible to make tangible, finite, and describable.

Drawing on these and other theorists, in *Deviant Matter*, I am trying to develop a language for what it feels like to face the aggressive and sometimes debilitating effects—that is to say, affects—that accompany hygiene as a normative political atmosphere and to begin to unwind hygiene's history and operating logics. Ultimately, I hope to expand what we mean when we say the word "hygiene": to understand it as a mode of governance that begins in science but ultimately finds resonance with diffuse forms of affective and aesthetic violence. "Moderation," "reasonableness," and "hygiene" describe affective and aesthetic orientations that accompany the everyday working of the state and nonstate actors who enact the quotidian work of administrative violence. Elsewhere, Tavia Nyong'o and I, writing together, called this orientation "civility": "Civility is not care, but it pretends to be; civility is the affective shape of administrative violence. It is the velvet glove around the iron claw; it is the rationality of logistics. Civility discourse enforces a false equation between incivility and violence that works to mask everyday violence as a civic norm. The violence that is polite is thrice as damaging as the direct attack because it gaslights as it wounds."[14] In the fourth of our eleven theses in that essay, we argued that a state can have a form and a feel: "Civility is a political aesthetic that obscures its politicity by asserting that it is 'only' an aesthetic or a style. It is thus an aesthetic that is served by the assertion that aesthetics and politics are separate realms. Civility, particularly as it defends the separation of aesthetics from politics—or history—within institutional structures such as the university, is ultimately invested in the work of defending civilizational racism."[15] We also questioned the inherent connections between rationality and the inherent good of the civic, the civil, and the work of the state; more precisely, we sought to outline how the state's claims to inherent goodness—through claims to reasonableness, rationality, and order—inherently function to obscure forms of violence. *Deviant Matter* builds out from these ideas. But while in the following four chapters, I explore the cultural life of different forms of deviance, specifically as they are embedded in forms of materiality that defy hygienic containment, in this chapter, I examine how hygienic civility came to be the normative affective orientation of bureaucratic functioning in the specific instance of the US Department of Agriculture, I do so to seek a clearer language to describe what it feels like to experience state and institutional violence at the affective (which is to say, at the aesthetic) level. What, in other words, is the sensory life of administrative violence; how does hygiene work its aesthetic logic against the embodiment of deviant peoples? And in what archives of practice might we find the evidence of these historical phenomena?[16] Does hygiene leave aesthetic traces behind? Are state archives aesthetic objects? Do state print cultures, like other forms of writing, render affective experience? Are they a genre? Does a state give off a feeling, and does that feeling have form? And, in particular, how can we account for the diffusion of state and other disciplinary power into other realms of living? How does a state come to *feel like a state* even when there is no particular singular actor or object to whom or to which one can attach that feeling?

Foucault, of course, laid out the idea of normativity as a practice of governmentality, and scholars continue to write the historical specificity of its applications across various historical periods and geographies.[17] In the context of the United States, Roderick Ferguson's work delves into the way demography, quantification, and taxonomization—which is to say sociology, statistics, and science—became the normative disciplinary frames through which the United States of America or, even more particularly, various agencies posed their policies as universally applicable to their citizens, simultaneously producing categories of criminal particularity and deviance through which they successfully reinstated and justified state racism in the postemancipation United States. Ferguson's *Aberrations in Black* documents how disciplinary sociology made heteronormativity an analytic tool against which the hygienic state consistently judged Black citizens to be culturally inferior, always already "deviant."[18] Given sociology's self-designated mission to both diagnose *and* correct a society's ills and given the centrality of the applied social sciences to regulatory and reform-focused state policies under Progressivism, it seems worth considering how the rise of the social sciences in the period from the last decade of the nineteenth century—when the first chair in sociology was filled in 1892 at the University of Chicago—also parallels the rapid growth of the state's investment in what a contemporary reader would recognize as modern scientific research.[19] Both of these disciplinary shifts were accompanied by two normative epistemes that we might also associate with particular norms of affective embodiment—rationality and objectivity—against which the deviant, particularly in the subject-object scene of sociological study, was posed.

* * *

The rise of a regulatory state—as opposed to a state system that relied largely on private litigation—followed the growth of the Department of Agriculture, and the USDA and its regulatory brethren were largely the product of progressive political movements. We might ask, What are the consequences of the alignment of progressive regimes with regulation, and how does regulation—in particular a regulatory culture that performed its entitlement to manage biopolitical life forces through a culture of scientism—effect an affective schema that might ultimately lay the foundation for the cultural and political struggles of the late twentieth and early twenty-first century?[20] As I discuss in the next section, I am interested in how the Department of Agriculture's expressly settler-colonial project—in relation to the expansion of US borders across the Indigenous nations whose sovereign lands were soon to become manageable, extractable "farmland"—might also be tied into this affective project. Is a science-driven expansionist project inherently driven by a logic of affective management, and does this have implications for thinking with matter? It is here that I want to turn to think more closely with the archive of the Department of Agriculture, surely the federal bureaucratic structure that most closely aligned itself with the growth of science as a state project.

The act establishing the Department of Agriculture was signed into legislation on May 15, 1862, five days before the passage of the Homestead Act and two months before the passage of the Morrill Act.[21] The Homestead Act laid out the terms by which "unsettled" land would be seized from Indigenous peoples and nations and handed over to "men who had not ever raised arms against the federal government"—not Confederates, that is. These men would receive the land for free provided they "develop" it. Passed at the same time, the Morrill Act made it possible for states to establish public universities and agricultural colleges funded by the development or sale of federal grants of land, provided that they were focused on agriculture. A natural complement to the Homestead Act, the Morrill Act marked the rise of large, state-sponsored, public postsecondary institutions whose primary focus would be training farmers—the men who claimed land through the Homestead Act—to increase agricultural growth, yield, and profitability for the nation through scientific management. The Morrill Act benefited all postsecondary institutions in the United States, as older eastern colleges and universities took advantage of the act to sell land in order to finance their own agricultural research centers.

Scholars of settler colonialism have noted the immediate and causal relationship between the passage of the Homestead and Morrill Acts and the displacement of hundreds of sovereign Indigenous nations. As the Pulitzer-funded "Investigating Land Grants to Universities" project documents, "The Morrill Act gave 79,461 parcels of Indigenous lands, totaling about 10,700,000 acres, to 52 land-grant universities to fund their endowments."[22] Native studies scholars have also documented the relationship between racial capitalism, settler colonialism, and the concepts of land ownership and value extraction embedded in the very project of agriculture in the West. Alyosha Goldstein writes, "Agriculture as a relation to land based on domestication, possession, and commerce has long been a means and justification for colonization in what is now the United States. This is an agriculture in which the sociality of land is illegible and epistemologies of conquest appear to evacuate land of its unruly animacies. State agencies, perpetually embroiled in partisan divides and bureaucratic convolution, serve both as mechanisms of dispossession and as occasional proxies for establishing ostensible limits to the most flagrant racist practices of contemporary capitalism."[23] As Goldstein demonstrates, capitalism's history of enclosure and conquest as expressed through western expansion deepened the relationship between whiteness and property by handing land to the "already-free" subjects in 1862 who were entitled to migrate west and claim land as their right, while most enslaved people were still not-free and therefore unable to access that same land. In doing so, the state facilitated an ethos of extraction—of profit, of energy, of capital—from the land but also secured land possession as a property of whiteness by only offering the right to extract to northern whites. Passed precisely during the moment that a war was being fought to ostensibly "free" the single largest source of forced labor in the history of the West but *before* many of those people were free, the Morrill and Homestead Acts glaringly reveal which racialized subjects were organically entitled to own and extract from the land that became the United States. The enormous scientific, educational, and administrative project birthed and put to the service of facilitating that extraction process only underlines the similar co-imbrication of modern scientific knowledge with whiteness itself.

That co-imbrication was not new to the mid-nineteenth century. The literature on the relationship between colonialism and science is now vast and rich, beginning with historical work into early-modern European exploration and continuing throughout the taxonomical and botanical exploration projects of the eighteenth and nineteenth centuries.[24] Many of these studies trace the centrality of plant and medicine bioprospecting to the race to colonize and then set up extractive economies from the Americas by European powers. Other work notes the centrality of scientific thinking (to botanical taxonomies, for instance) to developing and legitimizing ideas of racial hierarchy.[25] In the context of the establishment of the federal Department of Agriculture, science as an evolving body of knowledge was centrally linked to the settler-colonial project of the United States: as I have shown, the state specifically set up the Morrill Act to fund agricultural research and funded the "experiment stations" where agricultural data was both extracted and concocted in and through the displacement of sovereign Indigenous nations.

Londa Schiebinger makes explicit the links to these modern formations when she notes that from the seventeenth century forward, "botanical sciences served the colonial enterprise and were, in turn, structured by it. . . . The sixteen hundred botanical gardens that Europeans had founded worldwide by the end of the eighteenth century were not merely idyllic bits of green intended to delight city dwellers, but *experimental stations for agriculture* and way stations for plant acclimatization for domestic and global trade, rare medicaments, and cash crops."[26] Schiebinger's work is particularly notable for demonstrating how even botanical classification and nomenclature organized itself as a form of what she terms "linguistic imperialism," mapping and therefore colonizing the plant life of the Americas and other colonial and settler-colonial spaces simply by aggressively seizing the right to name them. "Never a modest man," Schiebinger writes, "Linnaeus fancied himself a lawgiver bringing order to the botanical commonwealth threatened by the 'invasion' of 'vast hordes' of foreign plants and their 'barbarous' names."[27]

While the project of naming new plant species might have seemed to be largely in the past, the Department of Agriculture's early documentation in the 1860s is similarly taxonomic, albeit scattered and disorganized in its early phases. The early print culture of the Department of Agriculture simply sought to centralize and quantify scientific knowledge and agriculture possibilities of the sizable portion of a continent, with the clear goal of normalizing and regulating the path for produce to travel from farm to domestic and international agricultural markets. Early annual reports from the department, each of them almost eight hundred pages long, do not include tables of contents and display no obvious organizing principle: articles describing the agricultural possibilities of various states are followed by essays on apples, horses, hogs, and machinery and some reports back from scientists such as entomologists. Indeed, Wilbur Atwater, later the first director of Agricultural Experiment Stations, commented on the lack of organization of these early attempts to chart the nation in print culture. He spent the early pages of the experiment station report trying vainly to establish what the print culture of the experiment stations office would be:

> This summary of experiment stations reports is itself an experiment. The object has been to reflect as accurately and fully as might be the accounts which the stations have rendered of their work. To this end, . . . a topical arrangement would perhaps be more logical, and may be followed in later publications. . . .
>
> It will also be observed that the widely varying ideas as to what the annual reports of the station should contain are reflected in these summaries. It seems desirable that the stations should reach some consensus as to what shall be included in their annual reports. Until this is done the compilations of station work made by this office can hardly attain a satisfactory degree of uniformity and orderly arrangement. . . .
>
> The reports of the individual stations herein given have been arranged according to States in alphabetical order.[28]

Uniformity, then, described as a project of orderliness, was a management goal of the departments and experiment stations but not one they reached right away. While the department grappled with taxonomizing its own taxonomies, from these early years, quantification still remained the primary work of the department, making order and quantification synonymous. And indeed, from 1862, in the first broadly circulated report of the secretary of agriculture, keeping track of levels of agricultural yield and rates of increase are central concerns of the department. In 1864, the commissioner of agriculture Isaac Newton (actual name) summarized the goals of the department as such:

1. The collection of statistics pertaining to annual crops
2. The preparation of tables of the exports of domestic produce and their value. The receipt, shipments, and prices of this produce at the cities chiefly trading in it.
3. The collection of information on general and important topics bearing on agricultural production
4. The preparation of monthly and bimonthly reports.[29]

All of this information, the secretary noted, would be tabulated and the annual reports completed when "returns" or profits were calculated of the prices for all goods, by November of that year. As one correspondent lyrically wrote of mutton sheep yields in 1867, "Profits are the golden beacon which guide the farmer's course."[30] The goal, the secretary states, was to give the farmer the information he needed to regulate his supply according to demand. In addition, the department sought to gather general information related to agriculture, for instance, about effective fertilization, animal husbandry, and so forth. And yet, unenumerated but throughout the report, the secretary also demonstrates that the department has a fifth and essential job: "No part of the duties of this department is more important or more laborious than that of collecting, compiling, and publishing the statistics of the agriculture of the country. This, after two year of experience has been systematized with thorough and comprehensive order."[31] He later continues, "These objects demand a publication such as the monthly and bimonthly reports of this department. . . . It is a laborious task because of the great variety of statical tables required, and the numerous calculations embraced in them; and it is a responsible labor, not only because of the knowledge of agriculture and statistics which it requires but on account of the effect which these tables exert over the commercial business of the country."[32] We are deep here into the archive of the "technologies of notation" that make up both governance and governmentality. It seems worth paying attention to Newton's repeated use of the word "laborious" (perhaps because "boring" was a term he might not have been allowed to use). Five years into the life of the Department of Agriculture, order, quantification, and management had begun to create their own affective and aesthetic effects: bureaucratic tedium.

Emmanuel Didier has demonstrated that the Department of Agriculture was one of the centers where statistical modes of governance developed in the late nineteenth-century United States. In particular, the department solidified the concept and practice of random sampling. While Didier tracks a more participatory version of statistics in the early work of the Department of Agriculture, he demonstrates how, across the periods between the 1880s and the Great Depression, the turn to "random sampling" of "representative groups" replaced participatory modes of governance and even participatory modes of information and statistical gathering. Instead, the department practiced a form of statistical expertise based on secrecy: "random" and "anonymized" data seemed to be in the service of a social "science" but obscured both the purposes and ends to which the data would be put. Interestingly, Didier aligns these "secret" or "confidential" methods with precisely the rise of objectivity that he charts: "Government action was from now on guided by the social sciences based on facts that could rightly be termed 'neutral' in the sense that they were factual and *free from all contamination by public opinion*. . . . Statistical objectivity is not a way of forgetting politics, of distancing oneself from partisan arguments, of letting nature eventually settle disputes between human beings. . . . Each method of objectivity brings with it a certain manner, in opposition to others, of bringing together the population, the government, and the means of knowledge—an operation that constitutes a political ideal."[33] Initially privately funded and then permanently funded by a state appropriation, the first agriculture experiment station at Wesleyan, established in 1872, concretized the centrality of science to the work of the Department of Agriculture. Much inspired by Justus von Liebig's agricultural experiment stations in Germany, which were committed to researching and improving European agricultural yield, this movement had chemistry at its center, and many of its most important actors were American scientists who had trained in Germany, the global center for the study of agricultural chemistry.

Wilbur O. Atwater, an agricultural chemist who had himself done postdoctoral work in Berlin and Leipzig after receiving a PhD for his nine-page thesis on corn at Yale University in 1869, was appointed the first director of experiment stations. In Germany, Atwater had made a study of Liebig's European experiment stations, and he modeled the US stations on them by similarly focusing their research on promoting agricultural yield and on supporting farmers with the best and most recent scientific information. Atwater began his work in 1875 at the Connecticut experiment station, and by 1889, he had been appointed as director of experiment stations at the national level. The first bulletin of the experiment station stated the problem thus: "The work being done by European stations is equally needed in the United States, and is already begun in obedience to an imperative public demand. The decay of agriculture in the older States, the deterioration of soils in the first-settled group of new States, the rapid absorption of public lands, and the increasing competition of Russia and India in the food-markets of the world, have strongly arrested public attention. The conviction has become general that waste must be checked and productiveness increased."[34] Experiment stations were initially funded by the land sales made possible by the Morrill Act and then by a special appropriations bill in 1875 that apportioned $15,000 to each state.[35] What seems to have changed with the rise of the experiment station is the centrality of scientific teams focused on developing fertilizer to the research and education project of the stations. Rather than simply tabulating yield every November (as earlier reports had done), by 1888 there were forty-five experiment stations, and most of them hosted a multidisciplinary team largely led by chemists but also including biologists, physicists, entomologists, and mycologists.[36] All of them conducted and published experiments meant to "increase production at a decreased cost, and at the same time to preserve the fertility of our soils."[37]

While the knowledge—never mind the print culture—produced by these experiment stations grew exponentially year by year, this expansion outward at the level of literal ground covered accompanied a biochemical focus on smaller and smaller units of analysis, such as soil health; led by agricultural chemists, the chemical composition of fertilizer compounds became of primary importance. Atwater in particular led the way, seemingly inspired by Liebig's own career trajectory, to connect the analysis of agriculture at the national level to understanding human energy at the individual level through biochemical analysis of food and energy production and expenditure. The human body, in short, become an object of statistical study, inserted into the larger machine of food and energy production that Atwater was also helping to manage at the agricultural scale.

Nick Cullather writes, "In the early part of the twentieth century, 'food' lost its subjective, cultural character and evolved into a material instrument of statecraft. To do so, it had to be quantifiable."[38] As his numerous publications analyzing food for both humans and as animal feed show, Atwater was at the heart of the emergence of the calorie into a tool for population management and in fact helped concretize the fundamental ideas of caloric intake that remain in use today. Writes Cullather, "Europeans first measured food in calories, but Americans constructed the calorie by giving it practical value, standardizing it and embedding it in systems of distribution and administration."[39] Under Atwater, the calorie gained traction as the premier mechanism for calculating human energy consumption and expenditure.

The calorie, thus, also became a primary mechanism for inserting the human body into what Cara Daggett has described as the Victorian period's "new energy cosmology": a period in which, drawing on newly articulated laws of physics, energy became visible as a quantifiable and measurable object. Further, Daggett argues, this new physics, which they called "thermodynamics," was both defined by and came to be put to the work of explaining and defining work itself. Atwater's own work at the turn of the twentieth century bears this out. Daggett writes, "Energy as we know it in the social sciences, as a sign for fuel, is a modern invention. . . . Energy has a long-standing moral and etymological connection to work, which gets imported into thermodynamics, with significant political effects. . . . As a Victorian science, thermodynamics lent natural, and even cosmological, validation to the industrial project and its celebration of work. Additionally, work, exemplified in the Victorian era by the steam engine, came to be governed as a site of energy transformation."[40]

At the heart of the idea of the calorie is the first law of thermodynamics: no energy in a closed system is lost; it is only ever transformed. While a calorie is strictly speaking the amount of energy (or heat) that it takes to heat one gram of water one degree centigrade, through Atwater's own work, the calorie came to be understood as, in his words, "fuel." As he said, speaking of the body, "The machine needs fuel": "Heat and muscular power, like mechanical power, light, and electricity, are forms of energy. The energy is latent in the food and is developed as the food is consumed in the body. We call it potential energy and measure its quantity as we measure quantities of heat or of mechanical power. In other words, the value of food for fuel is expressed in terms of potential energy. The quantities of potential energy in food materials are determined by the calorimeter."[41]

Atwater expanded on this connection between food and the laws of energy in another publication:

> The later development of experimental science has given us clearer ideas not only of the chemical, but also of the physical changes that take place in the animal and in the plant. To these processes it has become customary to apply the term metabolism. The processes of metabolism in the body are of two definite but closely allied kinds—the metabolism of matter and the metabolism of energy. . . .
>
> Food has two chief functions—to build tissue and serve as fuel. In the building of tissue from food and in the constant breaking up and repair of tissue we have to do with the metabolism of matter. In the service of food and of tissue material as fuel, to yield heat and muscular power, we have to do with the metabolism of energy.[42]

The question of metabolism, as Atwater indicates, brought together biology, chemistry, and physics as sciences interested in the nature and uses of energy. At Wesleyan, where he was a professor of chemistry, Atwater spent years doing experiments in what he called the "respirometer" or the "calorimeter," putting male subjects into a large metal box and measuring the amount of food and beverages that the subject consumed and then measuring feces, urine, and carbon-dioxide emissions to calculate how much energy was extracted from each food item, tracking and recording the efficiency of energy consumption. Drawing on Liebig's theories, "metabolism" became the word that describes the processes through which humans interfaced with, and extracted the fuel they needed from, the nonhuman world.

Against these extractable forms of matter, which Atwater and his colleagues in the USDA defined as "food," they came to see other kinds of matter—food from which energy could not easily be extracted, like bones or various forms of cellulose—as not nutritive and therefore waste. Additionally, bodily responses to food that interfered with efficient functioning, like the discomfort brought about from "fermentation" or "gas" in the intestines, or intoxication itself, were seen as signs of inefficient food absorption and therefore inefficient bodies: a good man, in other words, could hold his liquor and his gas. At a more popular level, however, and through another office of the Department of Agriculture, the Bureau of Chemistry, other kinds of consumable matter came under chemical examination and therefore regulatory purview, specifically medicine, narcotics, and alcohol, resulting in the first legislation meant to manage consumption at a national level: the Food and Drug Act of 1906.

The Food and Drug Act (FDA) was passed in 1906 as a result of a protracted battle in Congress between food manufacturers and food reformers. One of the early acts of the Progressive era, the FDA helped usher in the regulatory era of US government, shifting the nation's dominant juridical paradigm away from constant litigation and toward state regulation. It is important to recognize the taken-for-granted conjoining of food and drugs as it appears in the title of the law: food *and* drugs, a conjunction that points to how the USDA not only had extended its taxonomic work into the realm of consumables themselves but was beginning the work of separating those consumables into these categorical poles: food (energy) and drugs (medicine and narcotics). What the enormous retaxonomization project undertaken by state science ultimately did, then, was not only reclassify and reorder food and other consumable forms of matter in relation to what kinds of energy they might or might not produce but also ultimately work to legislate which forms of matter—drugs and other intoxicants—would be illegal in such a way as to facilitate the recapture of emancipated Black life and energy by the carceral state. And of course, what was also rendered illegal were those forms of energy that could not seemingly be recuperated by work.

For instance, and as I discuss further in chapter 3, at the turn of twentieth century, one of the key figures in the pure food and drug fight—the American Medical Association (AMA)—joined forces with elected legislators and the Department of Agriculture (specifically the Bureau of Chemistry) to pass a bill to shut down the enormous trade in patent or proprietary medicines. Largely narcotic or alcoholic concoctions available over the counter to any consumer, patent remedies advertised grand claims—curing cancer, venereal disease, sinusitis, flu, and various other ailments—and were enormously profitable and entirely unregulated. The Bureau of Chemistry and the AMA sought to make it illegal for patent remedy makers, food producers, and others to falsely label and advertise their products and to make false claims about the curative powers of their products and sought to require by federal law that food and remedy producers list all ingredients on labels. At the same time, the AMA simultaneously succeeded in seizing regulatory control over all medical advertising: soon after the law's passage, it became impossible to advertise drugs except in the *Journal of the American Medical Association*, and soon after that the AMA also claimed the right to classify and control dispensary access to what it termed "medicinal" or "ethical" drugs in the United States.

In order to pass the Food and Drug Act, the AMA also joined forces with a few other key groups. Temperance advocates were obvious partners, but the AMA also recruited Harvey H. Wiley, the first chief of the Bureau of Chemistry which was located within the Department of Agriculture. For almost thirty years, Wiley had waged such a vigorous campaign against "adulterated" or mislabeled foods that the Food and Drug Act was at times called the Wiley Act. Crucially, the AMA also joined forces with muckraking journalists, who were themselves waging a campaign to seize back editorial control of their newspapers and magazines from those same patent remedy advertisers.

In 1905, for instance, *Collier's Magazine* published a series of articles by Samuel Hopkins Adams in which he drew attention to the narcotic dangers of patent remedies such as Peruna, Paine's Celery Compound, Duffy's Malt Whiskey, Ayer's Sarsparilla, and Orangeine headache powder. Published in the year leading up to and during the congressional debates surrounding the FDA, Adams's nine articles accused patent and proprietary remedy manufacturers variously of making "dopes" of their consumers by promising cures that never came and of "doping" the consumer with various alcoholic and narcotic (and not at all medicinal) formulations, from the 28 percent alcohol in the Peruna Catarrh liquid to the 50 percent in Duffy's Malt Whiskey.

Establishing the line between alcoholic beverages and curative medicine was critically important to Adams, and the blurriness of that line caused him no small anxiety. In his major tirade against patent remedies, *The Great American Fraud*, Adams wrote,

> A distinguished public health official and medical writer once made this jocular suggestion to me:
>
> "Let us buy in large quantities the cheapest Italian vermouth, poor gin and bitters. We will mix them in the proportion of three of vermouth to two of gin, with a dash of bitters, dilute and bottle them by the short quart, label them 'Smith's Reviver and Blood Purifier'; advertise them to cure erysipelas, bunions, dyspepsia, heat rash, fever and ague, and consumption; and to prevent loss of hair, smallpox, old age, sunstroke and near-sightedness, and make our everlasting fortunes selling them to the temperance trade."
>
> "That sounds to me very much like a cocktail," said I.
>
> "So it is," he replied. "But it's just as much a medicine as Peruna and not as bad a drink."[43]

Most of the articles in *The Great American Fraud* detail either the misbranding or the doping practices of American patent remedies, such as putting opium and morphine in children's medicine.

The last article in Adams's series, however, made a very different, though related argument: it argued for the need to loosen the control that patent remedy manufacturers had on journalism through their advertising dollars, and it presented evidence that patent remedy interests had suppressed journalistic coverage of anti-patent-medicine legislation as well as any stories detrimental to or critical of their interests—fairly well-documented practices at the time. The patent and proprietary advertising budget was so huge and the industry advertised so broadly that it had become enormously powerful; often, according to Adams, patent remedy makers regularly forced editors and publishers to sign contracts limiting what publications would cover politically or argue editorially.

On a very basic level, these disparate interests came together because they were invested in something like what I have come to call "hygiene." But the archive offers an additional motive or interest that further clarifies what the aesthetic work of hygiene is: a large-scale effort to normalize what the journalists and editors aligned with the hygienists might have called "truth" (as in "truth in advertising"), what Wiley would have called "non-adulteration," and what we, belatedly, might call "realism," in its most limited definition as a transparent relation between language and what is empirically observable. The journalistic imperative to realism and truth—to not making "dopes" of readers—converged in this moment with the reordering of consumables into toxic and not-toxic, or "doping" and "pure" substances, drawing a direct line between this thin reading of realism as a claim to objectivity, truth, and cognitive sobriety itself.

In short, at the moment of the burgeoning consolidation of federal regulatory power and alongside the entry into the juridical sphere of a new microbiopolitics of matter, there emerged a larger shift in the dominant aesthetics of the moment and then, in turn, in a deeper penetration of the regulatory state into the cognitive and affective life of nation. This new microbiopolitics aligned itself with both the instantiation of a new administrative federal culture and a general aesthetic reorientation toward what we have come to recognize as realism or, as I discussed earlier, objectivity, rationality, and reasonableness. In this moment, then, we can trace a line from the entry of active and lively material life into scientific and popular discourse to representational and aesthetic structures, from macropolitical forms of administrative governance through to the affective and sensory modes—sobriety and intoxication, for instance—that define and discipline the citizenship form as well as its state-based analogs.

Latour here helps me to think further about this question of the relation between politics, affect, and aesthetics. In the introduction to *The Pasteurization of France*, Latour argues that a host of historical players who are primed for Pasteur's science make Pasteur's discoveries legible; their ability to use germ theory to their own political ends enables them to unify and advocate for their own social theories about hygiene, medical science, and social policy. Latour, discussing his own archive of scientific journals and magazines, writes, "The boundaries of hygiene are vague, and this vagueness is precisely what allows its practitioners to express more or less everyone's interests, and very soon, those of the Pasteurians. . . . Hygienists are all those who call themselves hygienists. Hygiene in the *Revue Scientifique* can be defined as a style."[44] In referencing "style," Latour is referencing a much older conversation in science and technology studies, reaching back to Ludwig Fleck's 1979 book *The Genesis and Development of a Scientific Fact.* Fleck argues that perception, particularly discovery, takes place with and against what he calls "thought-style," which he defines as disciplinary training and practice or "the developed direct visual perception of a form."[45]

Is what Latour identifies as a "style" the same as what we might call an "aesthetic"? And what might it mean to say not only that hygiene has a style or that social policy has an aesthetic but that hygiene itself works through aesthetic logics? What does it mean to claim that bureaucracy adopts a kind of formal consistency across time? In this chapter, I have argued that hygiene is a totalizing political project whose effects ranged across the scale from the total reorganization of the national as a result of westward settler-colonialist expansion down to the retaxonomization of many forms of materiality itself. What I have called "hygiene" impacted life in the United States at the level of the everyday aesthetics of governance largely by drawing on new norms of scientific comportment to organize and present itself. What is more pertinent to this project, however, is that by studying hygiene in its expression as a project of energy and resource management—or what I have also termed "securitization"—in and through the work of the USDA from 1862 onward is that in the department's relationship to matter itself, we can begin to see that the department's goal of managing population energy in and through consumables in fact ultimately presaged the criminalization of affective states like intoxication, leading to further energy capture in the form of criminalized populations, contained and extracted from, from inside a carceral state.

2

FERMENT

What does it feel like to live in a Pasteurian world? Fermentation initiates the second section of this book as a speculative figure for thinking through the imbrication of aesthetics, affect, materiality, and what I term, building from Black feminist and queer of color critique, deviant life. I begin with fermentation as my first materiality not only because research into fermentation was ground zero for the development of the history of microbiology as a scientific field—and therefore for the opening up of biopolitics to the scale of the microbe—but because fermentation's life as a chemical process is one phase in the series of changes that leads to, and from, two of the other three materialities that interest me in this book: intoxicants, which can result from fermented drinks and which early twentieth-century writers believed could also result from cheese; and rot or putrefaction, which we can understand as the underside of fermentation's productive and life-making possibilities. In chapter 5, I turn to a final materiality: gelatinousness.

In this chapter, however, we sink into a material process that carried forward a longer symbolic history related to the experience of group and crowd affect and whose descriptive power and symbolic associations were shuffled and reframed across the golden age of microbiology. Bruno Latour has already done some of this work in *The Pasteurization of France*, and I build on his work in this chapter. However, I am interested to trace the echoes of the Pasteurian turn in the US context specifically in relation to fermentation—and not primarily germ theory, as other scholars have most thoroughly done. This chapter thinks about energy and affective capacity in two sections. In the first section, I discuss the meaning and place of fermentation as a material process in the history of science by reading through an archive of newspaper, magazine, and scientific articles discussing Pasteur's ideas as they arrive in the United States; I also examine one of the relatively few of Pasteur's books that were translated into English, *Études sur la bière* (*Studies on Beer*).

In the second section, I look at an 1885 Louisa May Alcott story, "The Candy Country," to think about labor, energy, capacity, and materiality as they circulate around the idea of fermentation in the late nineteenth century, just as the microbiological and microbiopolitical turn was taking hold. This chapter thus further develops a method for reading materiality—here fermentation in particular—as both a descriptive and speculative trope for the affective sensation of living in a particular moment, a kind of ethnography of past sensory and energetic economies.

The Pasteurian turn has been taken up by many historians and philosophers of science: by historians of science documenting what has come to be known as the golden age of microbiology and by social historians who have thought through how infection became a working metaphor for race, particularly in the twentieth century. Much social history on race in the United States that takes up the microbiological turn investigates how the discourse of infection attached itself to immigrant communities, who subsequently saw strict policing on the part of public health officials. Nayan Shah's *Contagious Divides*, for instance, takes up the use of contagion and public health discourse to systematically disenfranchise Chinese San Franciscans in the late nineteenth and early twentieth centuries; Natalia Molina's *How Race Is Made in America* discusses the weaponization of disease to mark Asians and Latinx populations as "foreign" and "unclean" in early twentieth-century Los Angeles, while neglecting to address the real causes of illness, such as poor health infrastructure in Mexican American and Asian American neighborhoods. Most markedly, Warwick Anderson in his landmark *Colonial Pathologies* attests to "how the political rationality of American colonialism became manifest in a technical discourse on bodily practice, mundane contact, and the banalities of custom and habit, . . . in particular, that in framing disease potential, medical officers might also assemble a flexible, and sometimes unstable, framework for constituting racial capacities and colonial bodies."[1] Much aligned with my own arguments in chapter 1, Anderson outlines how a colonial investment in the aesthetics of hygiene created the conditions, in a sense, for feeling racial.[2] He notes his concern with the "typological construction of hygiene and civic potential for white Americans and Filipinos, that is, in the way hygiene once took specific racial form, and how this convenient racial biology came for a time to represent human destiny."[3]

In similar and aligned work, hygiene has been taken up as a central technology and social movement coinciding with progressivism deployed to the ideological ends of creating racial typologies and upholding white supremacy.[4] Affiliated with what Roberto Esposito has called the "immunitarian biopolitical model," this Progressive-era political model positions the new regulatory mechanisms of both local and federal government as defenses against the foreign or alien body, imagined as a virus.[5] Further, as Nayan Shah has demonstrated in *Contagious Divides*, a perceived lack of ethnic hygiene also poses the spatiality and domesticity of the migrant, the native, and the nonwhite as deviant and abnormal, outside of normative racial, gendered, and sexual regimes.[6] My work in this chapter builds on all of these scholars' work by turning to an earlier period and rethinking the rise of germ theory in terms of infection and contagion's secret stepsibling: fermentation. Engaging the new materialist and affective turn, I am also interested in thinking through fermentation's long history as a byword for political foment—in other words, as a figure for the multiplying possibilities of affect and feeling.

Ultimately my goal is to think with the possibilities—both speculative and historical—brought forward by ferment's changing presence in common parlance, in particular in popular print culture, as well as in science. I also want to develop the argument I have been making here about energy by putting the figure of fermentation energy as a nature-culture formation into conversation with biopolitical discourses: in so doing, I join with such scholars as Kyla Schuller and Greta LaFleur in moving discussions of biopower away from the past several decades of critical focus on what Foucault would call "anatomopolitics," or the work of disciplining the individual body, to biopolitics as a theory of the population, or in the terms of affect studies, of population *capacity*, understood as the imminent capacity for energetic outlay.[7] Fermentation here becomes a figure for what social theorists have called, variously, the "crowd," the "populace," the "population," or the "multitude"; more specifically, "ferment" here refers to what more recent theorists of the interpenetration of emotions with social formations have come to call "affect": a change in the temperature of a feeling that is also collective and social, feeling that is simultaneously physiological, located between and among bodies and subjects but somehow at the edge of what can be spoken. Here, following Patricia Clough and others, affect/energy is in fact a form of matter; matter, in turn, in its variously politicized nineteenth-century forms as ferment and otherwise, also catalyzes affect/energy.[8]

As historians of microbiology tell us, fermentation, specifically as it was theorized and explained in the research of Louis Pasteur during his time at the industrially focused University of Lille, is the primary process through which modern microbiological and bacteriological science came into being. One unconfirmed legend about Pasteur's turn to microbiology goes that Pasteur's 1856 work on sugar beet ferment for a French manufacturer of beet alcohol laid the foundation for understanding alcoholic and lactic acid ferment as caused by the *Saccharomyces cerevisiae*, or yeast, organism.[9] Whatever the events, it is clear that Pasteur's early interest in fermentation was driven by the imperatives of food manufacturing, in particular wine and later beer. Pasteur's work in understanding what ferment is and how the heating processes that later came to be called "pasteurization" could manage larger-scale fermentation-based industries entirely emerge from his conversation with these craft-based industries.

Through Pasteur's experiments on grapes and wine fermentation and later by finding ways to preserve broth solutions by limiting their exposure to oxygen and therefore both protecting broth from the invisible bacteria in oxygen that precipitate fermentation and decomposition and proving the experience of those bacteria, he disproved the mechanist theory of fermentation advocated by Liebig. Liebig had argued that internal chemical reactions inside matter itself caused what he termed "decomposition," a position also aligned with the theory of spontaneous generation. As Pasteur showed, yeast is a microorganism that devours carbohydrates—for instance, grape sugars—and produces carbon dioxide as a by-product. (One famous critical parody of Pasteur's research depicted effervescence as farting.)[10] What Liebig had thought of as decomposition, as a destructive and negative process, turned out to be, at least up to a certain line of consumability, productive, full of life and, in turn, a figure for beginning to theorize the place of metabolic processes in creating and transforming fuel into energy, at least at the level of the eukaryotic cell known as *Saccharomyces cerevisiae*, or yeast. I return to the idea of fermentation as energy shortly.

While the debates between Liebig and Pasteur are legendary in the history of science, research regarding the nature of fermentation was also at the heart of the major scientific debates of the nineteenth century, debates that were all variations on the same fundamental question: What is the nature of the energy that defines or fuels that which humans call "life"?[11] Ultimately, both Pasteur and Liebig were right: fermentation is in fact caused by microorganisms (Pasteur), but it also includes chemical changes that those microorganisms catalyze in the carbohydrates they consume (Liebig). However, Pasteur picked up on a longer tradition of scientists and philosophers who speculated that tiny organisms, at times called "globules" or "animalcules," were responsible for catalyzing the chemical changes referred to variously as "fermentation" or "putrefaction." In proving fundamentally that microorganisms cause fermentation and then decomposition and, later, in his work on anthrax that other microorganisms were definitively responsible for spreading infection, Pasteur shepherded a new set of modern characters—microbes—onto the political scene, not just as invisible agents in our bodies but, as Bruno Latour argues, as social actors. This scientific turn has often been referred to as the "golden age of microbiology."

I return to the question of metabolic life later in this chapter, but for now, I want to track the overlapping symbolics of ferment and infection, as they came to signify both multiplicity and the production and spread of both individual and crowd affect and energy; I also track how it was that these discourses moved from Europe to the United States to set the stage for the way "ferment" came to emerge as a figure available for imagining this new microbiopolitical order.

THE PASTEURIZATION OF THE UNITED STATES

In Latour's study of Pasteur's work in the context of nineteenth-century France, *The Pasteurization of France*, he demonstrates how the emergence of Pasteur as a heroic scientific figure was made possible by the many social actors invested in a theory that might actualize their plans for social improvement, which he calls "hygiene." Working through the body of the major French scientific journals variously published between 1870 and 1919, Latour sees Pasteur's work coming into the political, scientific, and social forefront of the time, not simply because of the force of Pasteur's genius or the power of his truth claims. Latour writes, "It is pointless to claim that Pasteur's discoveries were believed because they were convincing. They ended up being convincing because the hygienists believed them and forced everybody to put them into practice."[12] I want to linger here over another of Latour's claims about the Pasteurians and the social and symbolic revolution that was enabled by their scientific discoveries.

Written early in Latour's career, *The Pasteurization of France* (1984) marked the birth of actor-network theory—the ideas that multiple social actors produce the emergence of an idea (as opposed to "creative insight" or "genius") and, even more radically, that nonhuman actors, matter even, play a causal or at least agentic role in the laboratory theater of creation and discovery. This area of thought is well trod and forms one of the root sources of the multiple strands of new materialist thought that have emerged since. What interests me for the purposes of this chapter is Latour's discussion of the figurative language that accompanies the birth of bacteriology and microbiology. The parallels that Latour understands the hygienists to be drawing between microbes and sociality are illuminating:

> The hygienists were not alone in inventing new forces. There were those who manipulated fairy electricity, those who set up leagues for colonization, for the development of gymnastic clubs or for the promotion of the telephone, radio, or X-rays. The radical party, for instance, gained ground everywhere by forcing the traditional agents of the social game to take account of the dangerous labouring classes, whose actions and intentions were so little known. But it is with Freud that the resemblance is greatest. Like Freud, Pasteur found treasure, not in the parapraxes and trifles of everyday life, but *in decay and refuse*. Both announced that they were speaking in the name of invisible, rejected, terribly dangerous forces that must be listened to if civilization was not to collapse. Like the psychoanalysts, the Pasteurians set themselves up *as exclusive interpreters of populations to which no one else had access.*[13]

I wish to extend Latour here in arguing that this question of population—specifically in the figure of the underground multitude who are also refuse, trash, decay—is key to understanding the emergence of the microbe and its bacteriologist interlocutors into the social scene as Haraway's "natureculture" phenomenon, what she describes as "a synthesis of nature and culture that recognizes their inseparability in ecological relationships that are both biophysically and socially formed."[14] This emergence is not about a single or solitary actor but rather the emergence of *millions of actors*, and in this language of multiplication and multitude, we can begin to trace some of the formulations of microbiopolitical sociality and securitization that emerged during the golden age of microbiology.

More specifically, I am arguing here that the multitudinousness of these new actors comes to be understood as indexing energy—Latour compares historical actors who are "inventing new forces"—in its most material form as the capacity to work, to be put to work, or to have work energy extracted from people's bodies at the individual level but also at the population level. Pasteur and his bacteriologist colleagues—and relatedly the new visual technology of the microscope—made possible an understanding of the world as teeming with invisible actors that are invisibly multiplying and proliferating in numbers that cannot always be easily estimated but whose energy must be secured and directed: a population-level metaphor for the emerging biopolitical Pasteurian formations of the nineteenth century. As I will show, the emergence of the figure of microbial life in the world enabled microbes and therefore ferment (and relatedly intoxicants and rot) to become a scalable metaphor for energy. In this metaphor, both the teeming and multiplying bodies of tiny cells *and* the massed bodies of people were figured as analogous to each other; but also they became figures through which deviance was re-interpellated through the law, newly remade through its conversation with science and newly operating across the scale of its own affective and aesthetic microbiopolitical orders.

As I indicated in the introduction, I borrow the term "microbiopolitics" from the anthropologist and ethnographer Heather Paxson, whose work on the culture of raw-cheese artisans in the northeastern United States explores the idea of extending Foucauldian biopolitics into the microbial level. Paxson writes,

> If Foucault (1978) has argued that the nineteenth century saw the rise of *biopolitics*, the fashioning of new categories of persons to facilitate the statistical measurement and rational management of populations,

> largely via sex and reproduction, Bruno Latour, in *The Pasteurization of France* (1988), tracks a parallel history, describing the accommodation of microbial life into the very constitution of this social field. . . . Biopolitics, then, is joined by microbiopolitics: the creation of categories of microscopic biological agents; the anthropocentric evaluation of such agents; and the elaboration of appropriate human behaviors vis-à-vis microorganisms engaged in infection, inoculation, and digestion.[15]

Paxson continues, "Pasteurian practices configure microbes as elements to be eliminated so that human polities might be cultivated."[16]

Paxson's brilliant work in the contemporary era describes the alternative biopolitical imaginaries of twenty-first-century raw-milk-cheese makers in Vermont, who, following traditional and historical artisanal cheese-making practices, imagine ways of living and working in collaboration with microbial species that specifically refute the antimicrobial regime of pasteurization. In charting the domain of the microbial as a space through which "polities might be cultivated," Paxson is careful to delineate between her work and the work of other scholars in science and technology studies who variously consider the biologization of race alongside DNA technologies or who see "molecularization" as a political trend that, as in Nigel Thrift's work, seeks to penetrate and harvest human affective capacity as a space of control. By contrast and yet still building on Paxson's work, in this chapter, I seek to do exactly the opposite: I am interested in how the molecular is actually earlier worked through in the microbial and microbiopolitical turn of nineteenth-century science.[17] More particularly, I am interested in how these microbial figures for affective or energetic capacity become highly racialized.

Latour hints at the transatlantic circulation of Pasteur's work when he writes that the turn to the microbiopolitical, and the affiliation of microbial life with the multitude, took hold on both sides of the Atlantic. More recently, historians have shown that this phenomenon indeed circulated globally. As the historian Aro Velmet writes, "Pastorians," as Pasteur's followers were called, embedded themselves in, for instance, France's imperial projects:

> From 1890 to 1939, Pasteur Institutes spread from Saigon to the rest of Indochina, then to French colonies in North Africa—Algeria, Tunisia, and Morocco—and finally to French West Africa (Afrique Occidentale Française [AOF]) and French Equatorial Africa (Afrique Équatoriale Française [AEF]). Other scientists set up Pasteur Institutes beyond the empire, including in Constantinople, Rio de Janeiro, Athens, and St. Petersburg. Researchers at the institutes did groundbreaking work on the bubonic plague, malaria, typhus, sleeping sickness, and yellow fever, as well as on industrial agricultural methods ranging from treating rinderpest ("an infectious disease of ruminants, especially cattle") to inventing new forms of distilling industrial alcohol.[18]

Latour also notes that the Pasteurian Institute and its population-focused language also reached the shores of the United States. About the founder of the first US Pasteurian Institute, Latour says,

> At the time of the inauguration of a Pasteur Institute in New York, [Paul] Gibier writes: ". . . we shall see that the study of contagious organisms, which must be at the scientific base of hygiene, can and must bring considerable assistance to those who, finding that all is not for the best in the best of all possible worlds, are trying to improve the wretched condition of the disinherited."
>
> He, like a vulgar Marxist, attaches bacteriology to the class struggle.[19]

Paul Gibier, as Latour indicates here, was the founding director of the Pasteur Institute of New York, which took a leading role in treating rabies, or what was then known as "hydrophobia." Gibier was a French-trained bacteriologist, and by the time he arrived in New York, he had already written a dissertation on rabies and investigated cholera in Spain and Cuba.

The article that Latour cites here is Gibier's 1890 public address at the founding of the Pasteur Institute, which was reprinted in multiple journals. Although my particular interest is in fermentation and not infection, it is clear from these speeches that the two discourses haunt each other. Thus, it is worth taking a further few moments with Gibier's speech to expand the links between germs, as a multitude, and what I am thinking of here as populace energy, particularly in a figure present on the American scene. In his 1891 address, Gibier says,

> When, despite quarantines and other preventive measures, typhus, cholera, and a hundred other epidemic diseases appear in a city, the first victims are in the ranks of those whom poverty has condemned to unhappy and unhealthful existences. But those who have the happiness to lack nothing will be ill-advised to cry out in their selfishness: "What matters it to us! It is only the poor who die," for the contagion will not be slow in gaining strength in the field in which it was first planted. *The germs will multiply and acquire a sort of audacity*, and, after festering for a time in the dismal shadows of the poverty-stricken districts, they will be diffused in the light of day, and, *invading the favored localities, they will penetrate into the house of wealthy* and carry with them sorrow and death.[20]

Here we see that it is the threat not simply of class struggle but, in fact, of unsecuritized class energy, characterized as "multiple," "acquiring," and "audacious," that is of interest: Gibier implies that the project of hygiene is to contain a veritable bread riot of microbes whose increasing energy threatens the social order.

And indeed, this is also the language that Pasteur uses to describe ferment in his 1879 book *Studies in Fermentation*:

> Another equally exceptional characteristic of yeast and fermentation in general consists in the small proportion which the yeast that forms bears to the sugar that decomposes. In all other known beings the weight of nutritive matter assimilated corresponds with the weight of food used up, any difference that may exist being comparatively small. The life of yeast is entirely different. *For a certain weight of yeast formed*, we may have ten times, twenty times, a hundred times as much sugar, or even more decomposed, as we shall experimentally prove by-and-by; that is to say, that whilst the proportion varies in a precise manner, according to conditions which we shall have occasion to specify, *it is also greatly out of proportion to the weight of the yeast. We repeat, the life of no other being, under its normal physiological conditions, can show anything similar.*[21]

There are four things to note in the contrast between Gibier's statement on infection and Pasteur's statement on fermentation, published only twelve years earlier. The first is that having both emerged from Pasteur's labs and both relying on an argument about microbial life, fermentation and germ theory are persistently and tenaciously intertwined. The second is that both fermentation and germ theory rely, both as science and as they are imported as figures into social theory, on *multiplicity* and *excess* for their argumentative power. And the third point, as Pasteur definitively shows, is that this multiplying effect is also a source of wonder. Says Pasteur, "the life of no other being, under its normal physiological conditions, can show anything similar [to yeast fermentation]."[22] This is a grand claim indeed: fermentation is a metabolic process that performs a transubstantiation that exceeds in output that which is put to work as fermentative catalyst: more effervescence and yeast emerge than either the original amount of yeast or its fuel, sugar, a magical and seductive formula for a world bent on maximizing the relation between cost and profit. But the fourth phenomenon to pay attention to is that fermentation is as linked to *life* and *productivity* as germs and infection are linked to death, decay, and decomposition, except inasmuch as fermentation tends to signify *excess*.

Fermentation is typically narrated as part of the history of food and food science and has generally taken a minor role in the historical literature on microbiology, in which germ theory and theories of infection completely transformed medical practice and therefore public health. That relatively small exploration of fermentation, combined with the even smaller exploration of fermentation in the United States, warps our historical understanding. While beer, wine, and cheese were Pasteur's material introduction to the problem of fermentation, the US public learned about his fermentation research through the press and scientific journals reporting on European scientific debates and the growing public discourse about infection, disinfection, and contagion. The emergence of any one discipline is a somewhat difficult history to trace: if Pasteur's ideas gave birth to the fields of bacteriology and microbiology, we do not find journals of bacteriology and microbiology so named until much later. As one British historian of microbiology puts it, microbes became scientifically important to a wide variety of disciplines in the century after their "discovery": "serology, immunology, bacteriology, biochemistry, entomology, hygiene, tropical medicine and parasitology," as well as dairy bacteriology, wine and beer production, and agricultural stations studying soil fermentation and fertility.[23] Yet it was not until the 1940s, at least in Britain, that microbiology existed as a discipline, with journals, societies, and full-time posts. Thus, mentions of Pasteur's research do come up in nineteenth-century journals—for instance, in the *Medical News*, the *American Journal of the Medical Sciences*, the *American Journal of Pharmacy*, the *Medical and Surgical Reporter*, and *Scientific American*—but actual journals focused on microbiology or bacteriology did not exist in the United States at that time.

In US scientific journals, general-interest journals, and newspapers, the issue of fermentation arose in a more roundabout way. Ferment is alluded to most consistently in relation to the debates about spontaneous generation, namely, the question of whether life could emerge from inorganic or decomposed matter without what would later come to be understood as either bacterial or microbial cause. Further, the term "fermentation" was often collapsed with putrefaction and decomposition or rot as scientists worked out not only the overlapping biological processes that create and break down biological life but also where to lay down what is ultimately the line between these seemingly different processes. Meanwhile, public conversation around microbiology became increasingly specific to particular diseases and foods. In short, the conversation turned to hygiene more generally and the application of germ theory more specifically. My book is only a partial study, and I do not mean to imply that my own research represents the full picture of interest in fermentation in this period, as my inquiry has been limited to searchable databases of US journals.[24]

Many of these mentions in the journals arise more than a decade after Pasteur completed his initial research and certainly after his two major early articles on fermentation, "Mémoire sur la fermentation appelée lactiques" and *Memoire sur la fermentations alcooliques*, both published in the *Annales Chimie et de la Physique*.[25] As those titles indicate, Pasteur's initial research into these processes began because cheese and beer and wine manufacturers asked him for help in managing the fermentation central to producing their product; thus, Pasteur's initial work on fermentation was directed toward supporting industrial-scale food production. As Bulloch shows us in his classic history of microbiology, Pasteur's main experiments and research into these fermentation processes happened between the late 1850s and the mid-1860s, but he suspended this investigation until the early 1870s while he dealt with the anthrax crisis threatening France's silkworms. While Pasteur was initially disseminating this work, the United States was fighting in, and then recovering from, the Civil War of 1861–1865. As the United States recovered from the Civil War, Pasteur took up his work on fermentation again, publishing *Études sur le vin* in 1866 and then in 1876 producing *Études sur la bière*, the major work of his that seems to have been translated into English as *Studies on Fermentation: The Diseases of Beer, Their Causes, and the Means of Preventing Them.*

Neither Pasteur's early research into lactic acid fermentation nor his research on wine seems to have been translated into English at the time; however *Études sur la bière* was translated into English by a brewer and published by Macmillan of London in 1879 and does seem to contain passages from his previous books. In this rather large book, Pasteur documents in narrative and images the experiments through which he discovered that healthy beer is produced through the active harnessing and utilization of what Pasteur called "alcoholic ferments" and the management of what he termed "diseased" ferments. He writes, "The expression, 'diseased ferments,' is justified by the circumstance that the propagation of these ferments is always accompanied by the production of substances which are acid, putrid, viscous, bitter, or otherwise unpalatable."[26] In this phrase, we can see how fermentation and disease are already easily intertwined, even without recourse to theorizing infection and germs. Later, Pasteur writes, "During the process of fermentation, *the occult power of diseased ferments*, although it may escape the observation of the brewer, is manifested in a high degree."[27] While this is a translation, the original French is equally dramatic: "Dans les pratiques industrielles de la fermentation se manifeste également, à un haut degré, quoique à l'insu du brasseur, la domination cachée des ferments de maladie."[28] In other words, unknown even to the brewer, diseased fermentation manifests *a hidden dominance.*[29]

That "occult" energy, as Pasteur termed it, was understood as the yeast cell's power to increase, fertilize, and multiply, on its own terms. In his beer book, we see that power embodied in Pasteur's numerous images, many drawn by hand, of yeast as living in groups. In an image of healthy and diseased beer ferments in the beginning of the book, Pasteur describes the ferment that is drawn off beer as "increasing greatly during the process of fermentation."[30] In these images, as in many others, ferment is always multiple: each microbe is always a part of an ever-increasing crowd.

Similarly, Pasteur's many articles published in the US—some of them straightforward translations of his talks, others summaries of his debates with Robert Koch and other mechanists—always emphasize multiplicity and increase. In an essay titled "On Dust and Disease" by the English physicist John Tyndall, reprinted in May 1870 in the US journal the *Eclectic Magazine of Foreign Literature*, Tyndall wrote, "It was some time ago the current belief that epidemic diseases generally were propagated by a kind of malaria, which consisted of organic matter in a state of *motor-decay*; that when such matter was taken into the body through the lungs or skin, it had the power of spreading there the destroying process which had attacked itself. *Such a spreading power was visibly exerted in the case of yeast. A little leaven was seen to leaven the whole lump, a mere speck of matter in this supposed state of decomposition being apparently competent to propagate indefinitely its own decay.*"[31] While Tyndall here describes the mechanistic position, the imagery of propagation and a "spreading power" remains.

I am here building toward the argument that the discourses of population, of multitude, and of fermentative energy—that is, in the *fomentative* sense of "promot[ing] the growth, development, effect, or spread of (something material or physical)"—that haunt germ theory and the general discussion of microbes in this early period of the discipline (if it can be called that) are similarly attached to the idea of ferment.[32] The word "ferment" does not begin with Pasteur, and it is here that I become more obviously interested in fermentation as what Donna Haraway has termed a "natureculture" formation, in essence a site where both language and the natural world meet to act upon each other, a formation that takes up Latour's argument about the actant presence of the nonhuman world on the human world and uses it to complicate and rewrite poststructuralist theories of language.[33]

And yet, I am getting at something perhaps a bit to the side of Haraway's theory, something that might more approximately be called "matterculture." In circling fermentation, in approaching it through multiple interdisciplinary methods, I am trying to describe something about the materiality of the affective and sensory everyday in which these evolving matterculture formations get put to the use of describing the sensuality of being both human and material in the world. In this vein, ferment has a rich history. The *OED* traces the word "ferment" back to 1398 and offers numerous examples of its use specifically in relation to the material process. But it also notes that by 1660, the term appears in municipal records in its figurative possibility as a synonym for the exacerbation and inflammation of feeling.[34] In 1670, Milton used the term in *Samson Agonistes* as a figure related to festering, putrefaction, and heat:

> My griefs not only pain me
> As a lingring disease,
> But finding no redress, ferment and rage,
> Nor less then wounds immedicable
> Ranckle, and fester, and gangrene,
>   To black mortification.[35]

Ferment here reads as heating up, increasing in temperature: it is an affective response, both physiological and emotional. Interestingly, this use of ferment echoes across journals and newspapers in the period but specifically in relation to what we now call "group affect" or "shared feeling." For instance, in the nineteenth century, the word "ferment" appears in such cheap penny-newspaper passages as, "Battle Mountain, nearly the centre of the desert state of Nevada, is not a particularly attractive village. A railroad office and a freight depot, a row of business houses and saloons, and a cluster of unpretentious dwellings [unclear type] comprise its extent. At the time of which I write, some five years ago, it was a lively burg, however, and a rough one. A small army of teamsters and miners, and a coterie of three-card monte men who made it their head-quarters, kept the otherwise peaceful village *in a ferment of wild excitement*."[36] Here "ferment" refers to the feeling that possesses an entire small village, a possession even that is both unchecked and asocial ("wild") and shared, or mutual. Or, for instance, in the same sensational newspaper a year later, there is this story:

> VERY HARD CHEEK
> The little village of Lockington, O., has been *in a ferment* for some time over an affair of a very scandalous nature, the facts of which are as follows: About three months ago the wife of David Hayne, who ranked among respectable society, became too intimate with a man named Dillon, the result of which was elopement, and Hayne was left wifeless.[37]

Here again "ferment" refers to a hotting up, a scandalous feeling experienced by a group located in a shared space. Although I have limited myself to two anecdotes from the same newspaper, the *Police Gazette*, a sensationalist newspaper that profited from narrating vice, the same usage echoes across multiple newspapers in the century.

Still, what do we do about the fact that these stories—and their use of the word "ferment"—recur so often in this one gazette. Of course, given the fact that they are all from the same newspaper, we can assume that they were often written by the same author, although none of the stories are credited to an author. The sensational tone of the newspaper speaks to the popularity of crime writing in the period, but the reference to police also points to the link between management of the public good, named "police power" in classic political theory, and the figuration of lively matter/affect as unsecuritized crowd energy. But when we compare the *Police Gazette* to African American and abolitionist newspapers in the same period, there is an interesting shift: "ferment" moves from negatively connoting a state of unrest that is in need of swift resolution to a state that may well open up to productive and liberatory political possibilities. For instance, in 1831, William Lloyd Garrison's *The Liberator* printed a five-part series narrating the "history of slavery in Massachusetts." In the fifth section, the piece stated that, following a public scandal in which three Black Massachusetts freedmen were abducted and sold into slavery in the Caribbean, "the public indignation being greatly excited against the actors in this affair, and against others who had been concerned in the traffic of slaves, *it was thought proper to take advantage of the ferment, and bring good out of evil*. Accordingly, the association of the Boston clergy originated a petition to the legislature, praying for an act to prohibit the equipping and insuring vessels bound to Africa for slaves, and providing against the carrying of innocent blacks from home."[38]

Similarly, in 1849, the *National Standard* printed an editorial from Edmond Quincy (which was then reprinted in Frederick Douglass's the *North Star*) that stated, "We see in every direction the acknowledged indications that we have understood our business and done it well. . . . Slight quakings on the surface tell of more tumultuous heavings in the depths below. . . . The effects of long Anti-Slavery labors are beginning to be recognized *among the elements of political fermentation*. We have make [*sic*] the cauldron seethe, and it matters little what scum is first eliminated to the surface. *The agitation is the main thing*. If it be maintained the purification will follow by the inevitable operation of physical and moral law."[39] The reference to physical and moral law is key: in this sense fermentation can be understood as partaking of the larger symbolic economy that Cara New Daggett calls "energy metaphors."[40]

Daggett's work draws on a few decades of political theory examining the marriage of natural history and science to political economy. Beginning with Norton Wise and Crosbie Smith's writing on the relationship between work and waste, political scientists have explored how the scientific "discovery" of energy via the framework of thermodynamics—particularly in the form of the steam engine—came to be the primary language through which multiple symbolic ecologies were figured, including the statistical "sciences" of political economy.[41] As Wise and Smith show and Daggett develops, the secularization of Scottish Protestant values in the form of energy science—work/use is positive; waste/entropy is negative—became tied to the biopolitical project of extracting maximum energetic value not just from machines and the natural world but from the population of working peoples in an emergent and accelerating industrial age. In a sense, Wise and Smith were building a conversation parallel to Foucault's theory of the rendering statistical of the population by examining how principles of energy expenditure came to shape the meaning of waste as a phenomenon to be harnessed, marshaled, and directed.

Sharpening Wise and Smith's analysis and bringing the attention of political science to the crisis of the fossil-fuel-driven crisis of the Anthropocene, Daggett writes,

> Something happened to energy in the nineteenth century. . . . It was more than the advent of fossil fuel systems and an uptick in energy consump-

> tion; it was also the emergence of energy as an object of modern politics. In that birth, the expansive, multidimensional figuration of preindustrial, poetic energy was captured and yoked to a mania to put the world to work. Since the nineteenth century, the human relationship to fuel has been governed by this singular ruling logic of energy, which justifies the indexing of human well-being according to the idealization of work and an unquestioned drive to put the Earth's materials to use for a profit. Just as energy became tightly bound by the governing logic of work, so too work increasingly came to be governed through the metaphors and physics of energy.[42]

In Daggett's analysis, then, the "invention" of energy as an object of modern power formations—what she terms, riffing off Foucault, "energopolitics"—dovetails with a new language of labor, which itself draws on the theories of thermodynamics to naturalize a certain work regime. Certainly, Daggett's conversation with Foucault also invites comparison with the argument of Foucault's own mentor, Georges Canguilhem, that the mid-nineteenth century saw the arrival of "life" as an object of disciplinary interest.

In this (newish) thermodynamic regime, entropy—the energy that does not get used or captured—is the enemy of capitalist progress; the entropic, like everything else, is a potential source of energy that must and should be captured and vertically integrated into profit and labor extraction. Likewise, available energy or, in affective terms, *capacity* becomes a prized resource to be extracted from human, nonhuman, and animal bodies and put to use. As Daggett shows, the dominance of the thermodynamic model—with its waste-aversive ethos of efficient work-life use—spread beyond physics and into biology to become a theory of biological metabolism as well as a foundational capitalist metaphor. Of what use, then, was fermentation? And could, as abolitionists asked, fermentation's excesses be harnessed or directed? And what, too, of the fomentative possibilities of the crowd? How might they be contained or directed?[43]

"THE CANDY COUNTRY"

I turn here to a Louisa May Alcott story in which a young girl's relationship to various food objects and dietary regimes traces her growth into productive maturity, culminating in her "useful" mastery of fermentation itself. "The Candy Country" is fundamentally a story about biopolitical economies of energy. Narratively traversing three countries whose national identities are narrated as food objects—Candyland, Cakeland, and Breadland—the story scales the relation between the individual and the nation (or "population," in classic biopolitical terms) while also spatializing a narrative about progress into a young white girl's transformational journey across three different edible landscapes. On a simple narrative level, fermentation plays an important, even catalytic, role in the Alcott story, not only because life in Breadland is structured around "learning about bread and yeast" but because the protagonists—Lily, who learns how to make yeast bread, and a brown gingerbread boy variously named "Ginger Snap" and then "Muffin" when his reward of a yeast soul turns him into a white bread boy—are each changed when they are variously fermented or learn how to ferment. As we will see, however, this yeasty feeling is unevenly distributed—as unevenly distributed as the right to life itself: (to ruin the ending of the story right away) while Lily's encounter with yeast brings meaning to her life when her mastery of bread baking, in the ultimate stage of the story, allows her to become a "good Christian woman" and return home, Ginger/Muffin, by contrast, becomes a "white bread boy" and ultimately perishes, eaten by Lily.

In "The Candy Country," Alcott collapses the historical progression between colonial "discovery narratives," slavery, and the birth of industrial, even Fordist labor—a conjoining that makes sense when we consider that, as Sidney Mintz tells, they are historically linked as labor regimes.[44] Bringing this political unevenness and racist violence to the forefront, this last section of the chapter uses "The Candy Country" to think through the emergence of microbial life, in particular yeast and its fermentative powers, to ask what the presence of fermentation has to do with the symbolics of population; with economies of work, energy, and leisure; and in particular with the idea that affect is itself a kind of materiality. My goal is to link what I see as the biopolitical impulse of Alcott's story—in particular her differential and racially inflected distributions of "usefulness" in the story—to the representation of fermentation. In doing so, I want to query the relationship between race, new materialist theories, and biopolitical governmentality as it comes into view through Alcott's imaginative relationship to yeast. Doing so will bring into sharper view how fermentation circulated as a metaphor for labor, energy, and work.

Yeast was of course particularly important to the reformer Sylvester Graham, who argued that a bread-based diet would curb illicit sexual desires—in particular, masturbation. As I have discussed elsewhere, in his *Treatise on Bread and Breadmaking*, he laid out detailed notes on how to bake bread, bringing together his temperance and bread advocacy by forbidding such "vicious" ingredients as sugar, spices, and alcohol but also worrying that the overfermentation of yeast might turn bread sour or even alcoholic.[45] Graham is particularly pertinent to Alcott—and as we will see, Graham bread makes a personal appearance in the last country of the story, Breadland—because Alcott was a daughter of the reform movement: her father, Bronson, was an education reformer; his cousin, William Alcott, was a disciple and colleague of Sylvester Graham's; the two Alcott families lived together during the 1830s; and Louisa May, along with her sisters and mother, was subjected to the extremes of the Graham diet during her father's experiments with utopian community at Fruitlands, a formative experience that she later mocked in her satirical and autobiographical novella *Transcendental Wild Oats*.

Contained in a collection of short stories for children called *Lulu's Library*, "The Candy Country" tells the story of a little girl, Lily, who finds herself carried by the wind out of her everyday world. She lands in what we eventually discover is a series of edible nation-scapes: the Candy Country, Cakeland, and, finally, Breadland. Lily is called into the first nation, the Candy Country, by singing sugar birds:

> Sweet! Sweet!
> Come, come and eat,
> Dear little girls
> With yellow curls;
> For here you'll find
> Sweets to your mind.
> . . . .
> Our lily and rose
> Are not for the nose;
> Our flowers we pluck

To eat or suck.
And, oh! What bliss
When two friends kiss,
For they honey sip
From lip to lip!
And all you meet,
In house or street,
At work or play,
Sweethearts are they.[46]

We do not need to read deeply to understand the eroticism of this passage, which plays on Lily's name (and, perhaps also, the name of the protagonist of the Rose Campbell novels, published a decade earlier) and emphatically invites us to feed on lilies and roses—not only the flowers, perhaps, but the girls themselves: they are not for the nose, we are told; we instead pluck them to suck them. From there, the song segues quickly to the Candy Country's ambiently polyamorous everyday life, in which friends taste honey from each other's lips: all you meet, the song promises us, sweethearts are they—not just all but everywhere and anywhere: "house or street / work or play."[47]

Lily accepts the invitation. In her short stay in the Candy Country, she eats her way through the population, promiscuously sampling from every demographic. Each group tastes differently, we find:

> The young ladies were flavored with violet, rose, and orange; the gentlemen were apt to have cordials of some sort inside of them, as she found when she ate one now and then slyly, and got her tongue bitten by the hot, strong taste as a punishment. The old people tasted of peppermint, close and such comfortable things, good for pain; but the old maids had lemon, hoar-hound, fag-root, and all sorts of sour, bitter things in them and did not get eaten much. The dear babies melted in her mouth, and the delicately flavored young ladies she was very fond of. . . . Weddings were better still; for the lovely white brides were so sweet Lily longed to eat them.[48]

Within this candy demographic, selfhood is understood as essence in a purely literal form: to be of a kind is to taste of that kind, to be infused with a flavor that is distilled and concentrated—a cordial. Lily's polymorphously promiscuous tastes know no gender or age boundaries. But it is not really her perversity that is shocking about this passage so much as Alcott's frank sexual innuendo, particularly as it relates to the eroticism of eating—or is it drinking?—the male cordial, full as it seems to be of the vital spermatic liquids that Graham feared would leak away if the addicted masturbator and intemperate eater had his way with himself.

As Lily follows her cravings, sugar poisons her; she becomes peevish and bad-tempered, ultimately longing for "plain bread and butter."[49] When the Candy population rises up against her after she eats too many babies, brides, and old women—and worst of all, after she "calmly sits down on the biggest church, crushing it flat"—Lily abandons Candyland, "fearing some one would put poison in her candy."[50] Before escaping, however, she enacts the Enlightenment's classic revolutionary gesture and decapitates the king of the Candy Country, "[biting] his head off, crown and all."[51]

Lily escapes the toxicity of Candy Country and approaches the next fantasy nation-space, Cakeland, "over the mountains of Gibraltar Rock that divided the city of Saccharisa from the great desert of brown sugar that lay beyond."[52] As she approaches, the reader is invited to imagine the new space as an amalgam of North African desert and Columbus's never-reached Indies. Lily feels "a hot wind blowing toward her. 'I wonder if there are sugar savages here, roasting and eating some poor traveler like me,' she said, thinking of Robinson Crusoe and other wanderers in strange lands."[53] The fear of cannibalism, so consistent to narratives of Caribbean and African exploration, appears here as a fundamentally anti-Black sentiment, but as ever, this is a projection of repressed guilt: it is Lily herself who has just been banished for her cannibalism.[54]

Cakeland is described as a "very queer country": "Lakes of eggs all beaten up, and hot springs of saleratus [bicarbonate of soda] foamed here and there ready for us. . . . Every one cooked all the time and never failed and never seemed tired."[55] The first town she sees is a "settlement of little huts."[56] There, indeed, Lily meets Ginger Snap, a "Browny" and "queer fellow."[57] Cakeland is really an enormous industrial kitchen populated by brown cookie men and women who labor to send cakes and meals and cookies (which are, literally, aspects of their own bodies) through to restaurants and bakeries in the world that Lily has come from. Lily asks about all the cooking happening around them. Says Ginger, "'We cook for all the confectioners and people think the good things come out of the cellars under their saloons. Good joke, isn't it?' And Snap laughed till a crack came in his neck and made him cough."[58] Lily is fascinated with Ginger's work and asks him about it:

> "Don't you get tired of doing this all the time?"
>
> "Yes, but I want to be promoted, and I never shall be till I've done my best and won the prize here. . . . The prize for best gingerbread is a cake of condensed yeast. That puts a soul into me, and I begin to rise till I am able to go over the hills yonder into the blessed land of bread, and be one of the happy creatures who are always wholesome, always needed. . . . I leave my ginger behind when I go, and get white and round and beautiful, as you will see."[59]

Ginger Snap labors for a short while sending food through to the "real world" and teaching Lily to make gingerbread until

> just then the clock began to strike and a chime of bells to ring,—
> Gingerbread,
> Go to the head.
> Your task is done;
> A soul is won.
> Take it and go
> Where muffins grow
> . . . .
> In the sea of flour
> Plunge this hour.
> Safe in your breast
> Let the yeast-cake rest,
> Till you rise in joy,
> A white bread boy![60]

Ginger grabs the "silver-covered square that seemed to fall from heaven" and dives into an oceanic vat of white flour, holding the yeast-cake to his breast. The sea of flour then bubbles and roils and ferments "like a small earthquake" while the cake-folk and Lily watch until Ginger emerges as a "beautiful white figure on the other side of the sea" and takes off to Breadland.[61] The voracious Lily pursues close behind.

Crossing the mountains of Gibraltar Rock (a kind of candy) and a brown-sugar desert marks Lily's entrance into a landscape that is markedly not white, one clearly meant to mark the presence of exotic, spicy, and coerced nonwhite labor. There is, for Alcott, a common sugary connection between the monarchic and aristocratic state of the Candy people and the working state of the savage Cake people, a connection made manifest when Ginger tells Lily: "You'll get on better here with us Brownies than with the lazy Bonbons, who never work and are all for show. They won't own us, though we are all related through our grandparents Sugar and Molasses. We are busy folks; so they turn up their noses and won't speak to us at parties."[62] Thus, Brownies work endlessly and are spicy, primitive, and soulless until converted, or whitened, and made into bread; but both Bonbons and Brownies are unequal products of what we might identify as the imperial and slave-based trade in sugar and commodities. We begin to see the emergence of the modern and seemingly "postemancipation" state, however, when Snap is given a yeasty soul and departs for Breadland, "leaving his ginger behind." In Breadland, he is renamed Muffin and becomes, in a sense, a kind of whitened immigrant.

In Breadland, Lily arrives in an entirely new sensory ecology:

> A delicious odor of fresh bread blew up from the valley as she stood on the hill-top and looked down on the peaceful scene below. Fields of yellow grain waved in the breeze; hop-vines grew from tree to tree, and many windmills whirled their white sails as they ground the different grains into fresh, sweet meal, for the loaves of bread that built the houses like bricks and paved the streets, or in many shapes formed the people, furniture and animals. A river of milk flowed through the peaceful land, and fountains of yeast rose and fell with a pleasant foam and fizz.[63]

Breadland clearly stands as Alcott's projection of the reformist, progressive nation. There, "hearty and happy and with a lively yeasty soul," Lily lives on oatmeal and Graham bread and goes to school with white-bread children to study baking, brewing, and yeast science with a German professor, "a pleasant, plump lady from Vienna, very wise, and so famous for her good bread that she was a Professor of Grainology."[64] Yeast forms the central topic of the curriculum:

> The experiments with yeast were quite exciting,—for Fraulein Pretzel showed them how it would work till it blew the cork out, and go fizzing up to the sky if it was kept too long; how it would sour or flat, and spoil the bread if care was not taken to use it just at the right moment. . . . The children were very bright. . . . Hearty happy boys and girls they were, and their yeasty souls were very lively in them; for they danced and sang, and seemed as bright and gay as if acidity, heaviness and mould were quite unknown.[65]

Lily's time in Breadland ends when she makes the perfect loaf of bread, departing only then to take the bread home to show to her mother. When she asks to go home, she is told, "take the bread in your hands and wish three times, and you'll be wherever you say."[66] But when she asks to say good-bye to Muffin, he is nowhere to be found. Instead, she is told, "He was ready to go and chose to pass into your bread, . . . for he said he loved you and would be glad to help feed so good a little girl."[67] Ginger/Muffin, in other words, having already abandoned his brownness, more or less commits suicide—gives up his life, Christlike—in order to become the bread that will feed and physically constitute the moral and virtuous body of the white girl, who has herself abandoned the appetites that initially drove her to disrupt the heteronormative imperative. Blackness, albeit a Blackness fermentatively absorbed into some approximation of whiteness, thus fuels Lily's departure from fantasy and her reabsorption back into futurity.

Why is fermentation a transformational process that drives civilizational progress in this story, both at the scale of the individual—Lily's mastery of fermentation makes of her a "useful woman" and Ginger's actual fermentation negates his Blackness—and at the level of the population, in terms of the fermentative pedagogical project of the nation, Breadland, that concludes the historical and geographic progression of the story? As I have shown in the previous section of this chapter, fermentation theory was at the forefront of the growth of microbiology as a field in 1885; in entering this conversation, Alcott is in line with other white female authors of her period who engaged the burgeoning field of domestic science *as* science and advocated for women's rights to science education. But if we consider the various labor and energy regimes that Lily traverses, from candy to cake to bread, what we see is Alcott's investment in moving back and forth between population-level meditations—on the bodies, energy levels, and work philosophies of the varying nation-states and their various *kinds* of bodies—and a focused intervention into the particularities of white girlhood. In particular, we can see that her interest in *what living feels like* actually moves across scale not just from the population to the individual but indeed down to the emerging level of bacteriological, and therefore the microbiopolitical, as well. That this microbiopolitical move is not simply metaphoric is attested to in the ways that Alcott is attentive to affect as a kind of materiality in and of itself: sugar corrupts work energy, but fermentation is creative, productive, and pedagogical.

Yeast and fermentation thus become figures through which another erotics of everyday life emerges, one based in this new Pasteurian microbiopolitical order and determinedly set against the kinds of energy produced by sugar. Returning to the contrast with Candy Country, it might be useful to reconsider the relationship between sugar, energy, and labor. Sydney Mintz writes,

> Substances like tea, sugar, rum, and tobacco were used by working people in accord with the tempos of working-class life. Those centuries when England was transformed, albeit irregularly and unevenly, from a predominantly rural, agrarian, and pre-capitalist society were centuries of novelty in consumption. Sugar was taken up just as work schedules were quickening, as the movement from countryside to city was accelerating, and as the factory system was taking shape and spreading. Such changes more and more affected the patterning of eating habits. We have already seen how hot liquid stimulants sweetened with calorie-laden sugar, and tobacco, among other novelties, transformed meals and even the definition of the meal, while economic changes transformed the schedules of eating. . . . As the exemplar of luxuries turned into affordable proletarian goodies by dint of individual effort, sucrose was one of the people's opiates, and its consumption was a symbolic demonstration that the system that produced it was successful.[68]

Mintz was one of the first scholars of food to approach the shifts in palate that accompanied the transformation of labor regimes in the back and forth between slavery and industrialism as a question of human energy and the aesthetics of everyday human life, even though, as I have written elsewhere, he never quite allowed that connection to be the central problem of the book.[69] And indeed, other scholars have touched on the question of the relationship between sugar and aesthetics. In these formulations, sugar—its nature as fuel, as energy source—actually shapes the phenomenology of everyday life in relation to new labor and time regimes. Drawing from my reformulation of Mintz's ideas, my argument here is that Alcott essentially takes exactly the same understanding of the regime of sugar in nineteenth-century work life as a question of the sensory experience of energy itself, and she attempts to imagine the same for fermentation as a biochemical process. In doing so, her story helps raise the question, How biological is the biopolitical, after all? And how material is affect?

In "The Candy Country," we see Alcott's speculative imagining of this other aesthetic, energetic, and sensory order in that yeast is the catalytic agent that propels Ginger through the burbling primordial ooze of the white flour ocean and on to his later, whiter, incarnation as "Muffin," as well as his ultimate fate as a sacrificial figure who, as Alcott says, must not "have died in vain."[70] Yeast, however, is also the substance used to describe all the good children of Breadland, including Lily. These white-bread children have "lively," "yeasty souls" and go to school to experiment with yeast, learning to bake and to brew. Says Alcott, "they danced and sang, and seemed as bright and gay as if acidity, heaviness, and mould were quite unknown."[71] This is Alcott's fermentative everyday, and it is more than simply metaphor or analogy. For in linking the affective experience of being "hearty and happy" to having a "lively yeasty soul," she describes a structure of feeling linked to biopolitical belonging that is understood as joyful, creative, and—most importantly—effortlessly energetic and productive. In this fermentative regime, labor is never labored. That is, Alcott uses the by then widely known and understood theory of fermentation to talk about labor capacity, about the energy available for harvest in the service of "being useful."

The yeasty consciousness that Alcott strives for here is almost literally an ecstatic consciousness: Lily at one point feels as though "some sort of fine yeast had got into her, and was setting her brain to work with new thoughts."[72] This is an ecstasy, however, not in the sense of being transported beyond the body but in fact of being more deeply in it—of making "healthy bodies and happy souls by eating good plain food"—and of having one's body and self dissolved into the chemical and biological world.[73] We might characterize this ecstasy with one of Alcott's favorite words, one that Ginger uses to describe his destiny: "wholesome," a kind of completeness of self in which you are good to, and good for, the world—"good" being another keyword. The attainment of this sensation of being yeastily alive enables both Ginger/Muffin and Lily to evolve, to attain a higher state of being, but of course these are not the same states. For Ginger/Muffin, of course, to attain a soul is to be martyred, his highest calling. Says Muffin, now a white bread boy, "I [will be] eaten by some wise, good human being, and become a part of him or her. That is immortality and heaven; for I may nourish a poet and help him sing, or feed a good woman who makes the world better for being in it. . . . Isn't that an end worth working for?"[74] Ginger/Muffin, then, more than simply being martyred, is consumed: depleted and extracted of use, he becomes energetic fodder for Lily's return to normative time, as she in turn returns to the world to reunite with her mother and becomes, following Muffin's cue, a good and wise woman.

But we might also align this "wholesomeness" with another of Alcott's favorite words: "usefulness," or perhaps, borrowing a page from the geographer Nigel Thrift, "rightness." Thrift writes,

> I want to argue that, of late, as a result of the conjuring up of a particular sensory configuration of time and space in which commodities can unassumedly nestle, a different kind of efficacy is gradually being foregrounded. It is a form of efficacy that I will call "rightness" in that it is an attempt to capture and work into successful moments, often described as an attunement or a sense of being at ease in a situation. . . . The search after a certain sense of rightness has always been an intrinsic feature of the operations of capitalism, of course. . . . It is a Latourian sense of the world made incarnate by a co-shaping which is neither an intrinsic property of the human being nor of the artifact.[75]

This sense of rightness as a relation to the material world harnessed by capitalism to its own ends ties a new materialist reading of Alcott to our forgotten and neglected friend, old materialism. This reading surely resonates in a genre of writing—children's fiction—so deeply dependent on a magical relation with objects that come alive, a relation that has particularly been described as friendly to capitalism itself.

Candy Country is, in many ways, the new materialist's dream: the forms, beings, and substances living there bubble with vitality and agency, extending the qualities of humanness beyond our biopolitical protagonist, Lily. And we might link the baldly Christian symbolism that circulates around food and food people in the story—the fact that the whole story hinges on taking a laboring and newly ensouled Black subject into another (white girl's) mouth—to the more magical or, perhaps, spiritual thinking about matter that influences certain strains of new materialist thought. We are dealing, after all, with transubstantiation, with bodies and substances that, like the communion wafer, change into new substances. The idea that it is possible to attain, foster, and improve a soul is Christological, of course; the idea that improvement can be felt in that soul when the body is properly engaged in labor folds Christian materialism into an apparently secular-capitalist logic without ever naming it as such. It returns us to the Protestant labor-time energy metaphors of the nineteenth century, as explained and outlined by Daggett, Wise and Smith, and other scholars of eighteenth- and nineteenth-century political economy.

These logics, then, are both domesticated by Alcott within the language of kitchen alchemy, which, as the nineteenth century closed, was more and more infused with the language of science and which also engaged speculatively about what it might feel like to work, in a sense, without effort. Nonetheless, given the murderous ends that Ginger/Muffin meets, it is clear that Alcott chooses to do so only within the limits of her political imaginary, which cannot quite bring itself to imagine full humanity for Black subjects.

When Alcott uses the idea of the yeast fermentation that makes bread rise as an image to describe energetic and material transformation, she engages with a process that, as I have shown, had received quite a bit of scientific attention in the three decades preceding her story. Not only had Pasteur used his research into beer, wine, and vinegar fermentation to decipher the yeast organism's reproductive and fermentation cycles, but he also used the evidence of those cycles to disprove the doctrine of spontaneous generation and to argue against mechanistic explanations for ferment and decomposition, thus affirming the germ theory of disease. More than that, he showed that fermentation was the process by which the yeast organism metabolized glucose to produce the various gases that produce the leavening, flavor, and fizz that make alcohol and bread what we know them to be *and* also to create the energy that yeast cells need to survive. Fermentation, in other words, is about the production, transfer, and release of energy, and (to reiterate earlier arguments) the haunting of fermentation by the figure of multiplicity, of the crowd, of cells and animalcules that increase and grow and effervesce, making of it an energy metaphor that links individual bodies to population.

What, then, is the story that we might allow this substance to tell us not only about the haptics of "rightness" in the late nineteenth century but about the shifts in the aesthetic and sensory structures of this period? Even more precisely, building from my discussion of sugar, affect, and energy in the work of Sidney Mintz, what can be surmised from Alcott's intense interest in the energy and erotics of everyday life? Returning to my earlier discussions of the history of fermentation in relation to the thermodynamic work-energy metaphors of the period, Alcott's description of "wholesomeness" and "goodness" must also link to the experience of the biochemical and affective production and utilization of human energy within the possible distributions of sensibility made available by racial capital. Aligned with Alcott's commitment to exactly the sort of Protestant work ethic inherent to the energy metaphor outlined in Daggett's work, the word that Alcott uses to describe this capacity for labor is the "soul." The fermentative experience of white labor is both material and transcendent, but it is redeemed or at least made valuable by its being made useful and, by inference, by not being wasted.

Here it is worth returning to the questions of energy, capacity, and labor that framed my inquiry into fermentation as a historical phenomenon earlier in the chapter, but here in the context of the limited liberation project that has come to be described as emancipation and Reconstruction. Because again it is worth asking, What did it mean to reorganize the terms within which energy and labor were represented and imagined as an issue of racial difference in the second decade after the Emancipation Proclamation and during the decade following the failure of Reconstruction? What did it mean, in other words, to reimagine labor in the context of the presence of new, emancipated Black citizens whose labor had been heretofore stolen and extracted without recompense?

In organizing the telos of the story around "ensoulment" for both Ginger/Muffin and Lily, in the sense that Ginger/Muffin gets a soul, followed by being devoured by Lily, who comes more effervescently alive and then cannibalizes Ginger, Alcott allows this classically rhizomatic substance—yeast—to catalyze a vision of chemical interconnection between radically disparate bodies, bodies intimately separated by histories of racial formation, reimagined here as lying outside of heteronormative logics of reproduction but also contained within unsurprising and unimaginative racial regimes (thus further reproducing once again the liberated queer white subject at the expense of nonwhite peoples). As I mentioned in the introduction, the trenchant nature of this metaphor across time is visible in the fact that Durkheim, for instance, used the effects of fermentation—effervescence—to describe the shared and communal quality of religious experience, whose difference from the atomic and individual everyday, he theorized, led to the very idea of the sacred itself. And indeed Ginger's fermentative transformation into white bread takes place because he seems to have dissolved himself into a "great white sea of flour, . . . holding the yeast-cake clasped to his breast."[76] This transformation is also a dissolution; it is also a dissolution that takes place in the presence of an almost-worshipful community. Alcott writes,

> "I'm free! I'm free!" cried Snap, catching up the silver-covered square that seemed to fall from heaven; and running to a great white sea of flour, he went in head first, holding the yeast-cake clasped to his breast as if his life depended on it.
>
> Lily watched breathlessly, while a curious working and bubbling went on, as if Snap was tumbling about down there, like a small earthquake. The other cake-folk stood round the shore with her; for it was a great event and all were glad that the dear fellow was promoted so soon. . . .
>
> "He's gone to the happy land, and we shall miss him; but we'll follow his example and soon find him again," said a gentle Sponge Cake, with a sign, as all went back to their work.[77]

Thus, while fermentation here transforms bodies at the level of the individual, the narrative—in its insistence both on national typologies and on differences that sort themselves out along a relation to microbial transformation—is clearly thinking about population-level labor capacity.

The reader might wish to see in Alcott's story a wishful narrative about the fundamental biochemical similarities that link beings across difference, in which humans and nonhumans connect by a speculative relation to fermentation. But the sense of rightness, of aliveness, in the Candy Country can never be separated from each character's beginning and end points variously. As racialized humans or racialized objects, they are separated from each other by different relations to capitalism's commodity chain: the one a consumer, the other destined to be consumed; the one to live, the other to labor and (unbelievably, willingly) die.

This figuring of death from within the fermentation metaphor returns us to the politics of waste: What about the reorganization of labor, affect, and energy within this new regime of the biopolitical is beyond reclamation or use? (I return to this issue in chapter 4, on rot.) Here, in terms of the story, we might consider the gingerbread workers who do not graduate into edible whiteness, who remain strangely stuck between enslavement and the Fordist modeling of their labor. In this impasse, Alcott's narrative does not conform to the idea that industrialism displaces slavery; rather, it folds the two into the same state.

Thus, alongside reading the place of yeast in "The Candy Country" as being about a relationship between human and nonhuman objects and substances, we might better read it as occupying a particular place in the history of the relationship between human and nonhuman biological and chemical materials. Alcott's yeast imagery is a speculative image in the history of disciplining the various affects and bodily states produced by these vital materials, of navigating their status as threats to and agents for dominant modes and genres of bodily, psychic, and affective being. The sense of yeasty joy, of belonging, that Alcott attaches to Lily and Ginger/Muffin occupies a place in the history of science and the history of food, but—returning to Thrift's idea of "rightness"—it also occupies a place in the history of affect: it tells a story about the texture of feeling alive in a particular moment in time and therefore about life itself as it is engraved into, pursued by, and captured by the overlapping spheres of capitalism, politics, and culture.

3

INTOXICATION

In this chapter, I track the affective genre of intoxication alongside the rise of racial incarceration as it occurred in and through the rendering illegal of the forms of matter that came to be known as intoxicants. As in the previous chapters, the point, here, is to emphasize how one might use histories of matter and materiality as analytic tools that open up both the shifting landscape of biopower in the postmicrobiological era and a way into thinking with how engaging matter opens up the intersections between state biopower, aesthetic production, and affective normativity. In another mode, I am asking, How and why does intoxication—in some very particular forms—become anathema to the state, and what does that aversion reveal about the state's weaponization of its own modes of affective and aesthetic normativity against "deviant" populations, via a new microbiopolitics of matter following the late nineteenth century?[1]

In chapter 1, I traced the rise of civility and scientism as state affects against which various forms of deviant or unsecuritized forms of matter were held to be in need of criminalization and management. In chapter 2, I looked at how fermentation was taken up as a metaphor for the management of energy at the level of the individual and the crowd. Following on those two chapters, this chapter investigates how intoxication became symbolic of the disruptive excess of energy produced by fermentation's effervescent productivity and made visible as multiplicity. Additionally, this chapter explores the coproduction of white and nonwhite intoxication as separated and contrasted forms of affect and materiality: the one criminalized, the other sanctioned as both private pleasure and terrorizing racist disinhibition.

Although I do not take them up in detail, this chapter points toward two historical moments: first, the enshrining of Prohibition with the passage of the Eighteenth Amendment to the Constitution on December 8, 1917, which made all alcoholic beverages illegal; second, the War on Drugs that started during the Nixon presidency and reached its nadir during the Reagan presidency. Both of these historical events have been the object of an enormous body of historical research and critical race theory detailing the criminalization of African Americans as cocaine and then crack "fiends"; Mexicans and Mexican Americans as importers and purveyors of marijuana; Asians and Asian Americans as importers and users of opium; Native Americans as inherently metabolically inclined toward alcoholism; and working-class and rural whites as makers of bootleg liquor and inhabitors of liquor-centered sociality.

My interest here, however, is in tying these later forms of state violence and regulation to the historical shift that I have been exploring so far in the book: of the adoption of microbiological language into the biopolitical management of unsecuritized population energy, such that the resedimentation of racial and other forms of inequity particularly after the failure of radical Reconstruction took on what we might now recognize as a materialist figuration. As Michelle Alexander and other prison-abolitionist scholars have written, the growth of a profit-driven prison-industrial complex following the abolition of slavery was fundamentally a reestablishment of enslavement as a source of free or cheap labor, in the guise of a new carceral order. Of the Jim Crow era, Alexander writes, "Convicts had no meaningful rights at this time and no effective redress. They were understood, quite literally, to be slaves of the state. The Thirteenth Amendment to the U.S. Constitution had abolished slavery but allowed one major exception: slavery remained appropriate as punishment for a crime."[2] A fundamental argument of this chapter is that the War on Drugs, in its 1970s guise and again in its reincarnation as a legal push in the 1980s against the spread of crack cocaine, has earlier iterations in earlier prohibition movements that specifically targeted African Americans, Mexican Americans, and Asians and Asian Americans in regard to their putative relationships to particular forms of deviant materiality and affect, in particular intoxication.[3] More specifically, my argument is that we can deepen our historical understanding of this work by paying attention to how the earlier state securitization project, largely leveled at the microbial level, *also* played a part in this reorganization of matter and affect along racist lines. In chapter 1, I referred to this disciplinary regime and aesthetic as "hygiene," the normative and normalizing grind of everyday bureaucracy.

Both Prohibition and the War on Drugs, however, are decades away from the period leading up to the Food and Drug Act of 1906. At this moment, I want to pay particular attention to how these earlier iterations of prohibitionary legislation on the part of the state, which focused on a much wider variety of materials that included food and beverages alongside drugs (in part while seeking to create new taxonomies for consumable matter in and through microbiological means), anticipates later anti-intoxication movements through a concern with the nature of lively and intoxicating matter and its effects on humans. The question of energy returns here in that the state, undergirded by the logics of racial capitalism, needs to preserve an inexpensive or preferably free labor pool defined by race in order to maximize access to profit by creating new categories of criminalized (not productive and there unsecuritized) energy that can then be "fed," as it were, into the energy-harvesting machine that is carcerality. The overlapping of the state's interest in fermentative, intoxicating, and other forms of material-energetic capacity on top of reorganizing enslavement along carceral lines points us to how tracking energy in and through matter and materiality opens up congruences between scientific infrastructures and carceral logics.

Along these lines, the final focus of this chapter investigates whiteness and white intoxication as affective and aesthetic subject-genres that, in particular during the Reconstruction and Jim Crow periods, were paradoxically put to use in criminalizing Black intoxication. By way of setting the scene, I begin by briefly returning to the discussion of patent remedies and of the general medical and scientific anxiety around pure and adulterated foods. I then move on to discuss intoxication as a metabolic issue in the period. The second section of the chapter develops this argument by discussing a small set of ephemeral documents: two patent-remedy pamphlets. Finally, in the third section of the chapter, I turn to a cartoon serial called *Dream of the Rarebit Fiend*, first produced in 1904 by the pioneering artist Winsor McCay, which aesthetically and formally registers white intoxication as both freedom and a nightmare state. In this last section of the chapter, I also develop the links between fermentation and intoxication by showing how McCay's visual aesthetics rested on fermentative growth in much the same way as new microscopic and scientific media showed fermentative materials—for instance, the beer and cheese that make the eponymous rarebit of the cartoons—to be.[4]

INTOXICATION, REALISM, THE BATTLE OVER DRUG BRANDING

What is intoxication, and why are patent remedies part of the story of intoxication in the United States? I want to begin by thinking about intoxication as a genre of human feeling in which the categories of the material and the affective meet and are, at times, indissoluble. This idea finds its roots in the disability studies scholar Mel Chen's theorization of toxicity and intoxication as rhetorical figures and modes of embodiment that simultaneously confuse the subject-object binary and serve as recurring figures for forms of consciousness variously coded as disabled or racialized—in short, at the border of the human and the nonhuman.[5] But perhaps another way into this question is to ask its opposite: What is *not* intoxication, and what is not an intoxicant? While it may seem entirely too simple to ask such a foundational question, just that question was at the heart of the Food and Drug Act of 1906, an act (as I argued in chapter 1) that set the stage for a the juridical retaxonomization of consumable matter during and after the golden age of microbiology.

Alongside the imbrication of the new language of microbiology into the working of the state, this moment of enormous governmental administrative reorganization saw the enshrining of small-*p* progressive and benevolent values like temperance into large-*P* Progressive federal regulatory law. This shift to regulatory law was in part meant to intervene in the rampant abusive and anti-civil-rights laws being enacted at the state level after the failure of Reconstruction. The FDA, however, also reordered and redefined the relation between food and drugs and among food and drugs themselves, and in doing so shifted the ordering of correct affective comportment across the scale from the microbe to the state. These changes had specific repurcussions for the growth of which had specific repercussions for the growth of the carceral state. Prior to this new regulatory movement, the US in the nineteenth century was—because of the patent remedy industry and because of the unregulated drug market—a nation in which intoxication was an everyday and fairly prevalent experience. I, however, am more interested that this moment of redefining and regulating access to intoxicating and other consumables characterized by their lively materiality indicates a broader reorganization of the common senses: the conjoined ideological, aesthetic, and phenomenological quality of everyday life. The regulatory reordering of drugs and food, that is, is also about the categorical creation of intoxicants as illegal and controlled substance—and therefore the production of sobriety as a legally sanctioned affective state by the "Progressive" but increasingly carceral state.

Patent remedies are at the heart of this story because of their intoxicating powers and because of the power that patent remedy makers had over politics via their investment in print and newspaper advertising. However, patent remedies were not the only substance under examination at the time. As I showed in chapter 1, really every kind of food and drug and beverage was up for chemical examination and categorical definition by both the USDA and its Bureau of Chemistry. Tellingly, for instance, cocaine began to emerge as a kind of racialized matter in medical journals around 1900, specifically in debates about whether it should be available as an over-the-counter consumable, given some invented propensity of "the southern Negro" to consume it.[6] But scientists also debated whether water, for instance, was a beverage or a food. Apparently driven by mass food-poisoning incidents, they specifically questioned whether fermented materials were healthy and at what point ferment should be added or stopped. The question of the correct amount of additives or preservatives in industrial food was totally up for grabs for chemists and legislators alike. Preservatives, of course, were meant to guard against another form of toxicity: fermentation, which, as I discussed in chapter 2, was often confused with putrefaction and rot.

Fermentation, alongside distillation, was the central chemical process that produced alcohol—and therefore patent remedy—cultures, and (as I will return to with my discussion of the rarebit fiend) it was at the heart of dairy culture as well. The problem of controlling and directing fermentation, rot, and putrefaction and also of categorizing each of those processes differently also occupied a great deal of the food-purity conversation. Unlike the early periods of human history, in which fermentation had rendered liquid drinkable, in this period, fermentation increasingly defined food as dangerous or in need of management: Harvey Wiley of the Bureau of Chemistry himself included kefir and yoghurt under the category of possibly alcoholic beverages, and a large swath of the population believed cheese, in part because of its fermentative qualities, to be indigestible.

Indeed, fermentation was characterized as a danger to the body in part because it could occur inside the body, causing a condition that late nineteenth-century doctors termed "auto-intoxication": the body was poisoned—the "toxic" end of "intoxication"—by putrefied and fermented matter trapped inside the digestive process as a result of inefficient metabolism. The central figure and proponent of the idea of auto-intoxication, Charles Bouchard, drew a direct line between the emergence of microbial science onto the medical scene and the need for doctors to change their approaches to disease: "The physician ought not to allow himself to be absorbed alone in the research after a microbe. . . . Many diseases are produced by microbes, and these can only act by means of a deterioration of the health, resulting from various pathogenic processes. . . . While seeking the means of combatting microbes he ought and he will always be obliged to sustain the forces of the organism and make good its defense, inspiring himself constantly with this truth: before every illness there is a disturbance in life—for nutrition is life."[7] Bouchard's approach to auto-intoxication took on the findings of Pasteurian science—that microbes change matter through either ferment or rot but that they also infect—and made of them a different, two-pronged approach to medicine, in which microbial action within the body itself could become decidedly deviant: "What can bring about this disturbance—the first step to be overcome before becoming ill? It may bring about a change in the production or distribution of the forces which liberate certain substances elaborated by the living organism. It may modify the matter itself. . . . It may in short cause the appearance of abnormal substances through the *perversion* of the changes associated with nutrition. From absolute increase of normal matter, or the production of *abnormal* [matter], intoxication may be developed."[8] Perverted digestion, that is, leads up to the development of new substances in the body that may become toxic.

This threat of auto-intoxication meant that doctors should help patients gird up the body's defenses against other microbial attacks, but the other part of the threat was the possibility that fermented matter could infect the body from within, producing illness, debility, and abnormality because of ferment's putrefactive and intoxicating nature. These abnormalities might be brought about, in Bouchard's words, through faulty, inefficient, "deviant" metabolism that produced perversion from within.

This idea of faulty metabolism returns us to the earlier question of the thermodynamic energies of the body. If the ideal body-machine processed input and produced energy efficiently, it would minimize waste: to become auto-intoxicated was not to process food efficiently, to allow particular foodstuffs to become entropic and stuck in the gut, poisoning or intoxicating the body from within and making it vulnerable to infection from without.

It is worth returning again briefly to the idea of metabolism. Metabolism has a fascinating figural history in political philosophy, once again emergent from early nineteenth-century theories of thermodynamics: energy must go into a body in order for energy to come out, and metabolism describes the body's processing of energy input into output. Karl Marx saw the issue of metabolism, or *stoffwechsel*, as organic to human existence: humans must take objects from the nonhuman world into themselves in order to sustain their energy, just as industry must take in materials to produce products. This correlation, he argued, had become disordered under capital, leading to human alienation from the natural.[9] For Marx, then, metabolism was a physical process that explained both industry and human labor in and through the physics of thermodynamics itself.

Metabolism rose to prominence as a labor issue in the late nineteenth century as nutrition became one of the central sciences through which progressivism sought to intervene in human life as a question of energy capacity. As John Bellamy Foster has shown, Marx himself drew on Liebig's theories of the physical body, which explicitly embedded the first laws of physics into a theory of economics.[10] Charting the career of Wilbur O. Atwater, the historian Naomi Aronson writes that Atwater sought to raise money for his nutritional research by tying his work into the growing federal infrastructure dedicated to managing labor crises and unrest, including the multiple massive labor strikes of the 1880s and 1890s, as well as to the increasingly important Department of Agriculture.[11] She writes, "Atwater based his claim that nutrition offered a solution to the labor problem on two beliefs: first, that nutrition was fundamentally a science of work since it focused on the conversion of food energy to muscle power, and second, that there were social applications to be derived from the basic scientific principles."[12] For nineteenth-century scientists as well as political theorists, that is, efficient metabolism was one of the key method's through which the individual body was inserted, literally and figuratively, into an efficient capitalist economy. As ever, the USDA was ground zero for the development of these theories.

As I discussed at greater length in chapter 1, the calorie, meant to be a precise measurement of the amount of energy offered to the human body in any given food product, in many ways serves as the ultimate figure for rendering statistical the consuming and laboring body, to put the phenomenon in Foucauldian terms. Nick Cullather's classic account of the rise of the calorie notes,

> The calorie has never been a neutral, objective measure of the contents of a dinner plate. From the first, its purpose was to render food, and the eating habits of populations, politically legible. In this sense it was one of the lesser tools facilitating a widening of the state's supervision of the welfare and conduct of whole populations that has been referred to in different contexts as state building, modernism, or regulating the social. . . . The calorie was also a technology for classifying food within the inventory of resources (the "standing reserve") at the disposal of the state.[13]

In this sense, the calorie was, for the last two decades of the nineteenth century and the first part of the twentieth century, the quintessential metabolic form used to rationalize and measure the laboring body as a consuming and working machine. As Cherene Seikaly demonstrates in her historical study of food aid to Palestine, metabolic normativity was a primary technology through which such political phenomena as foreign aid, as well as the idea of development itself, was worked through.[14]

Thus, when Bouchard, speaking of auto-intoxication, discusses a "perverted metabolism" that might result in insanity or other effects as a result of auto-intoxication, he is contributing to the idea that bad digestion leads to inefficient worker bodies. In this symbolic economy, toxicity and intoxication are one and the same, but they do not so much mean drunkenness as poisoning from within. In fact, a working digestive system would *prevent* what Bouchard called "narcosis": "The substances which are generated in the intestines by putrefaction, and which are neither precipitated nor eliminated, pass on into the blood; but a natural effort to stop them is made by the liver, which partly prevents them from penetrating into the general circulation. . . . I know a patient who takes daily 20 grams of laudanum without ill effects. Is this because the poison is eliminated through the urine? If so, this should be poisonous. But it is not."[15] My point here is not to verify Bouchard's science. Rather, it is to point out that in this central account of auto-intoxication written in the wake of Pasteurian science, intoxication is a metabolic issue—an issue of absorption and bodily processing—that draws a direct line between the experience of a narcotic and a variously efficient or inefficient bodily system. Who then, we might ask, was entitled to narcotics and alcohol, and who was not?

THE RACIALIZATION OF INTOXICATION: THE CASE OF SWIFT'S (SYPHILITIC) SPECIFIC REMEDY

Swift's Specific Remedy was a somewhat alcoholic, putatively herbal liquid marketed as a broad cure for "blood poison" beginning in the 1880s, but a chemical analysis obtained by the *Journal of the American Medical Association* in 1912 found the compound to be 17.17 percent alcohol, 8.12 percent solids, and 0.16 percent ash; it was, in other words, about half as alcoholic as gin, traditionally about 35–55 percent alcohol. The historical archives of the Department of Investigations of the AMA contain a fairly thick file on Swift's Syphilitic Specific, in which it investigated the company's health claims, sent agents to its offices to inquire about its financial records, and in general treated and internally discussed both the company and the product as an alcoholic snake oil sold by money-seeking, dishonest quacks.

None of this effort seems to have impaired the success of this Atlanta-based patent remedy company still in business today. Swift's Specific (formerly Swift's Syphilitic Specific, hereafter SSS) advertised broadly, particularly across the South. The two pamphlets that I focus on here, *A Georgia Watermelon* and *A Georgia Possum*, were produced in 1891 and 1895, respectively.[16] Both pamphlets are small, cheaply printed booklets of about fourteen pages. They both feature original (albeit predictably racist) short stories by Joel Chandler Harris, one of the major southern regional writers of the era and then a well-known journalist for the *Atlanta Constitution*, the flagship newspaper for post-Reconstruction

New South politics.[17] To date, neither of these stories has received any scholarly attention.[18]

SSS Tonic, by its own words, was a decidedly southern remedy, as the regionalist titles of its advertising pamphlets imply; then, as today, however, it also had a national distribution.[19] With a home base in Georgia, SSS was during the postbellum period a major advertiser for the *Atlanta Constitution*, placing almost one thousand advertisements in the paper between 1881 and 1919.[20] Speaking thus from the belly of southern white political power in the postbellum period, the SSS pamphlets touted the tonic as a cure for every kind of ill, including scrofula, consumption, catarrh, rheumatism, cancer, and eczema. More covertly, SSS also marketed itself as a cure for syphilis, which it euphemistically referred to as a "blood disease" or a "contagious blood poison."[21] My goal is not to write about the history of those diseases or to ask whether SSS cured them (although we can be fairly certain that it did not); nor do I mean to fully abstract the distress pictured and narrated in these advertisements by rendering it purely metaphorical.[22] Rather, I want to think about the complex representations of illness, entertainment, crisis, and pleasure in these pamphlets as they are structured through the widespread understanding in the culture of the period that SSS, beyond its health claims, was a bottled cocktail disguised as medicine. How do we link this knowledge to both the looming criminalization of alcohol only a few decades later and the reorganization and reclassification of narcotics and medicine during the sedimentation of segregation and Jim Crow politics and after the failure of radical Reconstruction both in the South and across the nation?[23]

Reading these print documents at multiple hermeneutic levels, we fully access an unusual aesthetic of illness, debility, comedy, perversion, and broad comical criminality, an aesthetic similar to what historical scholarship on US advertising trade cards terms the "carnivalesque."[24] While most scholarship on the carnivalesque takes up Mikhail Bakhtin's now canonical Soviet-era rereading of François Rabelais's bawdy early-modern fictions in *Rabelais and His World*, in this chapter, I am interested in carefully relocating Achille Mbembe's rethinking of the carnivalesque as a disinhibited and terrorizing affective and aesthetic formation of the brutal neocolonial Cameroonian dictatorship.[25] Relocating Mbembe's more pessimistic view of the carnivalesque as a form of political terror into the context of the United States' particular formulations of inequality in and through intoxication culture positions these pamphlets in relation to a distant but also immediately recognizable political landscape: the emphatic reassertion of white supremacy via various forms of state and regional power at the end of the nineteenth century.

Both of the SSS pamphlets, about twenty pages each, are thin documents printed on inexpensive, acidic paper with chromolithographed (i.e., multicolored) covers. The interior is printed entirely in black and white, on paper that has by now turned completely yellow. On the first pages of both pamphlets, the left-hand page contains advertising text interspersed with numerous patient testimonials and small illustrations. The right-hand side contains the elaborate frontispiece for an illustrated story written by Harris. Both stories featuring a formerly enslaved African American character named Uncle Balaam, who recurs across many of Harris's books.

In the first pamphlet, *A Georgia Watermelon*, Uncle Balaam fantasizes about eating watermelon until it makes him sick. "UNCLE BALAAM SAT CONTENTEDLY," trumpets the headline.[26] Balaam sits at a railway yard in the heat of the sun, watching "a ventilated car" full of watermelons, when an acquaintance who works at the yard comes along to say hello. Uncle Balaam sets about to charm his young friend into stealing a watermelon. Their location is not stated, but clues in the text suggest that they are somewhere in Georgia, north of the Oconee River. The implied location sets up the conceit of technological progress: a few pages of the story are spent reporting Uncle Balaam's admiration of the possibility that one might now eat ripe watermelons out of season, as they are hauled up from farther south via these fancy new trains.

Beyond the advertised remedy, the pamphlet thus also seeks to promote southern goods like watermelon, which it then enriches in value via signs of the New South's industrial progress—namely, its connections to the rest of the country via railroad and its ability to ship ripening fruit, in modern ventilated cars, to regions where the fruit has yet to ripen. The scenario between the two men, Balaam the storyteller and the unnamed man (variously called "the other negro" or the "listening negro"), also stages the relationship between advertiser and consumer, as Balaam piques the railroad worker's interest and appetite:

"Dem yander millions," said Uncle Balaam, gazing at the freight car with half-closed eyes, "is cert'ny got de ole time look 'bout um. I look at um des now, an' seem like I kin smell de Maypop blossom."

"I wish you'd hush, Brer Balaam!" exclaimed the other negro, laughing.

"Yasser! An it look like I kin see de millions shinin' in de grass in de cool er de mornin', an it look like dey aint nobody watchin' 'cep'n a red-headed woodpecker in de top uv a dead pine."

"Oh go'way, Brer Balaam. You er gittin me all stirred up."[27]

"You er gittin me all stirred up"—the hinted invocation of desire in relation to food—raises the specter of overlap between gustatory and erotic pleasure.[28] But it is here framed, unusually, in the this seemingly innocuous moment between two Black men.

In the next few pages, Balaam continues to pique the railroad worker's appetite, drawing the responses, "I wish you'd hush!" and "I 'clar ter gracious [declare to gracious] Brer Balaam, you make me feel right quare."[29] Balaam tells the worker a story about going hunting for watermelons, an act duly pictured in the last illustration of the booklet. In Balaam's story, he seeks out and eats the perfect watermelon:

The other negro stood listening to Uncle Balaam with open mouth.

"I'l sorter poke roun in de grass wid my cane tell I come 'cross a great big million wid streaks on 'im. . . ." [said Balaam].

The listening negro moved a little nearer.

"Dey'd see me run my han' down inter de meat like a scoop an fetch myself a swipe cross de face an den dey'd hear me smack my mouf like a wagon driver poppin' a whip. . . . I'd make my way home an set in de sun an' nod. I'd nod if de bummel-eye bee didn't git me kase I'd have mo sweetness en me fum de juice er de watermillion dan one er deze yer sugar hogsheads."[30]

Here the sweetness from the watermelon mingles with Balaam's body, even as his eating is marked with the sonic echo of agricultural labor under slavery: the pop of a whip. Soon after, his body seems to merge with the melon in a dissolution provoked by sleep, sun, and food.

Balaam experiences the wages of his sin as gas or "biliousness":

> "An ef er get bilious I'd shuffle up ter town and git me———"
>
> Here Uncle Balaam made three crooked marks in the sand with his cane, thus:
>
> "S.S.S."
>
> "I'd git me dat an I'd take me a dram or two ou'n de bottle. . . ."
>
> "Brer Balaam," said the other negro, "des wait right whar you is I'm gwine ter git a watermillion. I des bleezter have it."
>
> "Go long den, honey," said Uncle Balaam, "When yo talk dat away, I ain't got time ter be in a hurry."[31]

The watermelon story offers a whiff of indecency and excess—getting the two men "all stirred up"—while casting SSS as a curative bit player in a decidedly intestinal drama, as a remedy for "biliousness" (then a catch-all term for gas, constipation, and stomach upset). This reference to digestive upset locates the promised "amusement" of the story in the narrative of bodily excess: an alcoholic circuit connects hunger, indigestion, and the latently libidinous language, each triggering "quareness." Sexuality already subtends the relationship between the patent remedy company and its consumers—as already noted, the middle *S* in SSS in fact refers to the remedy's earlier and ongoing life as a putative cure for syphilis—and indeed plays a decisive role in the history of SSS itself. What is relevant for the moment is that the term "quareness" cited in the advertisement works flexibly to encompass the range of ailments and physiological sensations that swirl around SSS, a remedy that would have been widely assumed to be alcoholic.

In *A Georgia Possum*, desire, drinking, and Blackness are similarly—though not identically—linked to theft and criminality. *A Georgia Possum* follows a comparable narrative trajectory to *A Georgia Watermelon*. Here, although the text never mentions the remedy by name, it recurs, as a kind of signature, in almost every image: nailed to a tree or veranda or hung on the wall as art (as were many chromolithographic prints and advertisements of the period). The *Possum* pamphlet again casts Uncle Balaam in a central role, this time in an explicitly Georgia setting. In the pamphlet, Balaam visits with Miss Becky, the white daughter of his former owner, to tell her that he has been threatened with being put in jail by his friend Aaron. His story begins with the two men sharing a meal: "*De way it come 'bout wuz mighty quare.* Fer one spell, me an dat ar n——r wuz eatin' out er de same spoon, ez you may say. Hit wuz Brer Balaam dis an Brer Balaam dat twel you'd er got de idee dat we wuz twinlets."[32] Aaron had invited Balaam over for a "surprise party" in which he challenges Balaam to a game of guessing what kind of "truck" or "meat" is cooking in each of two skillets: if he guesses correctly, he can choose which dish he will eat. While waiting for Balaam's answer, Aaron falls asleep. Balaam recounts, "Bimeby I made some ermark about sump'n, an' I don't git no answer. . . . [Brother Aaron] sot wid his mouf wide open an' soun' asleep. I say, 'Uh-uh, brer A'on! You can't fool me! You playing possum.'"[33] Looking into both pots, Balaam eats from the pot with the stewed possum meat while his friend sleeps and afterward places the leftover bones in his friend's lap. His story ends with Aaron waking up, realizing he has been tricked, and threatening Balaam with jail. Balaam concludes to Miss Becky, who is laughing, "Wellum, I'll say dis—ef dey er gwine ter slap n——rs in jail fer eatin' possum an taters de time's done come fer ol' man Balaam ter leave fer Affiky."[34]

Similar to the watermelon pamphlet, the possum pamphlet lays out the project of criminalizing Black men that went hand in hand with the resedimentation of white supremacy in the postbellum period. In these pamphlets, Black consumption is either extralegal or theft-like; however, the pamphlet contains the threat to economic order and whiteness by depicting Black domestic space and Black sociality as being economically and socially marginal, even deviant. Harris, of course, was both a journalist and an author and, as critics have documented, desperately sought to have his stories given the status of ethnographic documentation throughout his life. The 1895 *Georgia Possum* pamphlet opens by describing his writing as "characteristic dialect stories which so truly portray character life in the Southland." Thus, these stories toggle the generic lines between comedy, fiction, and a specious claim to ethnographic value, as indeed did most of Harris's work.[35]

Written by a major apologist for antebellum race relations and appearing in a pamphlet paid for by a patent remedy that had consistently advertised in the newspaper most closely linked to the post-Reconstruction vision for a southern economic revival, these pamphlets and their stories credibly connect to the larger political tensions set in motion by the failure of Reconstruction in 1877 and beyond. While the pamphlets and post-Reconstruction retrenchment may seem like wildly divergent discourses, the pamphlets and the *Atlanta Constitution* shared a vision for the New South's economic future. Editor Henry Grady monopolized the newspaper's editorial pages, arguing for the benefits of a commercial society across the postbellum South, emphasizing industrial progress over agriculture. In Grady's vision, this industrial society would become more efficient and less in need of labor power, setting into motion evolutionary forces that would make the South more urban and in general more like the North. Grady sought a political path in the South between the nostalgia and stasis of the Old South establishment and a vision of a modern and industrialized future. The New South position also advocated what its proponents claimed to be a middle ground in racial politics: a white moderate's project of gradual racial uplift, thus escaping association with slavery, the Civil War loss, and northern occupation of the South, that also distanced itself from the more radically egalitarian goals of the racially integrated Reconstruction state legislature.

The close ties among Harris, the *Atlanta Constitution*, and SSS raise the question, How might the circulation of Harris's stories, juxtaposed against the testimonials of illness (which I discuss shortly) within the Jim Crow South itself shift the story of intoxication and the history of the regulation of food and matter to US history writ large? It is here that I wish to return to the term "quare." The use of that term in these southern advertisements might bring to mind E. Patrick Johnson's now-canonical invocation of the Irish and southern Black vernacular origins of the term in his foundational "summon[ing of] quare studies as an interventionist disciplinary project," whose aim is "theorizing the practice of everyday life."[36] I am moved here not only by Johnson's grounding of "quareness" in the history of Black southern life and by his injunction to race queer theory but also by his call to attend to performance in the everyday, as a practice of both quaring queer theory and quaring disciplinarity itself. Such a methodology, I argue, necessarily shifts us away from a focus on representation linked to visuality and textuality toward what he terms "materiality" or "performance": the tense and ongoing work of living within the sensory orders of daily life. Put into conversation with Johnson's work, these pamphlets, as southern in origin as the term "quare," call to us to consider the historical work of "quare" itself. Deployed within the textures of the everyday in the postbellum South, "quare" underlines, as Johnson argues, the regional complexity of the history of race and sexuality as it subtends the work of narrating both wellness and illness in the United States. But the many levels and scales at which these pamphlets operate also symbolically point us to the tensions underlying the reorganization of everyday life in this period, in this region.

Uncle Balaam's quare appetite and its remedies are one such rehearsal, further quared in the material layout of the pamphlets. For both, Harris's stories lie on the right side of the pamphlet. On the left side of the pamphlet, the reader faces something quite different: advertising editorials for SSS Tonic interspersed with testimonials and small line drawings depicting the (seemingly myriad) illnesses, crises, and physical debilities of whites' bodies. The left side of the pamphlet tells a story about the United States in 1891 that seems casually disconnected from the Harris stories, which are meant to "interest, amuse, and delight." Instead, the advertisements include dozens of patient testimonials detailing illness and cure, like these from *A Georgia Watermelon*:

> I had an eating ulcer on my upper lip for eight years. . . . SSS cured me sound and well. . . .
>
> For years I have been constantly in trouble with . . . the breaking out of boils and carbuncles all over my body. . . . Nothing cured me but SSS.
>
> I had the worst type of scrofula [TB of the neck] from my infancy. . . . A friend advised me to take SSS. . . . The old skin peeled off and was replaced by a new skin.[37]

And my favorite, in *A Georgia Possum*, from poor Mrs. Bost of Statesville, North Carolina, reads, "I had catarrh twenty five years. Twelve pieces of bone, one of them over an inch long came from my nose. My front teeth dropped out. . . . I took four bottles of SSS and I improved from the start."[38] Against the tales of Black comic consumption of food, that is, the reader confronts white debility and illness, which can only be cured, it is implied, by imbibing alcohol.

Several qualities are notable here: the spectacularly confessional nature of the testimonials; their juxtaposition with the comedy of the Harris story; and the obsessive, gruesome, and relentless detailing of sensation, bodily deformation, loss of appetite, and weakness. Many, if not most, anecdotes feature open sores, ulcers, and boils ("Swift's Specific cured me of ugly and very painful boils and risings. I had twenty-three on my back and neck at the same time") and pieces of the body falling away ("My fingernails came off and my hair came out. . . . My blood was rank poison and my hair all gone").[39] Ultimately the narrative resolution is swift (e.g., "My father has been cured of the cancer on his face by use of nine bottles of Swift's Specific"), if obviously intoxicating.[40] These narratives return us to a cultural moment in which illness and disability were not just a part of everyday life but an occasion for treating pain with narcotics and alcohol—if not with SSS, then with another patent remedy. Even more, the pamphlets draw on a print genre that largely relied on rendering disability spectacular.[41]

SSS's central therapeutic claim was to be a cure for "blood poisoning," which doubled both as a disease in and of itself and as a cause of other diseases. In fact, as I already briefly mentioned, Swift's Specific Tonic was originally Swift's Syphilitic Specific.[42] By 1891, the company had shied away from publicizing the name of the disease that it claimed to cure, but even as the company dropped "Syphilitic" from the name of the medicine, its initials remained the same, the evacuated *S* pointing to the pamphlet's repressed content, a trace of its venereal history. Thus, in *A Georgia Watermelon*, the reader learns, "Swift's Specific was discovered by the Indians of America, who found numbers of their race afflicted with blood poison, which it is thought was brought among them by Columbus' men in 1492, and in the year 1824 the formula for this great remedy was obtained by white people in Georgia, since which time its record has been wonderful."[43] Race, then, is marked in this pamphlet from the first page of text forward; the "blood poison" here refers, at least in part, to the venereal diseases passed on from Europeans to Native Americans in the violent sexual conquest that formed a central tactic of settler colonialism.[44]

Whites were indisputably the remedy's primary customer base, as suggested both by the distribution of SSS's advertising and by the multiple drawings of white consumers, as well as by the history of patent remedy marketing itself.[45] Indeed, as Michael Cohen and other historians of drugs and pharmaceuticals have shown, not only were patent remedies largely marketed to whites, but they were also a central reason for the rampant rates of addiction among whites, particularly white women, at the turn of the twentieth century and particularly in the South.[46] Structured by the tension between the descriptions of disease and testimonials of recovery attributed to SSS and, on the opposing pages, the apparent comedy of the Uncle Balaam stories, these pamphlets configure health through the economy of racial metaphor. This economy, grounded in the performance of "authentic dialect," not only testifies to the inferiority of Black life but also actually sets the concision of the white narratives off in precise relief. This contrast at first leads to a surprising turn in the white biopolitical imaginary: the crisis state of whiteness in these pamphlets, which manifests a preoccupation with disability, invalidism, and degeneration among the postbellum white middle class, contrasts with the similarly disabled and yet hungry and desirous Black subject.[47]

If white consumers, covered in sores, suffer on without appetite, their skin open and broken, with bones falling out of their noses, the pamphlets script whiteness as recuperable, even transformable: white bodies, here so near to crisis and collapse, may be pulled back from the edge of death. All that is required is several bottles of SSS—and with them, a fantasy of medical sovereignty over the body. There is no such sovereignty for Balaam. He is never seen without his cane, never stops his everyday hustle for food. As such, these pamphlets barely conceal—indeed, overtly represent—that Balaam's and Aaron's performance of an excess of comic pleasure is a poorly laid veneer over what Lauren Berlant has described as the logics of slow death: "The physical wearing out of a population in a way that points to its deterioration as a defining condition of its experience."[48] And indeed, the recuperability of white health in the face of Black hunger definitively gestures to the entrepreneurial logic of laissez-faire that Michel Foucault lays out as the link between the shift in economic theory toward liberalism in the eighteenth century and the congruent birth of biopolitical state logics, in which some populations are designated as befitting of forms of death such as starvation, so that the state might excuse itself from assuming responsibility for hunger. Hunger, in the logic of liberal capital, becomes proof of the individual failure to properly manage capitalism, rather than proof of widespread scarcity. Survival itself is an entrepreneurial enterprise.

In the years between the passage of the Thirteenth and Fourteenth Amendments, in 1865 and 1868, respectively, and the *Plessy v. Ferguson* decision (1896), during which these pamphlets were marketed, whiteness seemed to be falling apart, to be seeking its remedies wherever it might find them. Henry V. Smith, of Belmont, West Virginia, attests in *A Georgia Watermelon*, "After taking seven bottles I was cured and sound and well. The old skin peeled off and was replaced by a new skin, as smooth and free from blemish as any person's. I have had no return or symptom of the disease."[49] Such is the intoxicating comfort of bodily sovereignty as it is promised to the entitled: the right to be boldly, freely exposed in the celebration of one's imperfections, one's vulgarities, one's pustules, broken skin, and nose bones; the freedom to drink seven bottles of alcohol and then emerge a new man.

As many historians have demonstrated, SSS Tonic was just one of a panoply of patent remedies circulating in this period. As powders or pills but most often as tonics and liquids, patent remedies were widely used as medicine, even as they were also accepted as a category of consumables that increasingly offered ways to imbibe alcohol and narcotics when local and state authorities attempted to control those substances. They often contained substances like cocaine, morphine, and opium and inevitably contained some amount of alcohol when they were sold in liquid form.

Perhaps the name for this genre—the aesthetic but also affective but also historical state meant to be invoked by the bacchanalian violence of the pamphlets—is intoxication itself, registered variously across a racial divide: one named as such and pathologized, the other enacted and unnamed, taken as natural entitlement. Taking the biochemical life of this tonic seriously, these pamphlets invite us to think on a broader level about the promise of disinhibited but sanctioned intoxication as one script that was offered by the product in relation to the racial drama that unfolds across its pages. Additionally, we might also consider the subtended conversation about syphilis that frames the circulation of the product itself; each of these gives the pamphlets a charge, a frisson, of unsanctioned and uncivil behavior. The materiality of SSS might be read not simply as subtextual but as explicitly linked to the racial fantasies and formations contained within and formally enacted by the advertisements: it outlines a set of still-sanctioned, intoxicated white behaviors, genres, feelings, and forms exactly in a period when other forms of intoxication were being outlawed and criminalized.

Let me return here momentarily to Mel Chen's work on toxicity and most particularly to their brilliant gloss on the relationship between toxicity and intoxication. Chen's work challenges us to follow the history of racialized disability, such as that of Down syndrome (formerly known as "mongoloidism"), through to other racialized forms of intoxication discourse, such as that of the metabolically challenged, alcoholically predisposed Indigenous person. Unpacking intoxication's racial history allows us to undo the ableist assumption of nontoxicity—of sobriety and rationality as a kind of model nonimpairment—as an intellectual and affective state affiliated with both whiteness and therefore able-bodied life.

I do want to be careful, in speaking of the unloveliness of these pamphlets, not to be complicit in discourses of ableism myself. In pointing to the terrorizing bawdiness of illness and disability in these pamphlets, my goal is not to contribute to the normalization, much less the moral economy, of health as it is and has been deployed against both currently able-bodied and disabled peoples. But I am trying to get at the wild permissiveness of these pamphlets to signal that their location in the early Progressive-era political economy of narcotic regulation underlines the relation between white disinhibition and Black terror that would, in following years, be expressed in the lynchings of African American people and in other forms of state and nonstate racist violence. The subsumption of white intoxication behind the category of the medicinal ultimately obscured and normalized the widespread practices of intoxication and addiction among white Americans.

What seems simply to be an outdated genre of advertising, selling an outdated medicinal product, then, unravels to reveal the shifting racial logics attached to particular classes of active, intoxicant materials, including medicine and narcotics in the late nineteenth century. One avenue of questioning that I could pursue here is about the parallels between the extensive culture of white pain documented in these pamphlets, the anesthetic quality of alcohol, and the contemporary epidemic of opioid use and death among working-class whites in the United States, particularly when we place that crisis in contrast with the crack crisis in African American neighborhoods in the 1980s, which received comparatively little public sympathy or compassionate state intervention. One parallel is that while patent remedies were not quite representative of mainstream medicine in this time—there really was no such thing as a medical establishment yet—many doctors did prescribe patent remedies to their patients, knowing full well that they were intoxicating. What this pamphlet does attest to, then, is how white intoxication was permitted and widespread, if not exactly celebrated, but also how closely the everyday life of white intoxication cultures coexisted alongside the production of Black criminality, which would soon become intimately and discursively attached to the circulation of narcotics. And we might also ask, Has white intoxication and even addiction historically functioned alongside white-supremacist violence? And if so, why? What terms do we lack here that might account for such coevality?

The logic of separate but equal, concretized in the *Plessy v. Ferguson* decision, plays itself out in the formal qualities of the pamphlet: the advertising on the left side and the story on the right seem on first glance to be antithetical, their juxtaposition symbolically charging the differences between them. The narrative forms themselves are not inconsequential. The white testimonials are brief and melodramatic and come to a swift, decisive narrative resolution: customers assert medical sovereignty over their bodies with the simplicity of a swig or two—or twenty. Practically presaging the 140-character tweet, customer testimonials name an issue, make it spectacular, and sum it up in triumphal healing. The Harris stories are more extended and end by invoking criminality or uncertainty: Will the watermelon thief be caught? Will Balaam be charged? Against the lone, disabled, and comic protagonist of the Balaam stories, the testimonial and advertising pages accumulate many small stories, evoking a multitude and a citizenry, loudly proclaiming both their physical tragedies and their entitlement to health; the Black subject is singular, isolated.

Even while divided by a fold in the paper, those opposing pages necessarily touch: in handling the booklet, the reader takes part in—enacts, perhaps—an intimate, interracial encounter. The reader initially flips open the pages of the booklet to stage a seemingly irrevocable difference: between Black and white subjects (and, indeed, between and betwixt male and female strangers who would perhaps not otherwise touch) posed on opposing pages. Each time a reader finishes a page, they turn to the next, pressing those pages together, forcing them into ever more intimate contact with each other even as a formal separation—a staple, a fold, and a bend—keeps them in separate compartments. These pamphlets render as inevitable both segregation and a forced and uneven intimacy between white bodies and Black subjects. Indeed, read strictly (that is, understanding the performance of reading itself in its strictest terms, reading from left to right, and turning the right page toward the left to read the following page), the Harris story actually folds over onto the white narratives, pressing Blackness down on the abject whiteness depicted there, further enacting the drama of white physical frailty and sexual vulnerability. These pamphlets thus work as what Robin Bernstein has called "a scriptive thing": an object that choreographs social and political relations by having the user of the object physically reenact (and thus give consent to) those relations.[50]

Crucial to my point here is the importance of material objects as archival remnants that retain the seemingly ephemeral traces of bodily practices, the hidden transcripts of everyday life. This sense of the kinetic as a register that does not or cannot adequately manifest itself in words—this engagement with performance and with the remains of kinesthetic cues and rituals—similarly echoes Berlant's understanding of aesthetics as "a relay through which the historical can be said to be sensed before it is redacted": the formal aesthetics of the pamphlets suggest political dimensions at the level of what can or might be felt before it can be articulated or as it is in the process of articulation.[51] Following Bernstein's reading beyond the kinetic, I also argue that these pamphlets also manifest Gilles Deleuze's understanding of Foucauldian biopolitics as a kind of material folding of the social into the body.[52] Between reading the pamphlet and imbibing SSS Tonic, that is, the reading subject is tantalizingly invited to rehearse and perform the racial erotics and logics of segregation itself, folding black page against white page and then spreading them apart again. However, subjects are also invited to fold the social into themselves, internalizing material relations by physically rehearsing them as form but then also ideally consuming the remedy itself.

In the SSS pamphlets, then, the formal aesthetic qualities of the pamphlet genre seek to align with and invoke the structure, sensory registers, and affective genres of everyday political life that surrounded it, as well as the qualities of the commodity advertised within. Each of these performatively brings to bear its own affective and political registers, and these registers, in turn, collude to assign feeling—psychological and physical—to different racial groups, aestheticizing the political and vice versa. Racial affect is here played out, choreographed even, via generic convention, making some lives tragic and others comic—and thus some pain legible and some not. More crucially, racial affect is materially invoked and practiced at the level of both text and form, with regard to both language and performance. One of those racialized affects is intoxication, which I am parsing here, alongside its affiliations with poor metabolism and impaired thought, as either white disinhibition or Black precocity and criminality. In and through SSS's performance of the allure of intoxication, we see the mutual imbrication of aesthetics and affective form, subjectivation, and biopolitical formation.

DREAM OF THE RAREBIT FIEND

If intoxication is the affective form that undergirds the SSS pamphlets, the Rarebit comics' depiction of intoxication is similarly symbolic of excess and unsecuritized energy, yet by 1904, intoxication has become completely associated with criminality. Here I wish to return to the discourse of auto-intoxication to understand how the human digestive system itself was understood as, in a sense, the body's own alcoholic still. The widespread popularity of that concept particularly circulated in relation to cheese and, in the period in which saloon and lunch chafing dishes became popular, in particular relation to Welsh rarebit, which is composed of grated cheese and beer, both of them fermented food products.[53]

An early science-fiction novel, published in 1902 by a lesser-known American writer named Harle Oren Cummins, predates Winsor McCay's comic strips by four years. Titled *Welsh Rarebit Tales*, the book consisted of fourteen short horror stories that, according to the introduction, were written after a Welsh rarebit party:

> Having run short of first-class plots, the club at a recent meeting decided to try a gastro-literary experiment. Knowing the effect upon the digestive and cerebral organs of indulging in concentrated foods before retiring, we each and every one partook, just before adjourning, of the following combination:

> 1 Large Portion Welsh Rarebit
> 1 Broiled Live Lobster
> 2 Pieces Home Made Mince Pie
> 1 Portion Cucumber Salad. . . .
>
> Partly as a warning to injudicious diners, we decided to publish the result.[54]

Cummins's stories range from frank reproductions of the main plot of Frankenstein ("The Man Who Made a Man") to nightmarish and racist accounts of Black circus snake-eaters kept employed by circuses through their addictions to alcohol ("The Strangest Freak"). At the center of almost every narrative is some account of eating or drinking in deviant ways; each outrageous story is a production of nighttime indigestion. The stories explicitly link eating improperly to a burst of imaginative energy that is both excessive (outside normative labor regimes and based in nightmares) and perverse (depicting physical deformity and racialized freakery).[55]

Whether or not Winsor McCay read Cummins's volume, his comics uncannily echo its concerns, and like the Harris pamphlets, McCay's *Dream of the Rarebit Fiend* allows us to draw connections from the reordering of matter, a result of the emergence of the microbiological world, through to the reordering and criminalization of sanctioned and unsanctioned affect and energy in the period. The artist and author of some of the most important cartoons, comics, and line-drawn animated movies of the early twentieth century, McCay is credited with inventing many of the visual innovations we now take for granted in cartoons and animation, including framed sequential movement.[56] He created *The Adventures of Little Nemo in Slumberland*, for which he is better known, and other important cartoons, and *Dream of the Rarebit Fiend* predates *Little Nemo* by a year. Published in the New York newspaper the *Evening Telegram* and later revived in the *New York Herald*, *Dream* first comes out on September 10, 1904. By 1905, the series was so popular that McCay published a stand-alone collection of the strips, and in 1906, Edwin Porter made (without McCay's permission) a six-minute gimmick film for the Edison Company entirely visually based on the strip. The *Dream of the Rarebit Fiend* comics represent intoxication as an increasingly criminalized affect that is, on the one hand, formally redolent of the visual and discursive cultures of fermentation that I discussed in chapter 2, while also linking those cultures to other products deemed dangerous by the state at the time, such as the patent medicines, nostrums, and quack remedies discussed in the previous section.

What is rarebit? Rarebit is a mixture of melted cheese and beer or ale—though I found an 1867 recipe with madeira—and sometimes with a bit of cayenne or mustard powder.[57] I have also found a few mentions of potash or bicarbonate or leavening agents added to the recipe, although that is rare. Rarebit was commonly served in a chafing dish and seems to have been often associated with gentlemen's clubs, chophouses, bars, and saloons. It seems not to have generally been heated to boiling, which would have left the alcoholic ingredients active. Rarebit is, in short, an ooey, gooey, sticky, somewhat alcoholic food, whose alcoholic qualities Edwin Porter at least underlined by showing the dish eaten with copious amounts of the same alcohol with which it was made (figure 3.1).

The introduction to the 1905 collection of the comic strip foregrounds the intoxicating and sticky sensory aspects of the rarebit. The author, perhaps McCay, wrote, "while one man's food is another man's poison, rarebit was a thing of dreams, clothed in gold and breathing a fragrance that fills the nostrils with a charm more bewitching than woodland odors, mellowed by the sole of good old ale embodying the sun-hued product of generous dairies."[58] Waxing lyrical that rarebit "trails its golden garments into dreams and opens up a wonderland in the space that lies between sleeping and waking," the introduction also argued that rarebits' power in "producing dreams [lies] in direct proportion to their tensile strength. . . . Its victims show a ruddy countenance and a confused method of locomotion. . . . Others boast that the rubber like substance which they have eaten will hurt no one."[59] The rarebit, for McCay, was then intoxicating, sensual, pleasurable, and also marked by a kind of material quality that resisted digestion and incorporation. I want to note, particularly, McCay's attention to the sensory qualities of the rarebit as both deformative and plastic in its textural qualities—able to stretch, bend, and persist—but then also deformative on an affective sensory level as well.

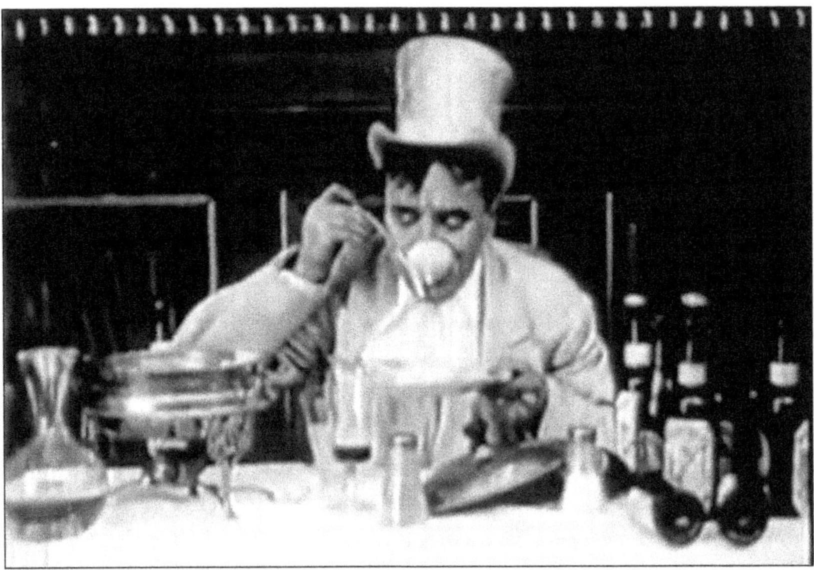

Figure 3.1. Still taken from Edwin Porter, *Dream of the Rarebit Fiend*, 1906, Edison Films.

Following on this material description, the *Dream of the Rarebit Fiend* strip is in part remarkable because while the dreams themselves become increasingly creative, undisciplined, and kinesthetically disorienting, the narrative template always follows a single and predictable formula: it starts with an everyday scene that rapidly turns bizarre, nightmarish, comical, and/or absurd; bodies perform outrageous, impossible, and sometimes terrifying feats or become outrageous and impossible themselves; in the last pane of the comic strip, the protagonist wakes up from what is revealed to be a dream and usually either decries the meal of rarebit or melted or fried cheese of the night before or swears that they will never eat it again because it causes them such terrible dreams (occasionally the food is lobster or fried cheese or mince pie, indicating a direct relation to Cummins's book). The comic, that is, is both outrageously creative in its imagination of bodily possibility and highly disciplined in its return to the everyday waking order. The preponderance of subjects of McCay's comic strips are white.

The very first *Dream* strip ever published introduces the subject of the comic via a dream about addiction: a man stranded at the North Pole without cigarettes craves them. He sees a man with rolling papers. That man turns out to have no tobacco. In the next pane, they are joined by a man with tobacco but no papers. They decide that they can die happy but then realize that they have no matches. They are then joined by a man with one match, which goes out in the wind. The dreamer then wakes up and lights a smoke in relief: "what a peacherino" dream, he says.[60] Subsequent strips elaborate on this theme but are more focused on other kinds of (often similarly addictive) consumption.

The formal and even at times formulaic consistency between the comics creates the sense of a kind of fungibility between the substances that McCay explores in the early versions of the comic strip. While the series begins with cigarettes, McCay's earliest rarebit comics also point to the fine line between alcoholic beverages and patent remedies. In one strip published a few weeks after the cigarette strip, one white gentleman challenges another to a drinking contest in a pub: together they drink thirty beers, forty-five quarts of rye whiskey, twelve gallons of brandy, and nine barrels of ale, which are administered by hose. Before they can drink in even more liquor, however, the dreamer wakes up and says, "Well of all the dreams! I wonder what my congregation would say if that was real?"[61] The line from cigarettes to liquor to patent remedies lays out illicit consumption as a central theme of the rarebit fiend strip. Yet by the sixth strip, rarebit-like substances start to tiptoe more obviously into the narrative: a man tries a hair-growing remedy that makes his hair grow so successfully that he becomes an exhibit in a vaudeville show. In the last pane, he wakes up and says, "All that mince pie with melted cheese does some funny things with you but I'm done no more for me" (figure 3.2).

With the eighth strip, the reader gets the first mention of rarebit: a man drinks homemade wood alcohol in a saloon and hallucinates animals surrounding him until, just as he is being suffocated by a large snake, he wakes up: "Oh I am at home, good! But I can lick the man who told me last night rarebits would hurt no one, oh!"[62] Similarly, in the tenth strip, a woman buys a bottle of fattening tonic for her husband and a bottle of weight-loss tonic for herself. She, however, begins to get fatter and fatter, and he begins to waste away. They then discover that they each took the wrong tonic. In the last pane, a child, who has been

Figure 3.2. *Dream of the Rarebit Fiend*, originally published in the *New York Evening Telegram*, October 14, 1904. From the complete DVD in Ulrich Merkl and Winsor McCay, *The Complete Dream of the Rarebit Fiend (1904–1913)* (Marienenberg, Germany: Beduinenzelt, 2007).

the observer in all of the pictures, turns out to be the dreamer, and the wife tells her husband, "Andy! I told you not to give that child any of that rarebit didn't I?" (figure 3.3).[63]

Finally, by the eighteenth strip, we are fully encheesed: a man flies to what he assumed would be heaven after dying in a car crash. (McCay hated cars and refused to learn to drive.) He then arrives in hell and is

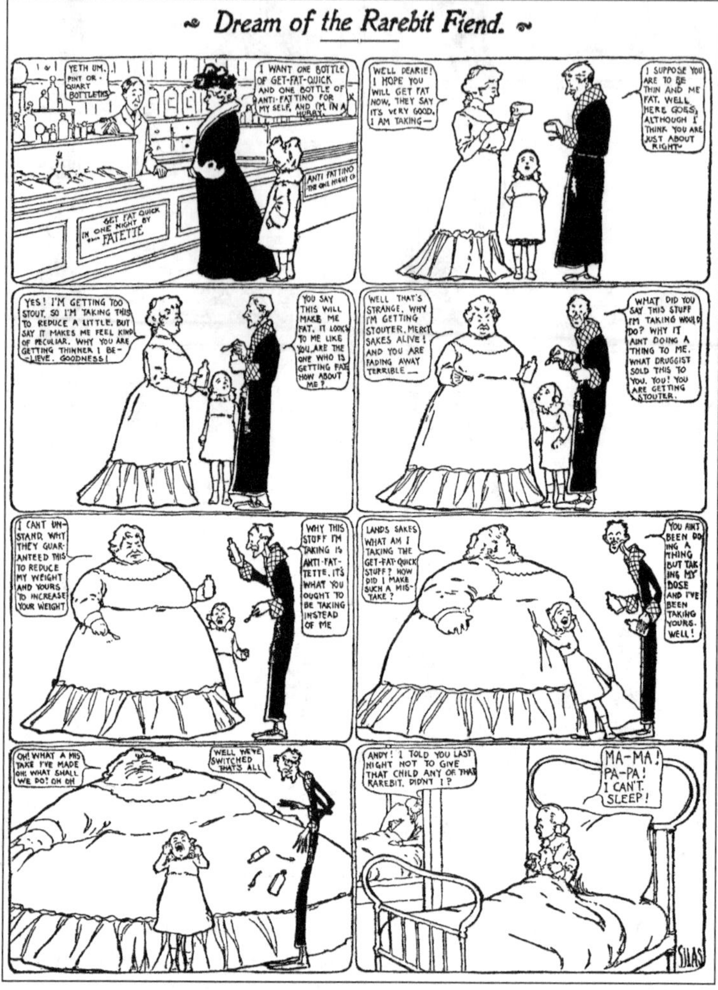

Figure 3.3. *Dream of the Rarebit Fiend*, originally published in the *New York Evening Telegram*, October 29, 1904. From the complete DVD in Ulrich Merkl and Winsor McCay, *The Complete Dream of the Rarebit Fiend (1904–1913)* (Marienenberg, Germany: Beduinenzelt, 2007).

sent into a world of cheese, presumably for being from New York. The cheese holds him down, sticking him to the ground so that he cannot leave and argue his case. A devil then comes to tell him to spin around a dozen times because the boss devil wants to see him melt. In the last pane, of course, he wakes up and says, "Oh! Oh! Well was I dreaming? Oh those rarebits are terrible things to eat, Oh! Oh! Oh!" (figure 3.4).[64]

Figure 3.4. *Dream of the Rarebit Fiend*, originally published in the *New York Evening Telegram*, December 2, 1904. From the complete DVD in Ulrich Merkl and Winsor McCay, *The Complete Dream of the Rarebit Fiend (1904–1913)* (Marienenberg, Germany: Beduinenzelt, 2007).

The naming of all of these strips as *Dream of the Rarebit Fiend*—even when the immediate cause of intoxication is not rarebit in the early days—points to a number of ways in which what would seem to us to be multiple forms of intoxication are in fact linked, whether the cause be beer, cheese, alcohol, cigarettes, or fattening or thinning medicines. At the same time, the term "fiend" hints at rarebit's similarity to or even categorical inclusion with other addictive substances. In fact, later, in the seventy-third comic (figure 3.5), a man seeks out a rarebit speakeasy and is rounded up and arrested in a "rarebit hutch" when police raid the place. Indeed, in this strip, the entire joke is that rarebit is somehow equivalent to an illegal intoxicant such that it needs to be sought out away from the eyes of the police.[65]

In another strip in which the protagonist ends up in jail, albeit in the dream, an obviously intoxicated man staggers through Manhattan, tearing up real estate and buildings (figure 3.6).[66] In the last pane of this strip, the rarebit dream is attributed to mince pie. But, most fascinatingly, the *Telegram*'s archive reveals that only four days previously—on January 3—a Peruna ad featured a massive body against an uncannily similar New York skyline, an image that is likely to have inspired McCay (figure 3.7).[67] (Recall that Peruna was over 28 percent alcohol and a favorite target of the anti-patent-remedy activists.) In both of these sets of images, intoxication produces a body that pushes against its own bodily limits, exceeding even the spatial structures of the city itself, before returning, as ever, to an everyday disciplinary containment—in this case, waking up from his dream in jail.

Taking seriously that *Dream of the Rarebit Fiend* was conceived of and written in precisely the same period that the Food and Drug Act was being written, debated, and passed, we see that the issue was not simply the rarebit itself—although clearly rarebit is not entirely occasional or cosmetic to the narrative—but the larger class of psychic and physiological, that is, affective, states that are provoked by the class of intoxicating, and in particular fermentative, substances to which rarebit and its ingredients (ale and cheese) at that time belonged. In short, the crude materiality of these fermentative substances, as it is inspired by the emergent visualities of the Pasteurian age, results for McCay in aesthetic commitments that he poses as the work of either the unconscious or the nightmare self, straining against the regulatory imperatives of the workaday world.

Figure 3.5. *Dream of the Rarebit Fiend*, originally published in the *New York Evening Telegram*, June 3, 1905. From the complete DVD in Ulrich Merkl and Winsor McCay, *The Complete Dream of the Rarebit Fiend (1904–1913)* (Marienenberg, Germany: Beduinenzelt, 2007).

Figure 3.6. *Dream of the Rarebit Fiend*, originally published in the *New York Evening Telegram*, January 7, 1905. From the complete DVD in Ulrich Merkl and Winsor McCay, *The Complete Dream of the Rarebit Fiend (1904–1913)* (Marienenberg, Germany: Beduinenzelt, 2007).

PROPRIETARY. | PROPRIETARY. | PROPRIETARY. | PROPRIETARY.

NEW YORK PROTECTED BY PE-RU-NA.

LIKE A DEMON grip has crossed the country leaving behind scores of physical wrecks.

Victims of catarrh of the head, catarrh of the throat, catarrh of the lungs, catarrh of the stomach, catarrh of the kidneys, catarrh of the pelvic organs, are to be counted by hundreds of thousands.

Grip is epidemic catarrh, and sows the seed of chronic catarrh within the system.

This is so true that few grip sufferers are able to make a complete recovery until they have used Peruna.

Never in the history of medicine has a remedy received such unqualified and universal eulogies as Peruna.

Pe-ru-na Recommended for Colds.

Mr. John F. Maher, 401 West Sixth street, New York city, writes:

A Prominent Dramatic Reader Restored to Health.

Miss Irene Ackerman, 20 W. 15th St., New York city, writes:

One Month's Treatment With Pe-ru-na Cures Nasal Catarrh.

"For nearly a dozen years catarrh has bothered me in one form or another.

La Grippe Cured With Two Bottles of Pe-ru-na.

Figure 3.7. "The Strong Hand of Pe-ru-na," *New York Telegram*, January 3, 1905, 5.

One can easily hypothesize that one of the major intertexts for McCay is early science film as well as magic lantern science shows. One well-known film was Charles Urban's *The Cheese Mites*, produced in England in 1903; in it, a gentleman using a magnifying glass to read the newspapers accidentally looks at the cheese on his plate and is shocked by the teeming life revealed. Scott Bukatman, in his book on McCay, expands on the prehistory of animation in scientific studies shot with Étienne-Jules Marey's "chronophotographic gun."[68] Science films, as media and science and technology studies scholars have increasingly written, formed an important subgenre of the larger genre that Tom Gunning described as "the cinema of attractions."[69] Moreover, the line between scientist and filmmaker was a fine one: even Auguste Lumière, of the Lumière brothers, was also a biologist who published in bacteriology journals, performed experiments on various forms of infected tissue, and developed various visual technologies to capture cellular change.[70] In conversation with these images—some of which I discussed in chapter 2 in the discussion of Pasteur's work on beer—it is at the level of the cell and specifically the fermentative cell as it is imagined as a site of energetic increase that I find myself thinking most about McCay's insistently repetitive comic strips.

As Hannah Landecker and others have documented, science films and magic lantern shows developed alongside other forms of turn-of-the-century popular entertainment, and Urban's London-based films were circulating in the United States by 1903. McCay himself had a thriving vaudeville career as a speed caricaturist, so he would have been well aware of all these media. This was also the age in which films and slides of biological material rendered at the cellular level became possible, particularly as experimental protocols in biology shifted from in vivo work, with living animals, to in vitro work, with cells "persuaded to live outside the body, glass-enclosed but always in full view."[71] While mid-nineteenth-century bacteriologists relied on slides of dry, stained cells to study cell structure, and Pasteur used photogravure, hand drawings, and microphotography to open up the visual world of microbiological life, by the 1880s, the German bacteriologist Robert Koch was leading the way forward in microbiological visual technologies by isolating anthrax bacilli in a transparent chamber, incubating the slides, and observing their growth from day to day, thus allowing for the elements of time and movement to enter the visual language of microbiology.[72]

Many of these media were initially in the form of sequential drawings, as in the case of Pasteur, whose initial training at the École des Beaux-Arts has been well documented, but later photographic slides showing images of various biological phenomena were available to the public in public expositions by scientific societies or described in newspapers and popular-interest magazines.[73] At issue in the films, as in the sequential photographs, was the period's fascination with movement and change, as well as with its new encounters with scale and time. Indeed, as Landecker shows, the cell was a primary unit for imagining visuality in this time. She writes, "The shot, then, is a cell; the montage, an organism formed by cell division; and filmmaking, embryogenesis."[74]

A great deal of scholarly attention has been paid to the intertwined histories of cinema and the sequential newspaper comic. Jared Gardner writes, "In the early years of the twentieth century, the newspapers and the cinema were indeed two spaces where a new moving script was being developed. . . . However, the crux of this relationship lies in the sequential comic, which for the first decade of film history provided the model, the theory, and the material to begin tracing out a new 'moving script' for camera and screen."[75] That Walter Benjamin, arguably the most astute and encyclopedic cultural critic of the twentieth century, largely missed the foundational importance of the comic form when looking at newspapers and cinema in the 1920s is not surprising. Even as Germany played a large role in the nineteenth-century origins of sequential comics, in neither Germany nor in the United States would the existence of comics register for the vast majority of cultural critics until the late twentieth century, except occasionally as a synonym for all that is ephemeral and disposable in mass culture.

One counter-example is Scott Bukatman's useful study of the close formal relations between Marey and his contemporary Edward Muybridge's experiments in motion capture and McCay's work in *Little Nemo Dreams of Slumberland*. Building on the earlier work of the comics scholar Scott McCloud, Bukatman writes, "By posing the dimension of time on a visible linear continuum, comics offer something different from cinema. Even after the reader has proceeded from picture to picture, the panels continue to relate to one another on the page."[76] In other words, comics more clearly resemble what Muybridge produced than what the Edison Company and the Lumières followed it with.[77]

Bukatman's study examines McCay's work in relation to themes of modernist visual and literary inquiry, such as the relationship between sensation and the city as well as the widespread contemporary discourses of neurasthenia, or nervous exhaustion. Bukatman also discusses *Dream* in relation to McCay's protofilmic engagement with motion and change between the cells of the comic, arguing that McCay's aesthetics ultimately break free of the limits of the comic-strip square itself. My interest here, while aligning with Bukatman's adoption of Anson Rabinbach's reading of the body as machine, turns to the smaller scale. I am interested in how the new microscopic level at which biopolitics was imagined also draws a line between the aesthetic and energetic economies of the comic and, for instance, microscopic slides. This issue is really one of scale: while scholars are attentive to the history of film in relation to scientific studies of human and animal motion, in relation to comics, scholars have rarely attended to the microbiological revolution taking place at the same time. Yet, as Olivier Gaycken and Scott Curtis demonstrate in their studies of early science film, fascination with what entertainment entrepreneurs called "The Unseen World" was widespread, and exhibitions demonstrating these microbiological worlds were wildly popular.[78]

Thus, in a 1903 article in the *New York Times* titled "Recreation with the Microscope," the author writes, "When the New York Microscopical Society was organized, about seven years ago, it was mainly for the convenience of physicians interested in bacteriological study. . . . But it was very soon apparent that many persons were interested in microscopical work aside from its importance to medicine. Members began to read papers on . . . the mosquito; on the digestive organs of grasshoppers, the potato bug, the locust boring beetle, the fermentation of beer and yeast, and the nutritive value of certain alleged health foods."[79] As the slide-lantern catalogues and film and vaudeville bills remaining from the period show, the microbiopolitical and early science-film age opened up the sense of an invisible world teeming with multitudes; other attraction films were similarly fascinated with the crowd, like those of Sagar Mitchell and James Kenyon, which showed workers leaving factories.[80]

Rarebit Fiend picks up on all of these themes, but to the sense of movement, McCay adds a fascination with frenzied and undisciplined multiplication. In a comic strip published on June 24, 1905 (figure 3.8),

Figure 3.8. *Dream of the Rarebit Fiend*. Originally published in the *New York Evening Telegram*, June 24, 1905. From the complete DVD in Ulrich Merkl and Winsor McCay, *The Complete Dream of the Rarebit Fiend (1904–1913)* (Marienenberg, Germany: Beduinenzelt, 2007).

for instance, a man takes a "Seidlitz" powder for his headache; the powder then effervesces out of control, spinning the dreamer through space. As panes four through ten show, the bicarbonate mixture explodes outward, ultimately taking over the banal human drama of the headache with the biochemical and determinedly biological, even abstract, imagery of rampant growth. Panes eight and nine in particular seem to signal the abstraction of cellular forms. In the last panel of course, the dreamer wakes up to bemoan "those blamed rarebits."

Similarly, in a comic published on April 15, 1905, a solitary gentleman goes out for a walk, where he is greeted by his exact "ringer" (figure 3.9).[81] In panes 2 through 9, his body multiplies until there are many identical protagonists vying for narrative control, and the multiplied self stages a continual dissolution and nondissolution of self from other. Each iteration of the protagonist uses the first person to refer to each of his other selves: "I shall kick myself out of bed if I don't let me"; "We are usses, mees"; "I will explain we are all me I am ourselves"; "we are a bunch of mees"; "I am we." Signaling a kind of cellular reproduction, the protagonist encounters a bud-reproduced identical self, one that ultimately constitutes a crowd.

In the proliferation of protagonists in this comic, we can see the echoes of such early cell photography and imaging as Pasteur's admittedly adorable sketches of budding cells in his 1885 beer book, and in this sense, the comic strips form a bridge between the drawing, staining, and histology microphotographies that dominated cell imaging in this period and the microcinematographic movies that emerged soon after. For example, as Landecker has shown, Julies Ries's set of photographic images, "Fertilization and Development of the Sea Urchin Egg," made and printed in Paris in 1907, tracks the proliferation and growth of a sea urchin embryo in serial fashion, embedding time in a serial visual framework.[82] While, as Landecker shows, the only evidence of this cinematic documentation of cellular reproduction is a print Ries made for subsequent publication, putting such early science microcinematography next to comics makes the parallel formal interests of the sequential comic and microcinematography clear.

Similarly, we can also see how the idea of reproductive increase was a concern of early cinema that is formally echoed in McCay's work through the comic's run from 1904 to 1909. In one comic from 1909, for

Figure 3.9. *Dream of the Rarebit Fiend*, originally published in the *New York Evening Telegram*, April 15, 1905. From the complete DVD in Ulrich Merkl and Winsor McCay, *The Complete Dream of the Rarebit Fiend (1904–1913)* (Marienenberg, Germany: Beduinenzelt, 2007).

instance, a young man becomes increasingly paranoid that his sweetheart has kissed the moon, at the same time as the moon begins to multiply in the sky (figure 3.10).[83] Similarly, in a 1908 comic strip a man applies a hair-growth tonic to his head only to have a bumper crop of mushroom fungus grow there, which his wife sells to their profit (figure 3.11).[84] McCay repeats the image in 1909 but with the protagonist growing heads (figure 3.12).[85] In all of these images, we can see a similar anxiety with fermentation's disproportionate expansion, albeit an anxiety tinged with aesthetic pleasure.

In *Theory of Film: The Redemption of Physical Reality*, Siegfried Kracauer wrote, "In its preoccupation with the small the cinema is comparable to science. Like science, it breaks down material phenomena in tiny particles, thereby sensitizing us to the tremendous energies accumulated in the microscopic configurations of matter. These analogies may well be related to the nature of film. It is quite possible indeed that the construction of the film image from shots of minute phases of movement favors the reverse tendency toward decomposing given wholes."[86] This fascination with cellular proliferation at the microscopic level clearly translates into *Dream*'s formal qualities, but there it is not simply an issue of stuffing more things into a comic cell but rather documenting and representing, in Kracauer's term, energy itself, as each figure becomes an accumulation of many selves that crowds, populates, and pushes at the limits of the comic's formal cell container. At the heart of this accumulation, as Landecker points out, is cellular reproduction: the ability of biological matter to proliferate and make more of itself, to produce excessively.[87]

Here, however, we must not lose track of intoxication, which anchors the narrative flow of every *Rarebit* comic. Fermentation's energetic life was directly linked, in scientific and pseudoscientific literature, to various forms of intoxication. Certainly, when it came to food and alcohol, fermentation's alchemical properties and its proximity to putrefaction produced a great deal of public and scientific curiosity, as scientists worked out how to pasteurize and manage healthy and unhealthy bacteria in cheeses and other dairy products. The sheer amount of scientific and popular literature on the question of fermentation and its difference from putrefaction can almost not be counted. As we have already covered, Bouchard claimed that such intoxication came from the intestines:

Figure 3.10. *Dream of the Rarebit Fiend*, originally published in the *New York Evening Telegram*, September 16, 1909. From the complete DVD in Ulrich Merkl and Winsor McCay, *The Complete Dream of the Rarebit Fiend (1904–1913)* (Marienenberg, Germany: Beduinenzelt, 2007).

Figure 3.11. *Dream of the Rarebit Fiend*, originally published in the *New York Evening Telegram*, July 16, 1908. From the complete DVD in Ulrich Merkl and Winsor McCay, *The Complete Dream of the Rarebit Fiend (1904–1913)* (Marienenberg, Germany: Beduinenzelt, 2007).

Figure 3.12. *Dream of the Rarebit Fiend*, originally published in the *New York Evening Telegram*, August 19, 1909. From the complete DVD in Ulrich Merkl and Winsor McCay, *The Complete Dream of the Rarebit Fiend (1904–1913)* (Marienenberg, Germany: Beduinenzelt, 2007).

> Two disintegrating processes are at work: *fermentation* of the carbohydrates from decomposition and *putrefaction* consequent upon the breaking down of proteids (proteins), a process which is attended by the formation of substances that give off an extremely unpleasant odor. . . . In one form of auto-intoxication poisons are formed in the interior of the cells of the body as a result of metabolism: in another they are formed within the intestinal canal from decomposition of putrefaction of the food as a consequence of the operation of formed and unformed ferments, . . . which allows of the production of toxic bodies from ingested food.[88]

Here we see that the line between fermentation and putrefaction is a very fine one, but further, we see that fermentative foods were still seen to be a danger, not simply because they were themselves fermenting but because they might continue to do so, turning to intoxicating rot inside the body. The primary threat here, of course, is that of toxicity: one may become toxic from ingested food, but as Bouchard proceeds to explain, one may also become manic, depressed, melancholic, or hallucinatory or fall into a stupor. In short, affective and psychotropic alterations, as a result of putrefaction-caused auto-intoxication, were to be expected. Fermentation and decomposition were the processes that created these new altered states: these newly visible forms of materiality leading directly to affective and energetic changes.

Relatedly, fatigue is a key theme in *Dream of the Rarebit Fiend*, and many of the strips end with dreamers awakening from napping on the street or on the job—even in addition to the foundational nighttime sleep narrative of the strip. Here I might follow Scott Bukatman to dive deeper into Anson Rabinbach's discussion of the relationship of the science of thermodynamics to nineteenth-century productivist work sciences to see how fatigue, like entropy and waste, became objects of interest in the many sciences that colluded with or drew on cinematographic technologies to study and quantify motion, with an eye to creating more efficient or extractive work structures. Where I would depart from Bukatman in his related reading of *Rarebit* is in his sense that one can entirely situate the comic strip in relation to the models of motion efficiency studies by the proponents of industrialism and productivism. Bukatman writes, "As the nineteenth century draws to a close, the body in comics is increasingly depicted as deformed by the machineries of

Plate 1. Installation view, Candice Lin, *A Hard White Body*, 2017. Bétonsalon, Paris, France. (Courtesy of the artist and François Ghebaly Gallery; photo: Aurélien Mole)

Plate 2. Installation view, Candice Lin, *A Hard White Body*, 2017. Bétonsalon, Paris, France. (Courtesy of the artist and François Ghebaly Gallery; photo: Aurélien Mole)

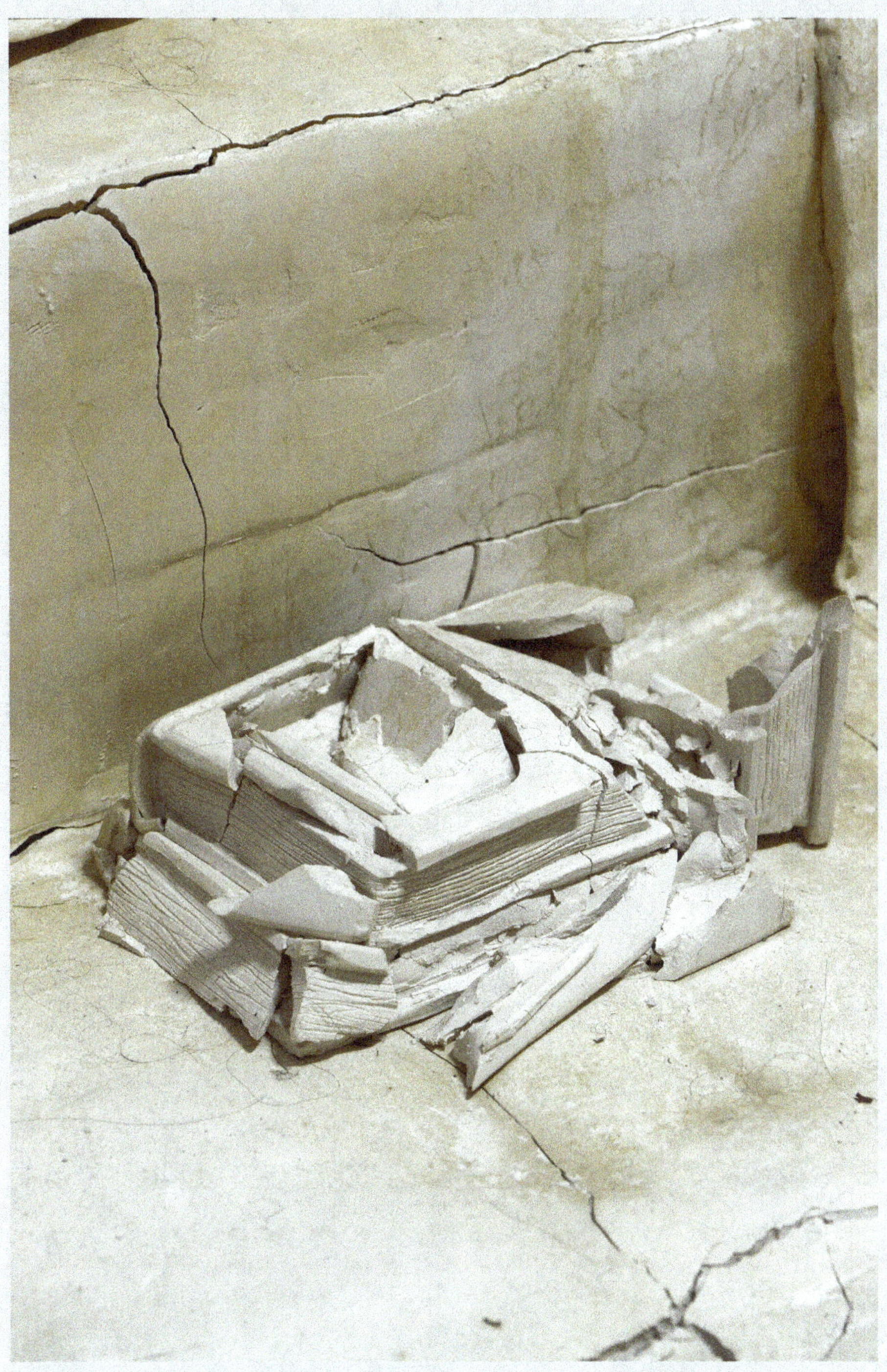

Plate 3. Installation view, Candice Lin, *A Hard White Body*, 2017. Bétonsalon, Paris, France. (Courtesy of the artist and François Ghebaly Gallery; photo: Aurélien Mole)

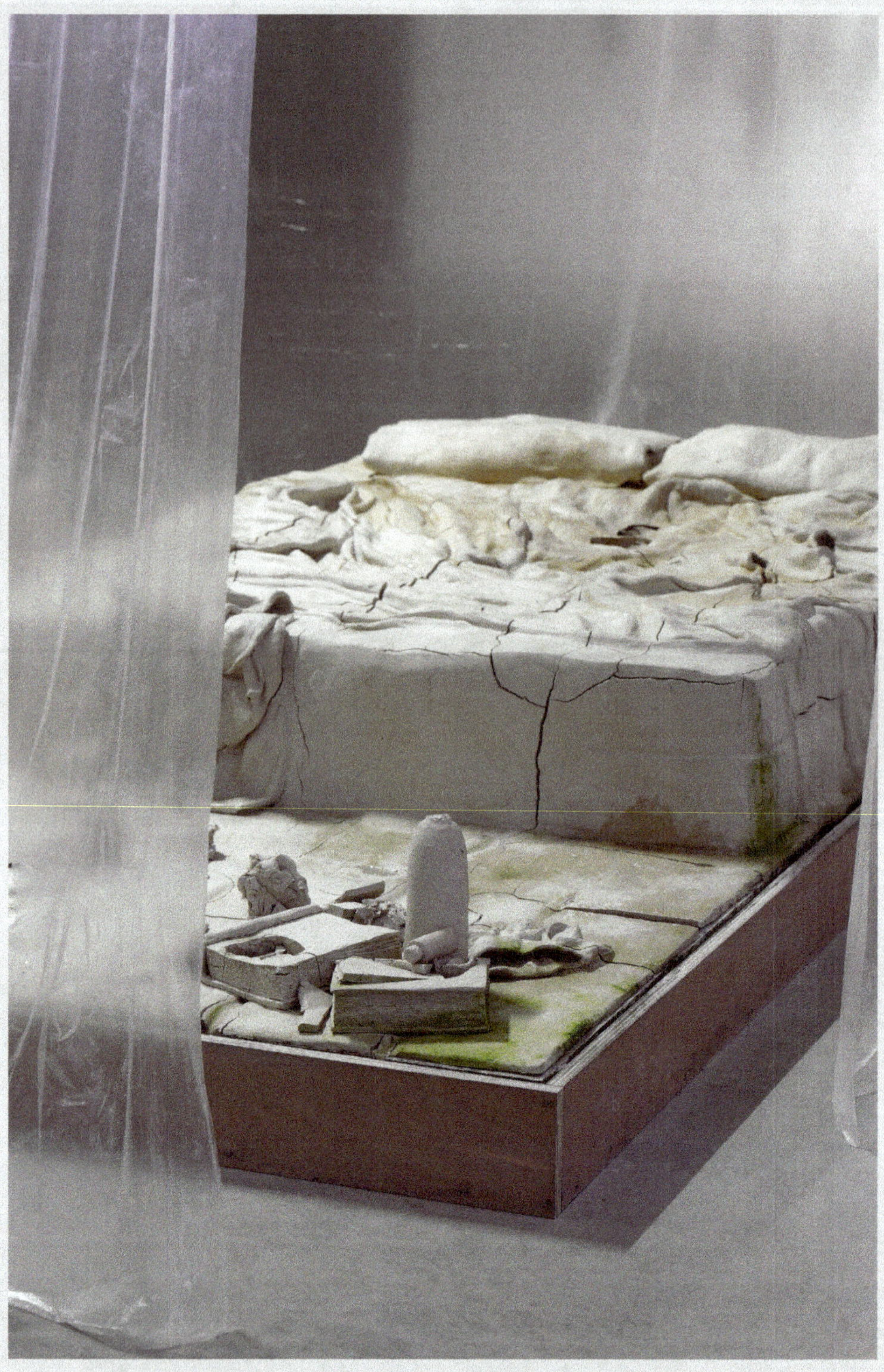

Plate 4. Installation view, Candice Lin, *A Hard White Body*, 2017. Bétonsalon, Paris, France. (Courtesy of the artist and François Ghebaly Gallery; photo: Aurélien Mole)

Plate 5. Installation view, Candice Lin, *A Hard White Body, a Soft White Worm*, 2018. Portikus, Frankfurt, Germany. (Courtesy of the artist and François Ghebaly Gallery; photo: Helena Schlichting)

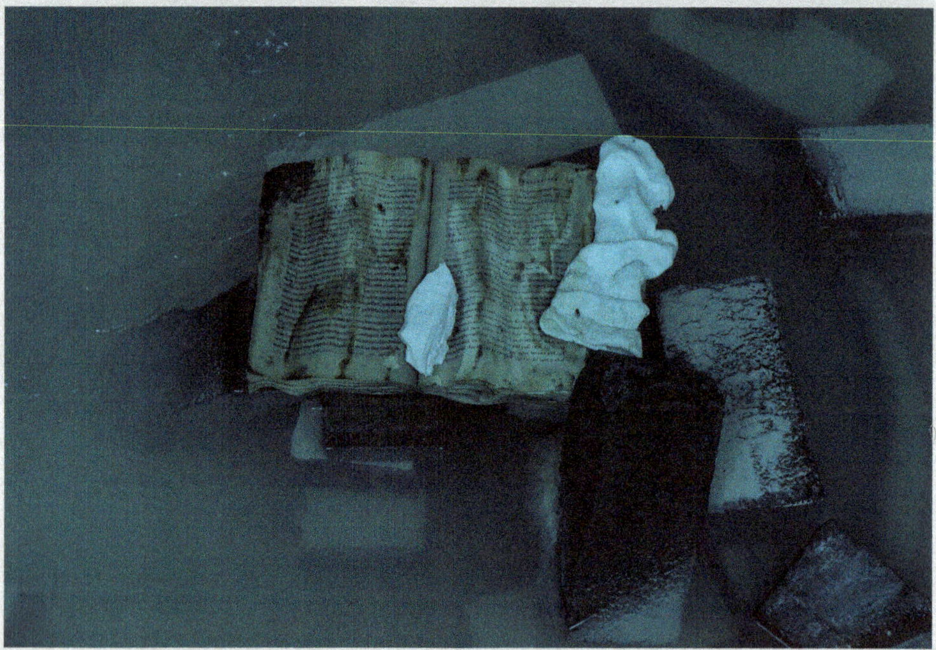

Plate 6, (*top*). Plate 7, (*bottom*). Installation view, Candice Lin, *A Hard White Body, a Porous Slip*, 2018. Logan Center Exhibitions, Chicago, USA. (Courtesy of the artist and François Ghebaly Gallery; photo: Robert Chase Heishman)

Plate 8. Installation view, Candice Lin, *A Hard White Body, a Porous Slip*, 2018. Logan Center Exhibitions, Chicago, USA. (Courtesy of the artist and François Ghebaly Gallery; photo: Robert Chase Heishman)

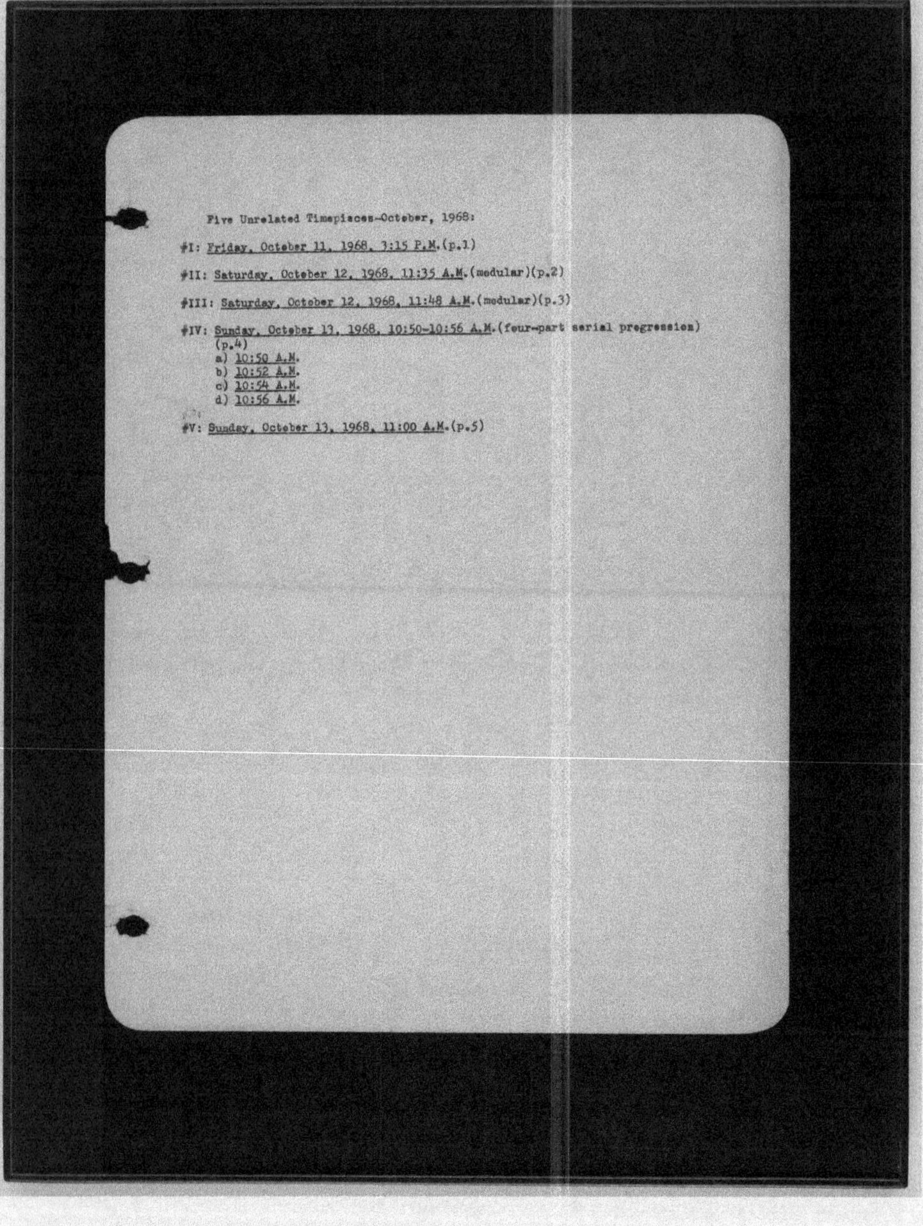

Five Unrelated Timepieces—October, 1968:

#I: Friday, October 11, 1968, 3:15 P.M.(p.1)

#II: Saturday, October 12, 1968, 11:35 A.M.(modular)(p.2)

#III: Saturday, October 12, 1968, 11:48 A.M.(modular)(p.3)

#IV: Sunday, October 13, 1968, 10:50–10:56 A.M.(four-part serial progression)
(p.4)
a) 10:50 A.M.
b) 10:52 A.M.
c) 10:54 A.M.
d) 10:56 A.M.

#V: Sunday, October 13, 1968, 11:00 A.M.(p.5)

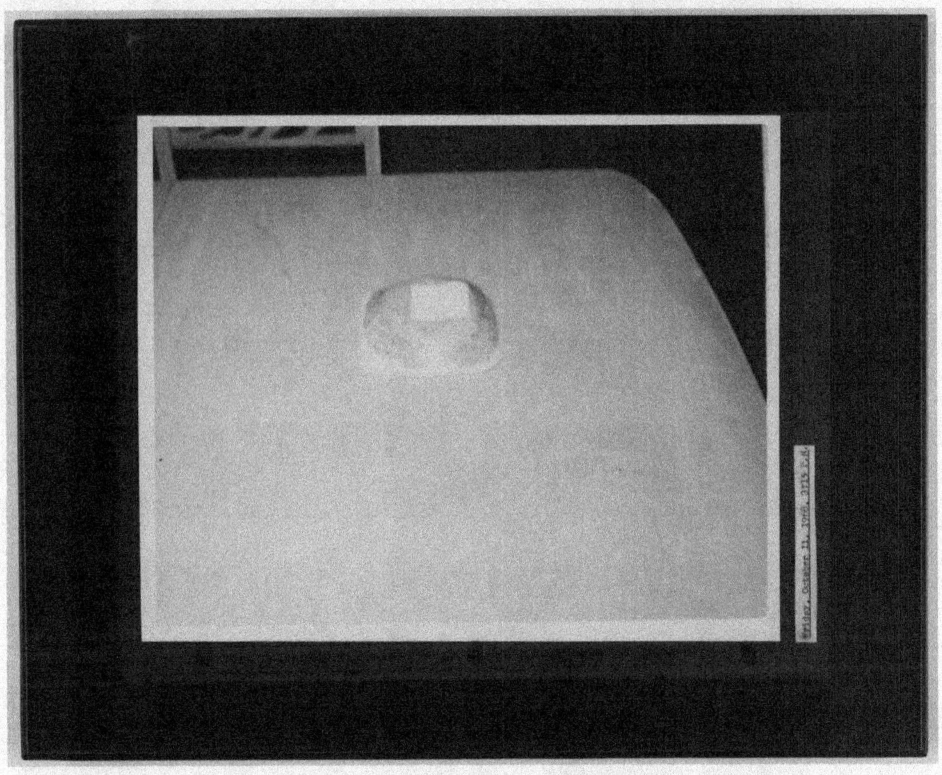

Plate 9, (*facing page and above*). Adrian Piper, *Five Unrelated Time Pieces (Meat into Meat)*, 1968, six pages, one typescript page, eight photographs and text mounted on black paper, each page 9.5" × 11.5" (24.1 cm × 29.2 cm) or 11.5" × 9.5" (29.2 cm × 24.1 cm). (Collection of Paul and Karen McCarthy. © Adrian Piper Research Archive (APRA) Foundation Berlin)

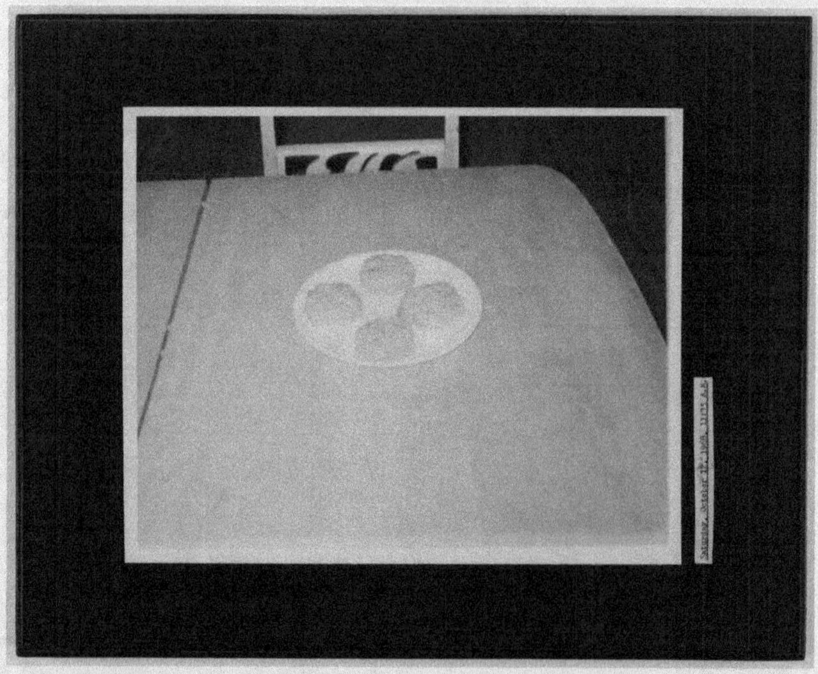

Plate 10. Adrian Piper, *Five Unrelated Time Pieces (Meat into Meat)*, 1968, six pages, one typescript page, eight photographs and text mounted on black paper, each page 9.5" × 11.5" (24.1 cm × 29.2 cm) or 11.5" × 9.5" (29.2 cm × 24.1 cm). (Collection of Paul and Karen McCarthy. © Adrian Piper Research Archive (APRA) Foundation Berlin)

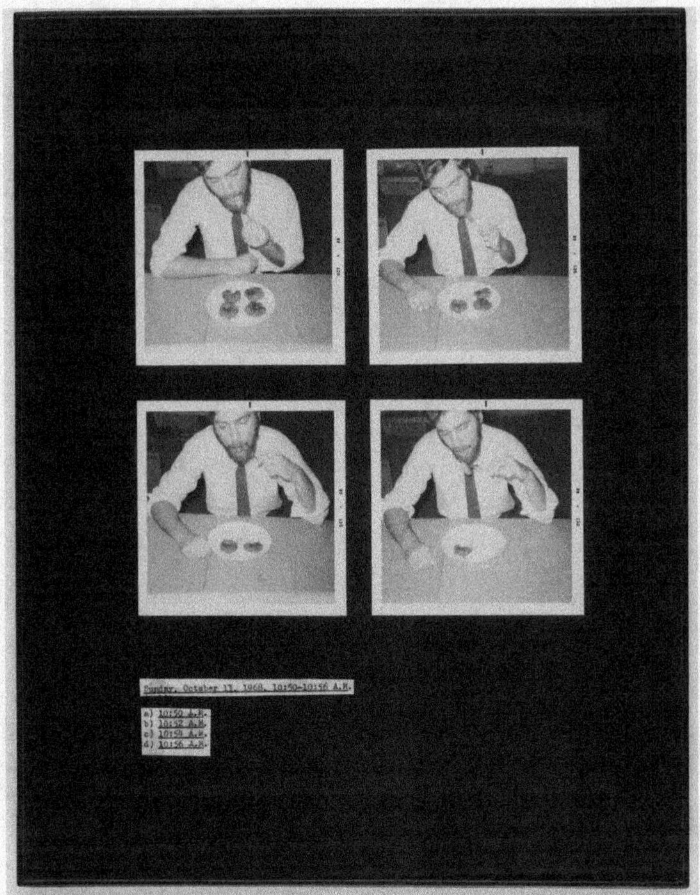

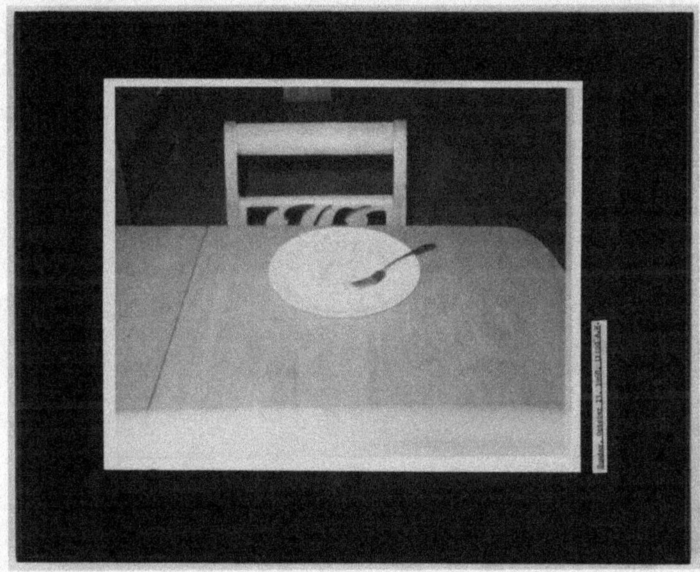

Plate 11, (*top*). Plate 12, (*bottom*). Adrian Piper, *Five Unrelated Time Pieces (Meat into Meat)*, 1968, six pages, one typescript page, eight photographs and text mounted on black paper, each page 9.5" × 11.5" (24.1 cm × 29.2 cm) or 11.5" × 9.5" (29.2 cm × 24.1 cm). (Collection of Paul and Karen McCarthy. © Adrian Piper Research Archive (APRA) Foundation Berlin)

Plate 13. Adrian Piper, *A Conceptual Seriation Arrested at Four Points in Time*, 1968, notebook with thirty-five pages: six typescript pages; twenty-five photographs and text mounted on colored paper; and cut-and-pasted text on four sheets of colored paper, each page 11" × 8.5" (27.9 cm × 21.6 cm). Detail: page 6. (Collection of the Adrian Piper Research Archive (APRA) Foundation Berlin. © APRA Foundation Berlin)

Plate 14. Adrian Piper, *A Conceptual Seriation Arrested at Four Points in Time*, 1968, notebook with thirty-five pages: six typescript pages; twenty-five photographs and text mounted on colored paper; and cut-and-pasted text on four sheets of colored paper, each page 11" × 8.5" (27.9 cm × 21.6 cm). Detail: page 16. (Collection of the Adrian Piper Research Archive (APRA) Foundation Berlin. © APRA Foundation Berlin)

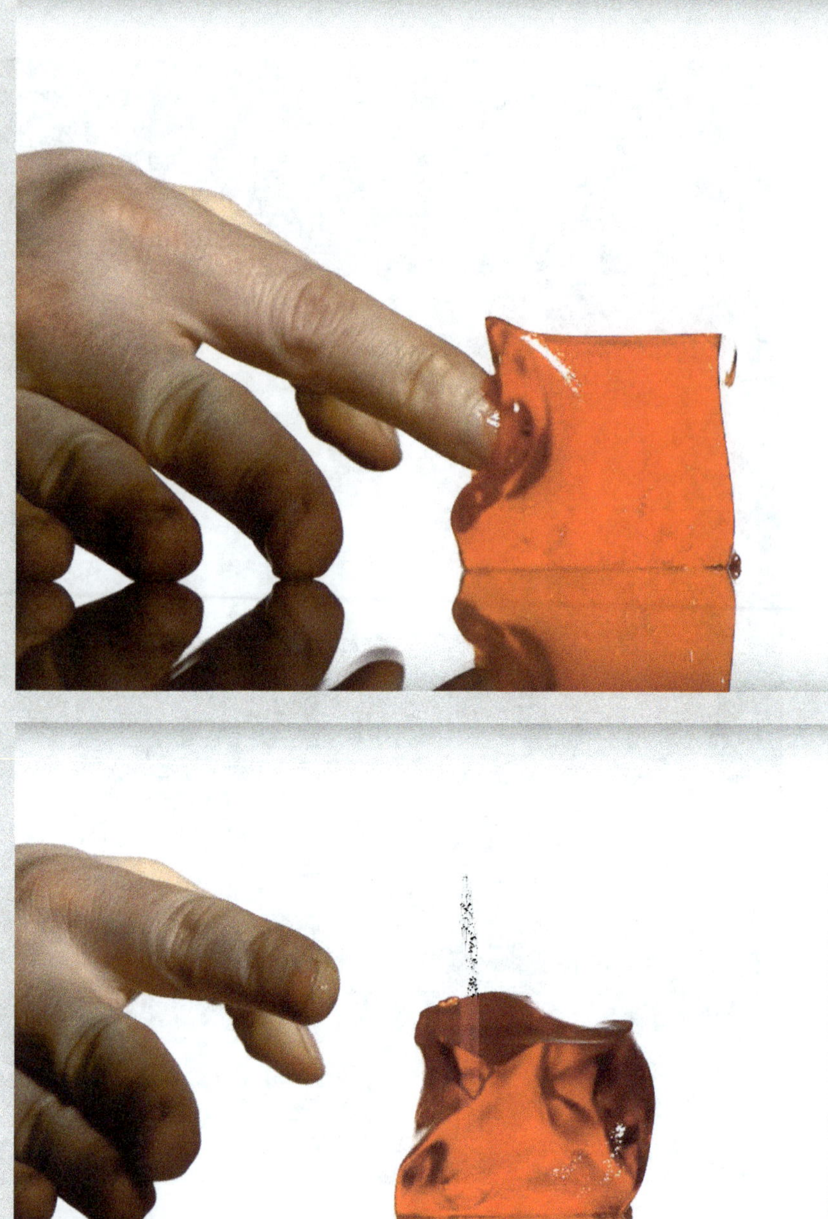

Plate 15, (*top*). Plate 16, (*bottom*). Still from ModernistCuisine, "Gelatin Cubes Dropped onto Solid Surface High Speed Video 6200 fps." YouTube, April 19, 2011, www.youtube.com/watch?v=4n5AfHYST6E.

Plate 17. Still from ModernistCuisine, "Gelatin Cubes Dropped onto Solid Surface High Speed Video 6200 fps." YouTube, April 19, 2011, www.youtube.com/watch?v=4n5AfHYST6E.

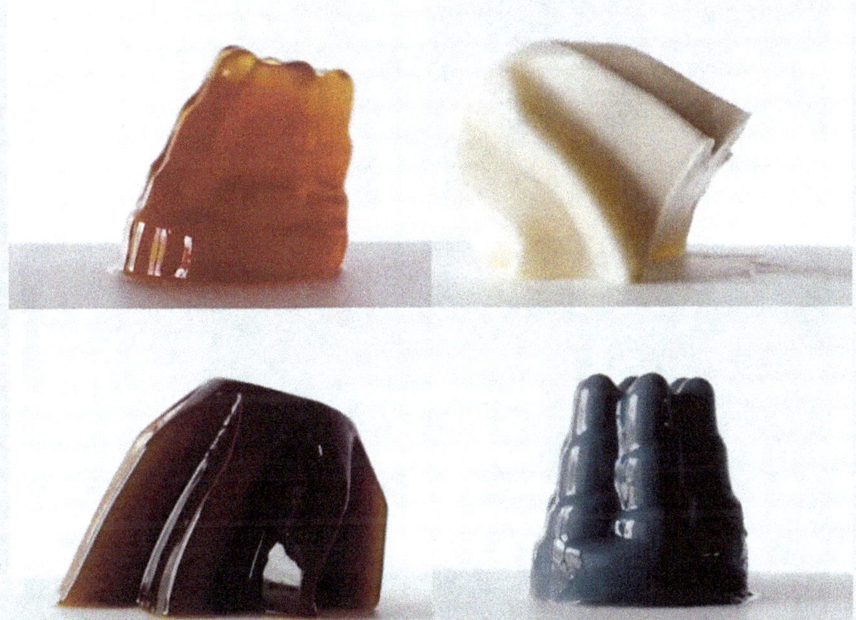

Plate 18. Still from "Jenny van Sommers: Jelly Roles: The Poetry of Puddings in Motion, with a Little Help from Bompas & Parr." Nowness, March 21, 2015, www.nowness.com/story/jelly-roles-jenny-van-sommers-bompas-and-parr?utm_source=YOUT&utm_medium=SM&utm_campaign=YT1001.

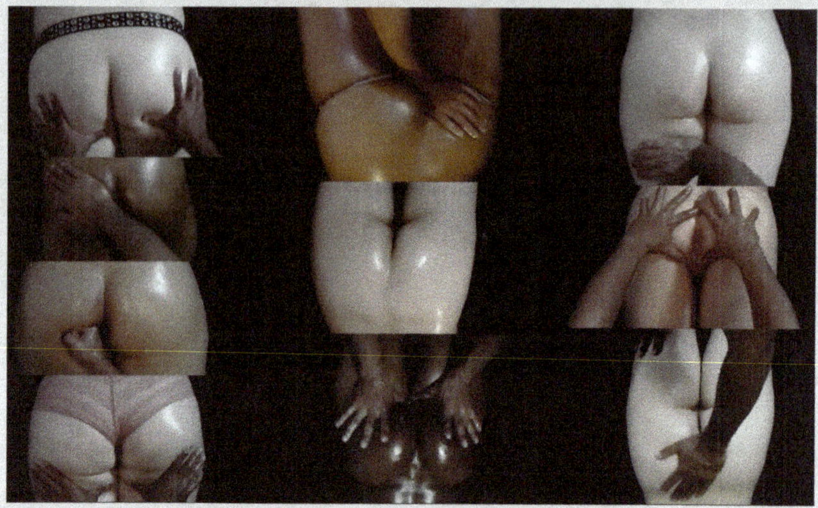

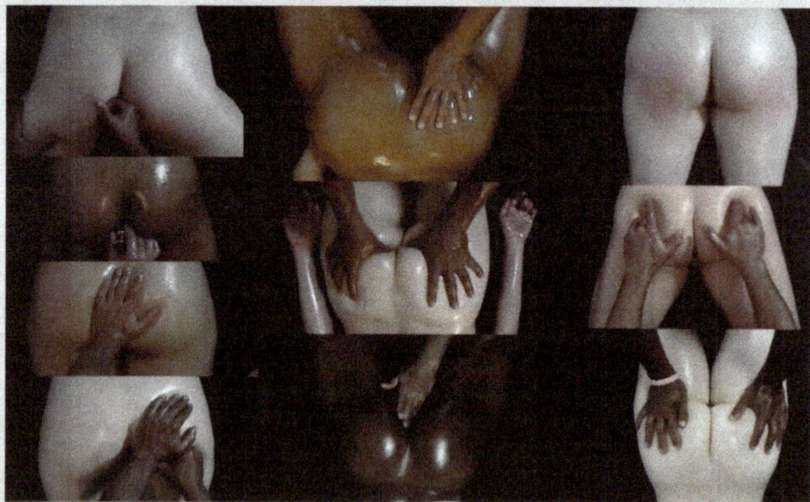

Plate 19, (*top*). Plate 20, (*middle*). Plate 21, (*bottom*). Stills from "Generous Gesture," directed by dirtysurface. (Property of dirtysurface, copyright 2013)

industrialism. A growing catalog of kinetic effects, including oscillating or blurred outlines and, of course, motion lines, conveyed a stronger sense of movement, but also conjured a body violently reacting to the power of technological might."[89] Rather, as I have been arguing, a more relevant scale is the microbiological, where questions of thermodynamics, waste, rest, and work were no less relevant. As Cara Daggett writes, "Energy and metabolism arose in the same decade, the 1840s, and were intertwined from the start. . . . By the early twentieth century, metabolism had become the central theme used to connect physics to biology. In 1913, Harvard biochemist Lawrence Henderson defined metabolism as 'the term applied to the inflow and outflow of matter and energy and their intermediary transformations within the organism.'"[90] Reframed through a metabolic and fermentative framework, the scale of *Dream* is visually focused downward to the cellular level but also scaled upward to consider energy as an accumulating population-level event.

I have argued that fermentation's status as an energy metaphor for populace- and crowd-level movement—for multitudinous, increasing, and unsecuritized energy—is acted out in McCay's own cellular aesthetics, but what I want to point to in *Dream of the Rarebit Fiend* is that fermentation here becomes even more specifically a way of talking about the emergent sensory and affective regimes, including labor regimes, of this period's new microbiopolitical frame. The nightmare work of the rarebit dreams, their hallucinatory movements, their association with rest or fatigue, makes of them a metaphor for what exceeds capitalism's thermodynamic logics of energy input / energy output. And while in the 1885 Louisa May Alcott story "The Candy Country," the protagonist, Lily, achieves usefulness in mastering and harnessing ferment, by 1904–1909, when McCay is writing his comics, ferment and its associated effervescent and intoxicating imagery have become a way of figuring what it feels like *not* to be captured by labor, at a microbiological, psychic, and physiological level.

I must attend to one last recurrent trope of the comic strips here, one that returns us to the earlier discussion of the Swift's Specific archive: the recurrence of criminality and imprisonment as a dream trope. In McCay's comics, most of the dreamers are white, but unlike the bifurcated racial drama of the SSS remedies, in which Black intoxication is criminalized by way of assenting to white intoxication and disinhibition, in the *Rarebit* comics, white people go to sleep in their normality, dream of being criminalized or deformed, and then wake up reaffirmed to their normality. Deformity in these cartoons is the nightmare state provoked by and defined by intoxication and visually inspired by microbiological proliferation, and perhaps we can begin to speculate here that, as the nation inched closer to national prohibition, deformity as uncivil aesthetics and uncivil affects became more openly understood as the antitheses of the concurrent imperative to the growth of the civil state.

My argument here does not counter the deep and rigorous vein of historical work that has attested to the racialization of criminality as well as affiliated and overlapping criminalization of disability during the post-Reconstruction and early twentieth-century period, although I want to be clear that the rarebit comic's representations of abnormally reproductive bodies seem to almost invert the idea of disability as inability to work and instead (but not unrelatedly) figure deformity as an excess of (repro)ductive energy. Rather, I want to point in these comics to the exceptional state of white intoxication and particularly to white intoxication's decriminalized containment in the dream life of the rarebit fiend. What McCay's work demonstrates, and most importantly what it reiterates obsessively across eight-hundred-plus comics, is that those intoxicated states must be understood as the nightmare vision of whiteness yet one that is recuperated and constrained, figuratively and literally, by the last, waking, pane of the comic. The whiteness of the dreamers, on the other hand, denies the racialization of intoxication contemporary to the period that was taking place in a juridical structure bent on containing Black freedom, energy, and labor inside prisons, at the same time as the nation moved toward national prohibition. In the world, that is, those nightmare visions were attached to the living conditions and, specifically, the carceral industry that would ultimately profit from the rendered and eternally renewable—because biologically essentialized—labor of African Americans, Native peoples, and other racialized subjects, institutionalized, imprisoned, and rendered deviant in the eyes of the state often because of their putative relationship to so-called intoxicating, soon to be illegal substances.

4

ROT

Let me begin with a proposition: whether or not we are able to find a solution to the ecological disasters brought about by human exceptionalism, it is possible, even likely, that there may be less than a century left of human life on the planet as we know it—and that only for those of us in the temperate zones. Another, hardly new, proposition: it is climate change that will bring about the practical end of human exceptionalism, namely, famine, drought, disease, and other expressions of planetary ecological disaster. Many humans and many other species are dying and are going to die. The world of matter is going to supersede our will to master it and in fact is already doing so.

This is not nihilism or accelerationism or giving up, however, so much as a wish to look directly at what is facing us and many other species and what has been facing us for quite a while. I cannot afford to give up; none of us can afford to give up. And we have an ethical obligation to resist what Donna Haraway witheringly refers to as "the affect of sublime despair" as much as we must abandon the techno-fantasy that the engineers will save our multispecies planet.[1] The question thus becomes, and here I take the lead from Haraway, What will survival look like in the trash heap of the Capitalocene, what she renames the "Compostocene"? From what methodologies and frames, with what writerly, aesthetic, political, technical, gestural modes will strategies for survival or, in the terms of both the Anishnaabe writer Gerald Vizenor and the Algerian writer Jacques Derrida, *survivance* emerge?[2]

I will mark here that I am not a fan of the term "Anthropocene" for the reason that I agree with many of its critics that it reinstantiates the very problem that it seems to seek to oppose: the murderous centrality of the human that has brought us to this point of ecological disaster, in which the horrible, greedy, invasive species called *Homo sapiens* has created the conditions for their/our own and many other species' extinction. I will admit that as a materialist, I like the idea of the Capitalocene or the Plantationocene a tiny bit better because it locates the driving energy behind our moment of urgency in the profit-driven logics that have brought us to this point.

And I, like many of us following behind the steps of the Black radical tradition—and here I learn from Cedric Robinson, Rod Ferguson, Grace Hong, Eric Williams, and Sylvia Wynter—see capitalism as fundamentally intertwined with the sorting of humans, matter, objects, spaces, language, and nonhuman species into the social and animacy hierarchies and cross-species assemblages from which, in Neel Ahuja's terms, the idea of the human would be abstracted.[3] So I would like to plant this chapter even more deeply in the fomenting capacities of radical Black, feminist, anticolonial, Marxist, queer, and Indigenous thought to return to the claim that the history of matter is the history of race. That is to say, the history of both the lines that divide and the spaces of contact between the natural and the artificial, the animal and the human, the subject and the object, is also the natural history of the organization of social value and indeed value itself in the West. But I also want to be attentive to the idea that the taxonomizing of humans and the obscuring of human/nonhuman assemblages are not outside this history but are in fact central to it—as the colonial history of science shows us. The matter of thinking beyond human exceptionalism must be taken up with not only speculative futurist but also parsed historical care.

One last concern: as Wynter teaches us, all of these histories also constitute the history of the modern, which, as Marx taught us, is also the history of "the forming of the five senses," a process that Wynter proleptically took to be neurologically plastic.[4] This chapter then follows Wynter and other Black feminists thinking with materiality to take the work of aesthetics seriously within the realm of the ecopolitical material present. In this chapter, I think about rot and decomposition as, to paraphrase of Cathy Cohen's words, both a figure for and a theorization of a "mobilized politics" of "intentional deviance grounded in limited agency and constrained choices."[5] In thinking with rotting matter, my goal is not to script a romance with other species, nonhuman animals, or matter but rather to both perform and investigate a thinking-with or a being-with nonhumanness that more approximates a disinterested but just cooperation or coexistence, rather than an affective investment that might reproduce some form of ownership. That investment takes its energy from my interest in deviance and abjection that drives queer-of-color theories as well as the push to counter the respectability that sits within particular conversations in queer and feminist African American studies and, more recently, in queer Latinx studies as well.[6] It is a being-with-difference that does not seek to lapse into melancholy passivity but rather relishes discordance, disruption, and, ideally, indecency.

In thinking with matter, however, I also seek to decenter the *cogito*, or the unitary thinking subject that has dominated humanist discourse for many centuries. My work in this book is not a postracial fantasy about matter and species nor only an argument about the status of the human (in the proposal that human exceptionalism must end); rather, it is a perversion and a degradation, a molding and decaying, of that problematic. I will conclude this chapter, then, asking a different question, one that Wynter asks across the body of her work and that Foucault named vis-à-vis the human sciences: What does imagining the end of human exceptionalism mean for imagining the end of disciplinarity in the humanities as we know it?[7] Is the one form of human exceptionalism linked to the other? How can we begin to imagine not just the end of human exceptionalism but also the end of humanistic disciplinary exceptionalism and its differential distributions of value as well?

Across chapters 1–3, I have taken up a series of materials, sensations, and affects as they are invoked in various works ranging across the nineteenth and into the early twenty-first century to think about how a set of nonhuman materialities attach to or are reengaged by various peoples who have been considered other-than-human and less-than-human across time. This book has thus argued for a cultural history of the relation between matter, aesthetics, and affect, shaped by and in the moment that state hygiene projects took up Pasteurian science. As I discuss in chapters 2 and 3 of the book, it is a critical historical fact that Pasteurian science, which both produced the germ theory of infection and entirely reframed the Western relation to lively biological matter and bacteriological life, took cultural and scientific hold in the United States immediately after the collapse of radical Reconstruction and during the rise of Jim Crow. During this period, as Michelle Alexander and Saidiya Hartman have written, Reconstruction failed, and slavery's afterlife gestated for its later reconstitution in the War on Drugs, in and alongside the sanctioned reorganization of enslaved labor that we now recognize as mass incarceration.[8]

What does rot have to do with this? Some images and thoughts to start with: When I started writing about food many years ago, I wrote an undergraduate paper that asked about the temporality of food photography and specifically about the illuminated foods in food magazines. One part of my argument was this: we are in a stage of proleptic mourning for the planet. Something about the frozenness of food photography, its sacralization of the natural world, of a set of objects and life forms that exist beyond and despite and before us but also, in the case of cultivated agriculture and food, with and because of us, really caught me. As many critics have written about photography more generally, the genre itself has always asked that its capture of life demands a turn to other terms: preservation, resurrection, death. The photography that caught me posed natural objects in illuminated white light and made deities of them. It preserved them in time and against time forever. And I felt intuitively that this could only be about the deep feeling lying underneath and between us all, that our ecologies were in peril and the reality of that was something that could not yet be believed.

Truthfully, this is how I see all of our food culture but especially the Western, especially Canadian and US, food cultures that capitalize on appearing artisanal, authentic, vintage, honest but also hyperspecialized in their relation to the matter we put in our bodies and call food or drink. I think that, on the one hand, the West's unconscious is preparing itself for a time when there may not be anything left and all we have is pictures of what those things were. I see Western food culture in this moment as an archive of everything that may go away, forever. But at the same time, because capitalism, that vampire machine, is always ahead of us, eating us alive, I see food culture's color-washed elaboration of consuming as a sacred, immanent act to be a way of making sure that what we crave, because and before it is going to disappear, has even more of an elevated exchange value.

It is out of that impossibly evanescently white food dream world that I began to think about rot. What will be left when all the food is gone? What is there for the hungry already? Garbage. And what is garbage but matter in phase change—that is, matter moving forward in time, not out of place but without place and out of use? When the 1 percent, who cannot even bother to pretend that they are not trying to use everything up and get off the planet, succeed in doing so—and could they hurry up?—what will be left is the garbage they leave behind, including us, and we will have to find a way to repurpose it, to live in it.[9] When we are talking about waste, we are talking about maldistributions of toxicity, concentrated among populations affiliated with, flooded with, and incarcerated for their mythical proclivities for intoxication, for obesity, for criminality; when we talk about poverty and race, we are talking about predestination for death, in Ruth Gilmore's terms.[10] These are the decomposed living, the walking corpses, the *zonbi* of capitalism, the unwashed, the masses.

Another word for rot is "ferment."[11] As I demonstrated in chapter 2, in the nineteenth century, scientists argued over the difference between fermentation and decomposition, over whether fermentation is an internal processes of chemical decay or whether fermentation and decomposition are catalytic chemical changes brought about by multispecies encounters between matter and alien bacteria and other living species. They asked, Is ferment alive? Is it life-producing, as it was for millennia when people fermented their foods to survive, to supplement their diets, and to manage the bacterial life in their water, or is it a kind of death, a toxin, like a rotting body in the water supply might be or like the offal and by-products from slaughterhouses was throughout the eighteenth and nineteenth centuries?

By the end of the nineteenth century, however, ferment and rot diverged: while ferment brings to mind productivity and effervescence and leads easily into a sense of a liveliness or of infectious feeling, rot (while similarly related to ideas of infection) is much more closely linked to death and to emerging environmental conceptions of pollution and waste. (Alongside, the miasmatic concepts of infection were increasingly discredited in the scientific literature, although not in the popular imagination.) I continue here to be interested in ferment and rot's overlap as biochemical and microbial processes that, as perhaps Mary Douglas would say in her work on purity and danger, differ from each other only as a matter of degree and, thus in their material interconnectedness, live at the intersection between a thicker concept of what life is, what death is, and where they meld.[12] Thinking with rot is about staying with the trouble, as Haraway puts it, about living with death turning into life and life giving way to death, the two of them producing each other.[13] It is, to think with Mel Chen and Jasbir Puar, from within and against the bio-necropolitical logics that have rendered minoritarian life and life worlds abject and to argue—without turning away from very real and material maldistributions of suffering—that because of that very abjection, those worlds may hold some of the epistemic wisdoms to save everyone. Rot, or maybe garbage more broadly (but what is garbage except that which does not need to be preserved but remains nonetheless?), is a both a phenomenon and a process. We cut the rot off food because it offends our senses—but is that not because Western senses have been schooled to the opiate sweetness of the fruits of empire, as Mintz and Wynter teach us, to the jagged energy of sugar- and caffeine-fueled labor?[14] Is it an environmental problem that the West is no longer schooled to the sour, the fermented, the sticky, gooey, pungent, and funky?[15] Let us intoxicate ourselves with the toxic.[16]

Rot, like the idea of waste to which it has been attached, provides much to think with: as funky ferment, it acts as a preservative, keeping food edible in hard times. I am thinking here of *smen*, the fermented and aged butter of the Amazigh peoples of the Rif mountains, used to flavor couscous; *injera*, the living sour flatbread of Habesha peoples of Ethiopia and Eritrea; *miso* and *nato*, both made from fermented soy; about the happy accident of vinegar that failed to become wine. But I am also following behind the anthropologist Anna Tsing's writing about mushroom ferment, about fungus eating its way across the forest floor, feeding on decay, fomenting change, even growing on the walls in the ruins at Chernobyl.[17] Jae Rhim Lee takes up rot for its life-giving properties in her organic death suit, built on the model of Korean sheet burial wrapping, which is meant to hold a corpse transfused with mushroom-impregnated liquid that then decomposes back into the soil.[18] So my question here, following these artists and scholars is, Can we hack rot to our own ends? Can we live in it? Do we have a choice?

HACKING ROT/DECOMPOSITION

> Hacking is a decomposition that explores and unsettles and perverts forms, or formaling. It is an active and purposeful misunderstanding, misreading, and misappropriation, but it is also a response to a call, a

> response that misappropriates a friend's argument, misreads his project; it is an experiment in nonsense, so no-sense. What it does is what it does: it doesn't promise anything. . . . There's no big theory coming out or before it. It's a kind of reading which is at once an imaging, in Benjamin's sense of the work done by the dialectical image and a composition as a description of the creative act, but it is also done as a decomposition of elements in the sense that the term has in chemistry. My decomposition of the arc of the form of the subject involves three moves: a translation, the first crucial move of which is the use of symbols of math and biology; a transposition, so once my terms become biological symbols I can then place them in an algorithm which is basically most of what I do, moving them from one place to another in that formula, so primarily a performance; and it is performance of a few simple mathematical signs that allows me to explode the arc of form of the subject through a series of transformations.[19]

Denise Ferreira da Silva's brilliant, speculative, and alchemical 2015 talk "Hacking the Subject" at Barnard College opens up and encapsulates the methodology I want to experiment with here: a thinking through and with biology that unmakes form, abstraction, and subjectivity as coeval concepts. In short, I begin with the figure and voice of the diasporic Black Afro-Brazilian feminist intellectual thinking at the edges of a Western philosophy predicated on the condition of Black negation, on Black thingness, and on Black no-thingness, for the very reason that I wish to follow on the crucial shift from ontology to ethics, from being to value, that she models as the condition of thinking from the outside of Man. The "no" that is the crucial shift from thing to no-thing is the space of nonrepresentation that Ferreira da Silva and many others thinking with her against Western humanism continue to hold open, "invaginations of a foreclosed universality, a heroic but bounded eroticism" that Fred Moten refers to as "black performance."[20] Not big theory, she is careful to tell us, but a doing, a performance, a speculation: "the constitutive outside," she tells us, reworking Judith Butler's account of subjectivation, that cannot be articulated but can be reached for, can be lived alongside, without mastery.[21]

Ferreira da Silva's talk, which she explains as a figural move through biology and mathematics, deploys a Black feminist calculus; it hacks both binary code and calculus against the very syllogistic philosophical relations (against the subjectivating forces of syllogistic thinking itself, that is, temporality, determination, mastery, and rationality) that produce Blackness as negation, as deserving of death within a contemporary racial capitalism that prizes the determining and determinative Enlightenment subject. That turn to matter and math derives its values and its ethics, as so many of us do today, in Hortense Spillers's biblical and always-insurgent 1987 essay "Mama's Baby, Papa's Maybe" (published three years before *Bodies That Matter* but not cited). As Ferreira da Silva and Spillers teach us in their parsing of the relations of Black womanhood as a raced nongender to the violent normalcy of white heterosexual gender binarisms—and here I am also thinking with Ferreira da Silva's consequent essay in *e-flux*, "1 (life) ÷ 0 (blackness) = ∞−∞ or ∞/∞: On Matter beyond the Equation of Value," and also in her more recent *e-flux* essay, "In the Raw"—Blackness as flesh materializes and embodies a capacity to tear the veil of transparency that circulates around abstraction, understood as a mode of extraction, and to disclose what lies at the limit of justice. Black feminist work—particularly in relation to the question of the object, to what she names as "this move to claim The Thing"—takes as its starting point an interrogation of the founding ethico-metaphysics, the fundamental physics, of Western thought itself:

> The call for Black Lives (to) Matter hides the question it answers: Why don't black lives matter? More precisely, it exposes how this question already contains the Kantian program and its equation of the universal and the formal—through articulating determinacy as efficient causation, or effectivity—which guides modern ethical, economic, and juridical formations. . . . In the famous statement that science is not interested in the Thing-in-itself (essence)—Kant defines the limits of knowledge as that which in things—now objects—is available to the senses (movements and alterations). Furthermore, repeating Descartes's assertion that the mind can only know with certainty that which is akin to it—that is, the abstract or the formal—Kant consolidates modern thought when he elevates the formal (as the pure or transcendental) to that moment that is before and beyond what is accessible to the senses. . . . Effectivity refers both to the senses' access to the things of the world (being affected or moved by them) and to the mind's capacity to resolve the manifold into

> the basic tools (categories) that the understanding has available for the "higher" moments of cognition—that is, abstraction and reflection—as well as for the task of knowledge—that is, determination.[22]

I want to make a careful transition here from Ferreira da Silva's work in critiquing abstraction through her parsing of the productive negativity of Black womanhood to think with her in her related exploration of Blackness as an optic through which both to revalue matter and materialism and to begin to perform the undoing of the homicidal humanistic logics we find ourselves in, which she names "formalism" or abstraction. Ferreira da Silva's turn against form as a kind of transcendental purity, in the service of Cartesian cognition projects, makes a link between her work in the vein of what we might call a Black feminist new materialism and another, less studied work of Hortense Spillers: her 1982 essay "Formalism Comes to Harlem."

It is tempting to read "Formalism Comes to Harlem" only in relation to the contemporary debate in which Spillers was participating, in which she is, at first read, fairly ecumenical: how to do justice to the work of African American literature within or outside the terms of Anglo-American literary critique. But I am interested in how we might carry that article forward in order to think about the relation between form, formalism, and some of the subtended critiques of formalist literary criticism in the Harlem essay that later emerge as a foundational manifesto of current Black feminist new materialist thought in "Mama's Baby, Papa's Maybe" (and also finds echoes in Houston Baker's idea of Harlem Renaissance writing as the "mastery of form" and the "deformation of mastery," or what Jackie Goldsby thinks of as James Baldwin's commitment to formlessness).[23] What, in other words, are the overlaps between what Ferreira da Silva identifies as the Kantian formalist project and what Spillers identifies as the literary formalist project, and how might we close the circle within this august intellectual matrilineage, the feminist new materialist project, in particular as it pertains to the overlapping life of race and matter and the current putatively neoformalist aesthetic moment in literature?

Building on these critics, I argue here that understanding form as a value through which to understand the aesthetic is, by definition, to work through a limited ontology within which only that which emerges into social—which is to say politico-aesthetic—legibility is valued. In another mode, turning to Jacques Rancière by way of Ferreira da Silva, I see the idea of form—and by definition much of the "new" formalism itself—as twinned modalities that concede to the sphere of aesthetics only those objects that can be interpellated as proper aesthetic subjects by politics. At times but not always, some of the formalist or new formalist positions figure themselves in opposition to a historical or a political or, insultingly, a "cultural" or "cultural studies" approach, thereby ignoring the past four to twelve *decades* of postcolonial, African American, Asian American and, other minoritarian theory; alternately, they flatten out all historical criticism into a frankly unethical straw-man misreading of the historical as base determinism. Ironically, these positions pose themselves in a salvific relation to literature itself while paradoxically masking their own collusion with the field of politics—which is to say, in this historical moment, benefiting from the field of the urgency of institutional and material maldistribution. In this way, the disciplinary study of aesthetics prioritizes and chooses for itself only those phenomena recognized as valid, as holding proper aesthetic citizenship, asserting an aesthetic and political relation that posits the line between those two fields as stable.

As I have argued across this book, the projected stability of that line works to obscure how, in fact, the idea of aesthetics works, at the broadest level, not only to mete out death but to uphold the legitimacy of the political—specifically statist politics. As I argued in the introduction, these formal projects constitute what Wynter has called "Aesthetics 1," when she writes that "The work of Aesthetics 1 is to secure the social cohesion of the specific human order of which it is a function." Wynter scathingly defines "Aesthetics 2" as "the imperative enactment of each governing code of subject/abject, of symbolic 'life' and 'death,' . . . of the very condition of existence of all human forms of life . . . from which the . . . ethico-aesthetic practices of literary and film criticism emerge."

What, then, does it mean to propose a critical modality that seeks to attend to form's decomposition?[24] When Ferreira da Silva writes, "Hacking is a decomposition that explores and unsettles and perverts forms, or formaling. . . . It is also an experiment in nonsense, so no-sense," she echoes the movement of Spillers' formalism essay, which operates as a dual argument, particularly considered in relation to her later work in "Mama's Baby." As Spillers shows us in her reading of temporality in Toni Morrison's *Song of Solomon*, form takes place in and through but not entirely determined by the historical relations between language and experience. On another level, however, Spillers speaks decidedly against the analysis of form as it is enacted via "the contemplation of smaller and smaller units of symbolic reference":

> Morrison and Ellison, among others, sense too keenly, perhaps, the requirements of their own imposed alienation to raise [language] to an act of form. For them language withheld for so long, by law, from the African/American as the origin of his human power, does speak. The suppressed subject now mobilized toward historical movement particular to itself is not, in this case, an optional principle of composition. It matches . . . an original scene, primal and sacrificial, when living ancestors lost life, lost language. In either case, the signifier is not empty. More precisely, it fixes a decisively unambiguous change in the state of nature.[25]

Not composition but decomposition; death, a change in the state of nature; language emerging from the loss of life that was also the loss of language, a birth emerging from a death. Thus, these antiformalist positions are not only an argument made against the dominant logics of the present but also a critique of the present understood within the colonial frame that produced the death projects called chattel slavery and settler colonialism. In Langston Hughes's words, as Spillers quotes,

> "What's the difference," [straight man] asked, "between Re and Be?"
>
> "A lot," said Simple, "Re-Bop was the imitation like most of the white boys play. Be-bop is the real thing like the colored boys play. . . . From the police beating Negroes heads. . . . Every time a cop hits a Negro with his billy club, that old club says, 'Bop! Bop! . . . BE-BOP! . . . MOP! . . . BOP!' . . . That's where Be-Bop comes from, beaten right out of some Negro's head into them horns and saxophones and piano keys that plays it. Do you call that nonsense?"[26]

Writes Spillers, "Moving through layers of American culture . . . toward the metrical near-unity of re and be. . . . The French school would have a field day here."[27] I do not think of deconstruction as the French school so much as I think of it as the North African school, especially in its earlier iterations. Leaving that aside, I want to tie the loose end between Simple's question, as phrased by Spillers, and Ferreira da Silva's question: Do you call that nonsense? Do you call that decomposition? What is the form—or is it the nonform or is it the unform—of the nonsensical, the decompositional, the imagistic, the perverted, the Be that is also the Re? Hughes is thinking with jazz, deep in the tradition of African American literary production, as well as the criticism of that moment that pulls from the historical synchronicity between music and literature in African American and diasporic epistemologies. But I want to follow Fred Moten and Ashon Crawley's lead here to think more broadly with the sonic—the sonic that is also an instantiation of a performative dissent from the commonsensical, breaking through the disciplinary energy of intextuation, into the speculative material ontologies of survivance, persistence, despiteness. The turn to the sonic for me accords with Rancière's sense of politics as that which disturbs the "sensus communis"—in other words, dissensus. A world-historical shift, that is, may be brought about by reordering the senses themselves in their deep relation to the ordering of species, worlds, and the valuing of various humans as well.

Here I offer two other questions which I think need answering: first, How, following important work in Black feminist and queer of color new materialisms, might we conceptualize the undoing of form as a central investment of a humanistic studies? Or, in Ferreira da Silva's words, how might we reach toward that which is external to form, its constitutive outside here understood as matter? Second, which I take to be the most critical question here, In what archives, histories, shapes, sounds, material lives, and affective traces can we discern the unform, or the decomposition, with which to degrade the limits of the here and now? With what otherwise methodologies can we access them?

By example, here I would like to turn to a passage in James Baldwin's *Giovanni's Room* and then think about a responding artwork by the alchemical interdisciplinary artist Candice Lin. *Giovanni's Room* holds an important place in the Baldwin canon both as his second novel and as a text that has at times offered a challenge to Baldwin critics because of Baldwin's seeming absenting of race from the narrative: the protagonist,

David, is a white American, and his lover, Giovanni, is Italian.[28] In the passage I want to look at here, David has woken up after his first night with Giovanni and remembers the night before:

> Giovanni had said something in the taxi about his room being very dirty. "I'm sure it is," I had said lightly, and turned away from him, looking out of the window. Then we had both been silent. When I woke up in his room, I remembered that there had been something strained and painful in the quality of that silence, which had been broken when Giovanni said, with a shy, bitter smile: "I must find some poetic figure." And he spread his heavy fingers in the air, as though a metaphor were tangible. I watched him. "Look at the garbage of this city," he said, finally, and his fingers indicated the flying street, "all of the garbage of this city? Where do they take it? I don't know where they take it—but it might very well be my room." "It's much more likely," I said, "that they dump it into the Seine."[29]

What is garbage doing in this passage, and how might Baldwin's intervention lead us to think more historically with the politics and aesthetics of the discarded? At a first level, at the level of analogy, we see in this passage an affiliation with abjection that has long pursued gay life, particularly in white gay male modernist frames, with which Baldwin was obviously well familiar: the queers are the discarded of the world and also simultaneously, as putatively nonreproductive subjects, the most decadent, the most aesthetical of modern citizens (we can easily turn to Dorian Gray here). Rot haunts the queer, the degraded: even decadence is a word that finds its roots in the English word "decay," as many modernist queer theorists have pointed out.

When Giovanni says, "I must find a poetic figure," the taxi is moving toward his home, where, we assume, Giovanni and David will touch for the first time. But of course we do not see or hear or feel them kiss or touch or fuck; rather, David wakes up the next day remembering the conversation about garbage from the night before, which he characterizes as "bravado and cowardice" in "a figure of speech."[30] This passage displaces sex and instead turns to movement—movement through Paris streets, the movement of garbage along and in rivers, the movement of rivers through cities, of water through earth, matter in movement as it decomposes and ferments—to mark the limits of representation within Baldwin's aesthetic terrain. The metaphor holds in the next paragraph:

> But I sensed, when I woke up and looked around the room, the bravado and the cowardice of his figure of speech. This was not the garbage of Paris, which would have been anonymous: this was Giovanni's regurgitated life. Before and beside me and all over the room, towering like a wall, were boxes of cardboard and leather, some tied with string, some locked, some bursting, and out of the topmost box before me spilled down sheets of violin music. There was a violin in the room, lying on the table in its warped, cracked case—it was impossible to guess from looking at it whether it had been laid to rest there yesterday or a hundred years before. The table was loaded with yellowing newspapers and empty bottles and it held a single brown and wrinkled potato in which even the sprouting eyes were rotten. Red wine had been spilled on the floor; it had been allowed to dry and it made the air in the room sweet and heavy.[31]

The decaying matter that flows through these passages, which is to say the biodegradation of carbon-based material, whether it be human or animal body or vegetables whose sprouts fail to proliferate or the ferment of a wine long past its drinkable date, its sugars expelled as a scented miasma, seems to get clogged and stuck in Giovanni's room, as though it were itself a bend in the river. But even stuck in Giovanni's room, matter continues to phase-change, shifting color and material form, falling apart as an expression of death-in-life or life-in-death.

What the text tells us will be a "metaphor" or poetic figure also comes to us in physical gesture: in the spreading of Giovanni's fingers, fingers rendered heavy to make their motion, figuring poesis, making aisthesis even more "tangible" by using gesture to figure the unfinishedness of touch. At the same time, the seemingly arrested futility of the gesture registers a kind of inability to become form—to be completed. Failure is an often-cited queer modality, as many artists and theorists, including Jack Halberstam, have attested. I want to reject a totalizing nature of failure as a reading, a reading that instantiates fullness or completeness as its other.[32] Instead, I want to try out the idea that those images in movement—in particular the movements, across multiple scales, of discarded decaying waste, movement with the commercial and infrastructural heart of Paris, movement of the taxi through Paris and past the river waste—is the figuration, or perhaps defiguration-in-process, that matters here because it insistently poses the stuckness of Giovanni's relation to aesthetic possibility as a biopolitical problem, as an incompleteness or a gestural futility that takes up the brokenness of state infrastructure as the condition of trying to live otherwise. Giovanni's gesture also sketches life lived in the interstices of the stateless, citizenless condition that is Black queer and queer of color life as fundamentally antithetical to full social legibility and therefore to form itself. Here as ever, I ride with Cathy Cohen to think with deviance as a mode of resistance that troubles agentic liberal willfulness and that therefore reveals state-sanctioned narratives of normalcy and the good life as the terrorizing projects that they actually are, particularly in their ongoing violence against Black and (exponentially) Black queer and trans life.[33] What lives on this complex passage—one that should contain queer touch, that turns away from the sensory totality of two men fucking, giving consent to each other, perhaps, to fuck and to be fucked—is a failure to represent, to abstract into a poetic form that can live on the page. And we can say the same of Baldwin's absented Blackness as well: Blackness is both too much and not enough for this novel, the violence of the American scene forming the inexpressible condition of the novel's emergence.

What do both David and Giovanni look to instead? These passages turn to the street that flies by and then to the river and then to decomposing waste in Giovanni's room to think with that which cannot be rendered "poetic": aisthesis here growing out of the decaying presence of garbage and rot, of the world and of matter in movement and in decomposition. From within those terms, what takes place—and also what fails to materialize between David and Giovanni—flowers out of Giovanni's refusal to concede the space and scale of the everyday to the hygienic imperatives, such as state-sanctioned heteronormativity, that sanitize pleasure and kill what makes life worth living. This passage stands in, I think, for the poetic project that Baldwin wrestles with in *Giovanni's Room* and that, in his genius, he allows to rest in its troubled incompleteness.[34]

INFRASTRUCTURE

Rot, decay, waste, and disease: the decomposition of the remains of human production and consumption has been a problem of city engineering and political hygiene—which is to say of state infrastructure—for over two hundred years, beginning with the health crises brought about when butchers and slaughterhouses dumped animal waste and neighborhoods deposited human sewage into major city rivers such as the Thames and the Seine; in the United States, the Mississippi received waste all the way up to Illinois and south to Louisiana. In 1873, a lawsuit, brought forward by Confederate lawyers on behalf of white butchers in Louisiana against the hygiene bills proposed by the "mongrel" Reconstruction legislature, made its way up to the Supreme Court and became the first case to evacuate the rights and privileges clause of the Fourteenth Amendment. The *Slaughter-House Cases* decision of 1873, which has been described as the worst Supreme Court decision ever made, still stands as precedent for states' rights today, blocking national civil rights legislation at every turn and giving states police power over their internal functioning in such a way as to block federal intervention at every turn.

It is worth taking a slight detour in order to explore this history more fully. In 1862, General Benjamin Butler entered into New Orleans with the conquering Union army, where he occupied it, much despised and hated, until the end of the Civil War in 1865. One year into the war, New Orleans was a key win for the Union army because it was the port from which the Northern army could control traffic on the entire Mississippi. Directly following the abolition of the trade in enslaved peoples—but before the abolition of enslavement itself—in the neighboring state of Texas, beef had become a booming industry; in New Orleans particularly, there was local hope that industrial-scale beef slaughter and transportation would replace the trade in enslaved Africans as the primary industry through which New Orleans might maintain its wealth as a city. Originally inhabited by the Chitimacha Indigenous peoples, New Orleans was colonized in the early eighteenth century by the French. As Ari Kelman writes, the tension between the many drawbacks of New Orleans's site and its situation—its strategic geographic location and its environmental challenges—have fundamentally shaped the political history of the city.[35]

While the bends in the Mississippi may have made building ports and military defense sites easier, as became clear across the centuries following French colonialism, the curves in the river actually created enormous problems for public hygiene. First of all, the entire city of New Orleans sloped downhill and thus away from easy drainage. Additionally, because of the intensely soft ground beneath the city as well as consistent seasonal flooding, the entire infrastructure of public hygiene in New Orleans depended on overground sewage drainage, for both excrement and the city's daily garbage, which would then drain into the Mississippi and Lake Pontchartrain. The growth of the beef trade in the first half of the nineteenth century exacerbated this generally lax relation to public hygiene: unregulated, butchers indiscriminately dumped offal, bones, carcasses, and hides into the streets and into the Mississippi from the slaughterhouses randomly located up and down the river.

Fascinatingly, installing sewage infrastructure and regulation in New Orleans came to be seen as an imposition, variously of the occupying Northerners or of the radical Reconstruction legislature. Discussing the need for reform in 1868, an editor of the *New-Orleans Commercial Bulletin* wrote, "Unless the butchers shall convert the radical legislature to the idea that it is better to make ox-tail soup of all the river water that we drink, the removal of the butcheries below the city limits may become a law. . . . It would be a very hard case if we were compelled to drink this oxtail soup of the butcheries the rest of our lives."[36] Without proper infrastructure, the river, that is, came to be a rotting, stinking, gelatinous mess, full of animal waste, much like the collagen-rich poor people's soup that the editorial called to mind.

Yet for the remaining unrepentant Confederates, even a rotting river was better than being occupied by the Union army or told what to do by a mixed-race "radical" legislature. During the war, the occupying Union General Butler cemented his extremely unpopular status in New Orleans—he was nicknamed "Beast" Butler—by immediately setting up a public health and hygiene infrastructure that he policed with a heavy hand. Writing about the occupation of New Orleans in the *North American Review*, Butler later wrote that "the streets were reeking with putrefying filth, and the smells from the decomposing matter were, to a Northern nose, unbearable. Everything had of custom been thrown into the streets that the inhabitants desired to be rid of, and lay there seething and rotting. The canals and all their tributaries, the drains, were covered with green slime so thickly that the water was not visible. In the pools were dead animals floating about, with every other description of animal decomposition."[37] Butler's infrastructural advances between 1862 and 1865 were picked up on and continued by the Reconstruction legislature immediately following the end of the war in 1865. The legislature, which was also the first racially integrated legislature in the South, followed such riverside cities as Chicago, New York, London, and Paris in setting up a single industrial clearing house for butchers to centralize and regulate waste disposal—thereby hopefully curbing waterborne illness by cleaning up the garbage-infested waters. The charter founding the local monopoly, called the Crescent City Slaughterhouse, dictated that all butchers and slaughterhouses in the New Orleans area had to do their slaughtering in the same site for a reasonable fee and, further, that their disposal of animal waste and animal parts would be legislated by the state government.

John A. Campbell, a lawyer and former US Supreme Court justice who had quit the Supreme Court to join the Confederacy, challenged the Crescent City charter as part of his broader postwar campaign to do everything in his power to undermine and block every bill passed during radical Reconstruction, by the new "mongrel" legislature. For the most part, Campbell filed nuisance suits against the Reconstruction legislature, largely against any effort to racially integrate the state, including public services like education. The new slaughterhouse arrangements would have opened access to butchering to Black butchers, thereby increasing competition in what had mostly been a white trade until then. By taking up the cause of a largely white group of butchers who objected to the centralized slaughterhouse, Campbell attempted, in the words of the historian Michael A. Ross, to "turn the Fourteenth Amendment on its head": Butler claimed that the Crescent City monopoly abridged the poorly written and vague privileges and immunities clause of the Fourteenth Amendment by prohibiting New Orleanian butchers from exercising their businesses as they wished.[38] In a flattening out of antidiscrimination language that seems more than familiar today, Campbell used amendments meant to protect freedmen and women against those same people, by claiming protection for an inherently protected class in the name of "freedom."

Campbell's case made its way through the Louisiana courts and all the way up to the US Supreme Court, where Campbell's former colleagues saw him coming. In a twist of fate with disastrous consequences for racial justice for the next 150 years, the Supreme Court, led by Justice Samuel Freeman Miller, ultimately decided to deny Campbell's argument with a majority decision in 1873. The decision instead upheld the state's, which is to say Louisiana's, right to regulatory power because, historians have argued, of Miller's fundamental belief in state citizenship and his belief that hygienic measures needed to be locally governed. Legal historians have long debated the sitting Supreme Court's intent in this decision, which in effect began the chain of events that led to the failure of Reconstruction as state policy in 1877. While earlier legal historians have read more sinister motives into the Miller decision, more recently historians seem to have come to a consensus that Miller's intention was to uphold Reconstruction—he had after all abandoned the South and moved to a "free" state before the war. However, he failed to see that only four years after the 1873 decision, Reconstruction would falter and fail and the handing over of police power to the state's legal structures would work against all of the gains made in the twelve years after the civil war.

My own interest in these cases is somewhat different. I am not so much interested in tracing the twists and turns of the historical actors' intentions and effects—although I think that no doubt there is quite a bit to unearth in the suspicion that white butchers would have worked hard to foreclose or retaliate against competition from Black butchers in the form of an integrated slaughterhouse as well as an integrated competitive marketplace. As Koritha Mitchell argues, Black success has always been met with retaliation.[39] I am more interested in the effects produced by the calcification of this one specific form of state regulatory power, which emerged as a question of states' rights in relation to environmental pollution (rot, decay, and its polluting and dangerous toxicity in the Mississippi) and public welfare (the need to control communicative diseases such as cholera and yellow fever in Louisiana): What are the effects, in other words, of the sedimentation of this one particular form of state regulatory power known as police power around the hygiene project? The fact that the lawsuit was launched against an interracial state legislature by a Confederate general for white butchers only thickens the plot because it seems to indicate that anti-Reconstruction forces might rather protect unsanitary conditions in the water system than be engaged in an interracial business project. This, then, is the real hygiene project, the actual goal: Jim Crow segregation as desirable and in the public interests above and against better health for more citizens.

Working from legal historians' claim that the *Slaughter-House Cases* decision turned the tide against Reconstruction and gutted the federal government's power to enforce the intent of the Thirteenth and Fourteenth Amendments, my more precise assertion, then, is that this gutting of the Reconstruction project happened as a result of *Slaughter-House*'s specific hygienic imperatives, which we might better understand as based on folk theories of racial infection instead of scientifically investigated germ theory. By upholding the Reconstruction laws meant to ameliorate the political conditions for formerly enslaved peoples, the *Slaughter-House* decision laid the groundwork for the particular technology through which state racism later occurred. To restate, in the Court's decision, Justice Miller and his colleagues ultimately laid the ground for the state's ability, in and through the logic of public welfare, to supersede the federal government's right to intervene in the name of extending civil rights. By affirming the state's right to govern over and above the Constitution, the *Slaughter-House* decision of 1873 laid the groundwork for a new and rearticulated form of racism: hygiene-oriented administrative violence, sometimes paradoxically connecting the microbial level, at which biopolitical power was primed to intervene, and the various forms of infrastructural violence that targeted African American citizens and others in the name of public welfare.

As I began to discuss in chapter 1, the legal name for such power is "police power," which *Black's Law Dictionary* defines as "the function of that branch of the administrative machinery of government which is charged with the preservation of public order and tranquility, the promotion of the public health, safety, and morals, and the prevention, detection, and punishment of crimes."[40] The English jurist William Blackstone defined police power much more sweetly if far more intrusively as "the due regulation and domestic order of the kingdom, whereby the inhabitants of a state, like the members of a well-governed family, are bound to confirm their general behavior to the rules of propriety, good neighborhood and good manners, and to be decent, industrious and inoffensive in their respective stations."[41] By contrast, Jeremy Bentham defined police as "in general a system of precaution, either for the prevention of crime or of calamities. Its business may be distributed into eight distinct branches: (1) Police for the prevention of offenses; (2) Police for the prevention of calamities; (3) Police for the prevention of epidemic diseases; (4) Police of charity; (5) Police of interior communications; (6) Police of public amusements; (7) Police for recent intelligence; (8) Police for registration."[42] In Bentham's definition, we see that the definition of policing is simultaneously malleable, hard to define, and expansive, making such distinct terms as "offenses" and "public amusements," "prevention of epidemic diseases," and "registration" fungible and clustered around two poles: preventive and punitive.[43] In Foucauldian terms, police power is a "network of branched lines of regulation practices."[44]

Police power, in short, comes to look something like local political sovereignty or, in more common parlance, regulatory jurisdiction or regulatory power, with the proviso that the phrase continues to carry forward a sense of regulation and intervention *for community well-being*, the classic positive justification attached to biopower itself. The links between public order and public health return us to Rancière's invocation of police power as that which orders the distribution of the sensible in order to manage the field of legible political citizenship. In Rancière's formulation, aesthetics is a sensory project deployed to guard the borders of what *counts* as political belonging, speech, or activity, the interior of which is regulated by police power.[45]

Thinking solely with the *Slaughter-House Cases*, we can see that rot, decay, and decomposition constitute part of a material history entirely imbricated with such state imperatives as the ordering of space—which is to say managing contact across racial and species lines. This, then, is some of the history through which Giovanni's stilted and unfinished gesture toward the garbage of the Seine, and through which Baldwin's engagement with the remains left in Giovanni's room the morning after their encounter, signifies. The unmanageability of matter, its deviant refusal to be contained by state hygiene, marks, in a sense, the environmental presence of race and racism in *Giovanni's Room* as well as state neglect as a sign of its bio/necropolitical ordering imperatives. Race and racism are, in Christina Sharpe's terms, the weather, an environmental condition that marks where and how state infrastructure imposes and breaks and how those breaks create ruins from which otherwise life is theorized. But queer desire here, enveloped and expressed, signified and worked through, grows in the ruins of state abandonment: unhygienic and unsanctioned, alive and persistent.

To adopt a deviance-centered methodology that attends to and dwells within what is broken in the service of an otherwise is to propose that thinking with rot, with movement and decay, is to think queerly with matter, to refuse to abandon the matter that does not matter, to be attendant to its aesthetic possibilities, its discordances, its commitment to what is wrong in the pursuit of what is right. In this reading of *Giovanni's Room*, rot alerts us to the historicity of matter, its embeddedness within regimes of the aesthetic that also condition possibilities for the field of politics. Thinking queerly with rot also returns us to the conditions of the ecological present, in which staying with the trouble in Haraway's terms means sitting with the reality that living with toxicity, with the rotting remains of human consumption, is the only way forward, is in fact the very terms on which any otherwise infrastructures will have to be rebuilt. As I show in the final sections of this chapter, it is to this possibility, taking Baldwin as a point of departure, that Candice Lin responds.

A HARD WHITE BODY: CANDICE LIN'S DEVIANT ROT

When I first visited Candice Lin's studio in 2017 (about ten blocks south of where I used to live in Altadena), I was not really up to the complexity of her work. Mostly I let the sounds and smells of the studio—its alchemical properties, the vinegar odors emerging from the bottles filled with ferment—settle in my memory. It is only now, after I have caught up with her archive and her materials, that I think I can begin to find my way through to the work itself in its varied and multileveled totality. Lin's work is layered and complex: each installation gathers and weaves together stories, archives, histories, and bodily traces of figures that have come before us, whose historical shapes call out to our own still-submerged raced and gendered formations; those shapes and histories track across multiple expressions of the installation. Lin's work asks how objects carry or have been made to carry the history of race. What has drawn me to her *Hard White Body* series is precisely its decompositional structure: the way material breakdown is embedded in the tripartite structure of the show but also how her engagement with abject materiality is in part an ethical commitment to cocreating with lively matter.

The installation called *A Hard White Body* took place in three cities—Paris, Frankfurt, and Chicago—across thirteen months, following a temporal and material trajectory in which each installation literally decomposed into the others. What was a sculpted, pristine, and large installation in Paris broke down into sectioned piles in Frankfurt; by the time the work arrived in Chicago, it was not only broken into tinier pieces but soaking in a slurry of water and urine, the broken ceramic work and paper archives of the first installation decaying and molding into a rotted pool.

While I focus largely on the third installation, I want to follow the evolution of the work across its three sites. The first installation, at the Bétonsalon in Paris, centered on a white ceramic reproduction of *Giovanni's Room* that draws on the passage I explored in earlier in this chapter (figure 4.1). The installation began in September 2017 with an opening party attended by the artist in which guests were given beverages and then asked to urinate into a urinal located at the front entrance; white ceramic funnels were supplied to people with vaginas to allow them to pee standing up (figure 4.2). When the liquid was gathered, tubes then ferried the collective urine over to a distiller, where it was infused with herbs and then purified, the "cleaner" liquid ferried up into pipes and the distilled urea left behind in the machine. The extracted liquid was then again moved through pipes on the ceiling over to the ceramic bed, and from there, the liquid rained down on the bed within the plastic sheets, a literal golden shower, albeit somewhat "purified."

The first expression of Lin's installation, in Paris, was also full of archival material, stationed throughout the central room for visitors and viewers to peruse and read. The documents put two disparate figures, each of them a figure of gendered, raced, or sexual dissidence, into archival conversation: the eighteenth-century French female botanist Jeanne Baret, who traveled dressed as a man, collecting and documenting botanical life in the eighteenth century; and James Baldwin, the Black author and one of the greatest political essayists of the twentieth century, who himself spent many years in France.

Another material, ceramic, also anchors the show. Lin has noted that ceramic takes on a symbolic relationship with cleanliness and purity, both because of the whiteness of the material and also because of its historical associations both with China and with its uses in nineteenth-century science as a material through which to filter impurities. Hygiene

Figure 4.1. Installation view, Candice Lin, *A Hard White Body*, 2017. Bétonsalon, Paris, France. (Courtesy of the artist and François Ghebaly Gallery; photo: Aurélien Mole)

Figure 4.2. Installation view, Candice Lin, *A Hard White Body*, 2017. Bétonsalon, Paris, France. (Courtesy of the artist and François Ghebaly Gallery; photo: Aurélien Mole)

and its opposites, then, aesthetically frame the exhibit. In the book that accompanies the Bétonsalon exhibit, Lin reflects on golden showers as an erotic practice—the purified liquid after all showers down onto the ceramic bed—and on deviance as a formation that links raced gender to queer, gay, and lesbian desires. The links between multiple queered erotic and racialized encounters are allusive and shaped by a politics of matter. She writes,

> One of the first sexual encounters in my teenage life was with a long-admired elf girl in the same Catholic high school. Her name was J. . . . On our second date, I said, "have you heard that R. Kelly likes to pee into the mouths of fifteen-year-old girls?" and she said, "well, I am fifteen." And I said, "okay." It tasted like salt and shrimp and her mouth opened like a lamb's. I wanted to squirt milk into it; I wanted to lead her to slaughter. She complained that I splashed in her eye, but I knew she just wanted to deflect from the uncomfortable eroticism of it all.[46]

Urine's liquid pungency is central to the eroticism here: the tension between purity and infection, the aesthetic and sensory opposition between hygiene and kink or deviance, expressing itself in the congress between bodies, coagulating into the meanings circulating around the living biochemical matter that traffics and carries illicit touch. The material—salty, marine-like piss—is where bodies touch; it is the quality of disgraced touch itself. Lin writes,

> James Baldwin describes Giovanni's room as being underwater, as being almost marine. "Life in that room seemed to be occurring underwater . . . and it is certain that I underwent a sea-change there." When he returns to Paris after being in the USA—under water, under siege, bombings and bullets, at funerals, talks, meals and protests—he notices the Arab cafes are emptier. Certain friends, or perhaps it's a stretch to call them that, are no longer anywhere to be found. "Have you seen ______?" he asks about an acquaintance—a "beautiful stone hustler," his "favorite money-changer and low-life guide." But he gets no answers and no one will meet his eye. Not unlike the time he is jailed for accidental complicity in stealing a hotel sheet and realizes it will be a long time before he is missed, before anyone, any distant friend, notices to ask, "Haven't seen Jimmie in awhile, have you?"[47]

Recall that Giovanni sees the excrement-filled Seine river as a failed poetic figure for the encounter between him and David. In this passage, Lin moves from *Giovanni's Room* to Baldwin's later discussion of the conflict between Algeria and France and the place of Algerians in Paris life, deepening the relation between the forms of racialization enacted in the installation, made locally pertinent to Paris. As Lin documents in photographs she took as she broke down the installation in Paris, the liquid distilled from the donated urine was showered onto the ceramic representation of the eponymous room of Baldwin's *Giovanni's Room*, cracking the ceramic, changing the purity of its whiteness to a muddied yellow and brown and instilling the entire exhibition space with a fermented urine smell.

Rot also recurs when Lin writes of Jeanne Baret:

> Disguised as a man, she lived with [her lover] Commerson on a ship named the Étoile for three years in the captain's cabin, with its low 5' ceiling, packed tight with specimens of foreign flora and fauna, filled with the smell of vinegar, sea salt, acidic vomit from the nausea of seasickness, the mildewed smell of her linen bandages wrapped tightly around her chest, the rotting smell of Commerson's leg, which ulcerated and grew dark with gangrene. But this molding leg became an excuse for her to share the safety of his cabin. . . . So Jeanne Baret moved from sleepless nights listening to the creak of communal hammocks hung all around her, gripping her loaded pistol, to relative safety—a dank and airless room. Giovanni's room is also described as a tomb under water, not unlike the stuffy hull of the ship with its stale air of preservation, not unlike the bottom of the Seine.[48]

Rot, then, as waste, and discarded matter, as the material expression of deviant desire, form the through line for all the interwoven narratives that make up *A Hard White Body*: it signifies to *Giovanni's Room*; it signifies to Jeanne Baret's body, as well as her gangrenous lover with whom she lived as another man; it is invoked by the artist's narration of her own sexual awakening. Yet decomposition is also a formal practice for the project, as the installation breaks down over time, ultimately dissolving into a slurry. The line here between the material and the metaphoric is fine to nonexistent. Because the *Hard White Body* installation stayed up for many months at the Bétonsalon gallery in Paris, the acidic and bacterial effect of the distilled liquid fermenting on white ceramic began to show, reenacting the rotting waste of the literary scene: the ceramic began to crack, mold began to grow on the sculpture, and at one point even mushrooms (or at least some kind of fungi) appeared (figures 4.3 and 4.4). This excursion through the Paris installation allows for a richer understanding of the tripartite work of the series as it took place in Paris, Frankfurt, and Chicago, across thirteen months.

Figure 4.3. Installation view, Candice Lin, *A Hard White Body*, 2017. Bétonsalon, Paris, France. (Courtesy of the artist and François Ghebaly Gallery; photo: Aurélien Mole)

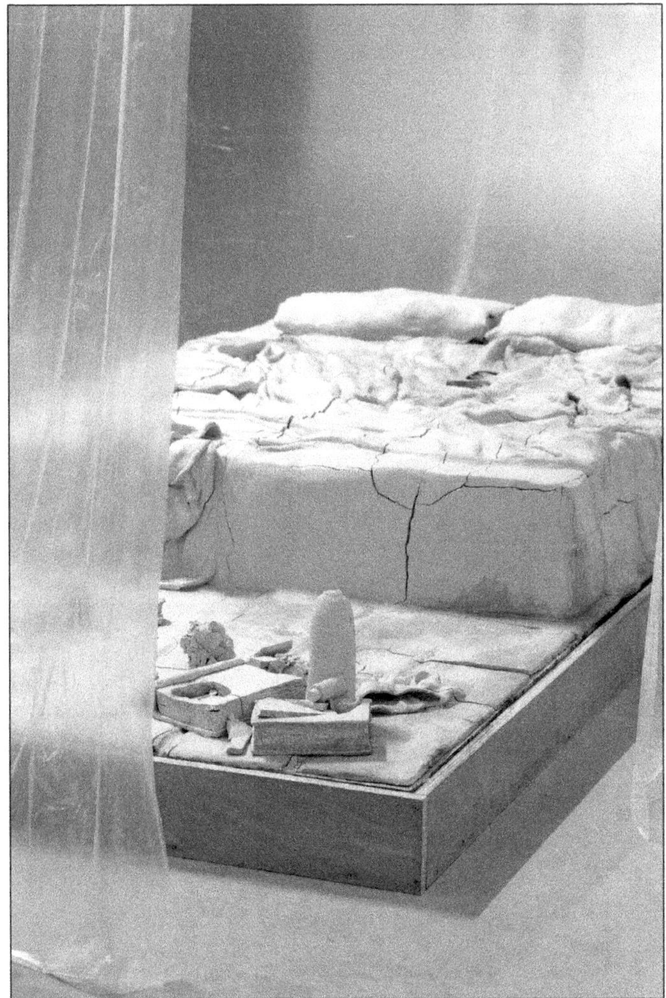

Figure 4.4. Installation view, Candice Lin, *A Hard White Body*, 2017. Bétonsalon, Paris, France. (Courtesy of the artist and François Ghebaly Gallery; photo: Aurélien Mole)

By Frankfurt, the installation became *A Hard White Body, a Soft White Worm*, and the ceramic bed featured in the first exhibition was broken down into piles, the matter of the first installation rearranged—decomposed—into new formations (figure 4.5). Above the reordered stations, a large sheet of plastic screened a video installation with a soundtrack murmuring a monologue on low, barely discernible volume.

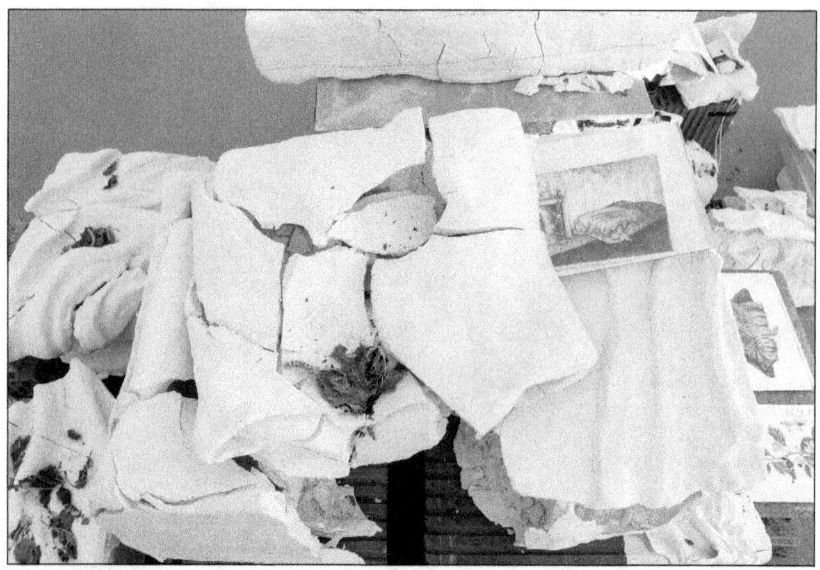

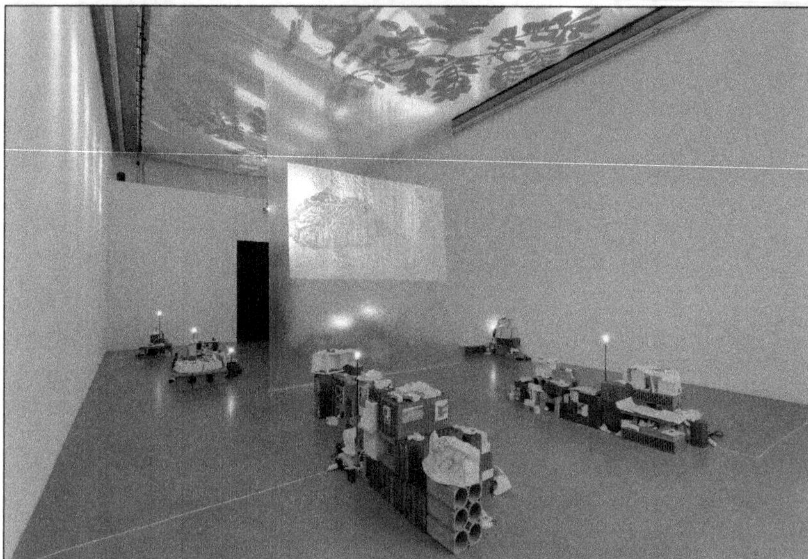

Figure 4.5. Installation view, Candice Lin, *A Hard White Body, a Soft White Worm*, 2018. Portikus, Frankfurt, Germany. (Courtesy of the artist and François Ghebaly Gallery; photo: Helena Schlichting)

By the time the exhibition got to Chicago's Logan Center, Lin had broken down the installation into even smaller parts. I spent the last two days of the exhibition in Chicago videotaping and photographing the show, sitting around the installation at multiple angles, trying to get close to what objects remained. At the heart of this exhibit was a large pool of water where the remains of the previous exhibits lay, soaking in a murky liquid. The main room of the exhibit was illuminated with a green light. Some of those objects sitting in the pool included Giovanni's shattered but reconstituted ceramic bed and pamphlets from the 1893 Chicago world's fair, including one advertising the ceramic water filter named for Pasteur and his assistant Chamberland. Molding and decomposing books sat on bricks, as did lists written by Jeanne Baret, medical bottles, ceramic underwear and socks, drawings of Giovanni's ceramic bed, and jars with herbs inside (figures 4.6–4.8).

Over the center of the pool, the plastic sheet from the Frankfurt exhibit hung with the same video projected onto it. The monologue again ran at a low volume. To the side of the main exhibit there was a new installation in another room, specifically addressing Chicago and the cen-

Figure 4.6. Installation view, Candice Lin, *A Hard White Body, a Porous Slip*, 2018. Logan Center Exhibitions, Chicago, USA. (Courtesy of the artist and François Ghebaly Gallery; photo: Robert Chase Heishman)

Figure 4.7. Installation view, Candice Lin, *A Hard White Body, a Porous Slip*, 2018. Logan Center Exhibitions, Chicago, USA. (Courtesy of the artist and François Ghebaly Gallery; photo: Robert Chase Heishman)

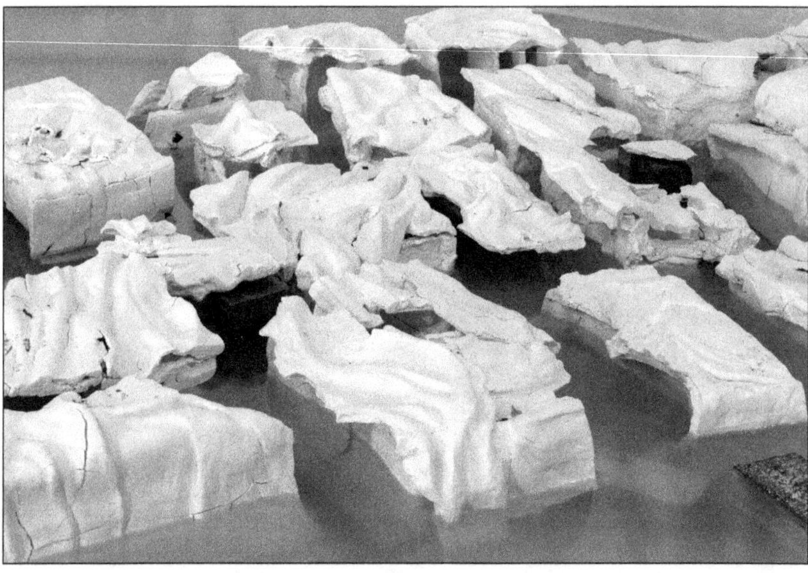

Figure 4.8. Installation view, Candice Lin, *A Hard White Body, a Porous Slip*, 2018. Logan Center Exhibitions, Chicago, USA. (Courtesy of the artist and François Ghebaly Gallery; photo: Robert Chase Heishman)

trality of the world's fair to the circulation of race and hygiene narratives as well as technological and scientific innovation. In that side room, the distillation machine from the original installation continued its work, piping liquid up through a copper coil and into the main exhibit, where it dripped into the pool.

A Hard White Body is a meditation on how the history and living practices of humans seen as "deviant" overlap with the histories and living practices of deviant matter. The material processes deployed by Lin pollute seemingly pure materials for each installation, actively degrading them and involving them in such "deviant" practices as erotic urination (golden showers); meanwhile, the overlap between rot and sexual deviance recurs in her invocation of such figures as Jeanne Baret and James Baldwin.[49] Drawing on her archival material, Lin's installation also documents how nineteenth-century bacteriologists used ceramic's porosity and cleanliness to filter their materials; ceramics were later marketed as a domestic water-filtering technology at the Chicago's world fair. Lin's installation and written material, on their own but also in their conversation with Baldwin, tell us that the history of matter is populated with gender-nonconforming and nonheteronormative bodies and that matter itself comes to take on—itself theorizes—the counterdisciplinary ways that these humans sought to express or represent queer world-making practices. As she shows, they did so in and through their aesthetic, scientific, and erotic relations with matter, plant life, objects, and other nonhuman phenomena.

ADRIAN PIPER'S SERIAL DECOMPOSITION

I want to close this chapter with a short discussion of rot in the work of the conceptualist artist Adrian Piper. In particular, I am interested in two early pieces of Piper's that engage decomposition as a process central to her own fascination with objecthood. The first piece, *Five Unrelated Time Pieces (Meat into Meat)*, took place between Friday October 11, 1968, and Sunday, October 13, 1968. In that sequence, Piper, who is vegetarian, documents her preparation and serving of hamburger to her then-partner. The first photograph shows a package of supermarket-wrapped ground beef lying on a pale wooden countertop; it is 3:15 p.m. on Friday, October 11, 1968 (figure 4.9). At 11:35 a.m. the next day, we see four

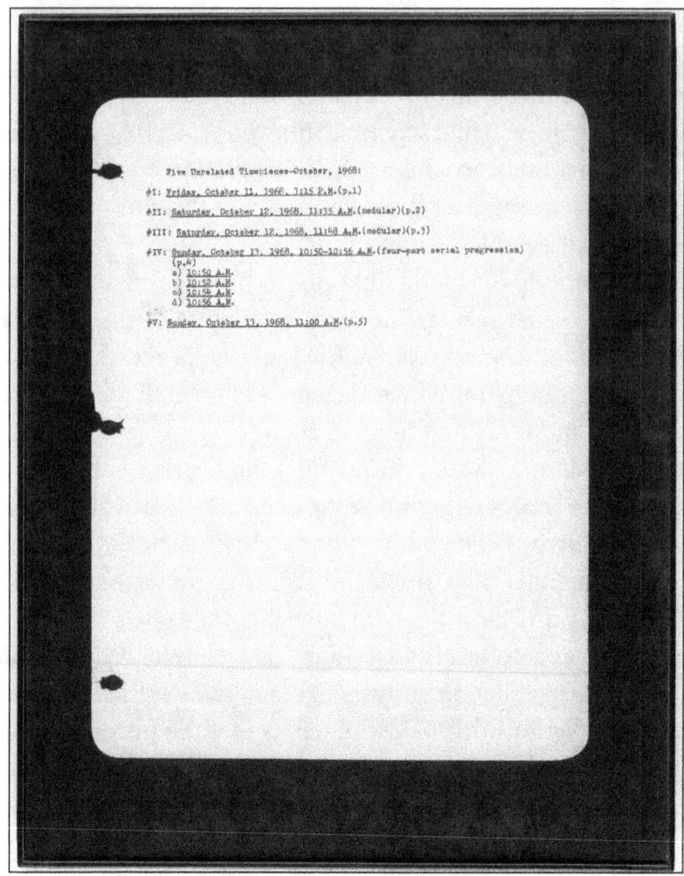

Five Unrelated Timepieces–October, 1968:

#I: Friday, October 11, 1968, 3:15 P.M.(p.1)

#II: Saturday, October 12, 1968, 11:35 A.M.(modular)(p.2)

#III: Saturday, October 12, 1968, 11:48 A.M.(modular)(p.3)

#IV: Sunday, October 13, 1968, 10:50–10:56 A.M.(four-part serial progression)
(p.4)
a) 10:50 A.M.
b) 10:52 A.M.
c) 10:54 A.M.
d) 10:56 A.M.

#V: Sunday, October 13, 1968, 11:00 A.M.(p.5)

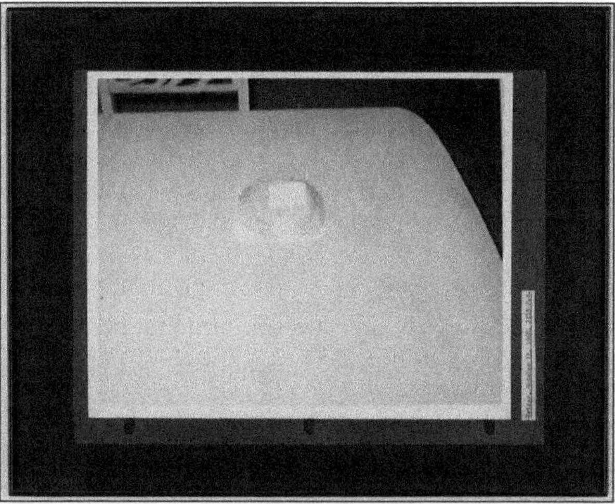

Figure 4.9. Adrian Piper, *Five Unrelated Time Pieces (Meat into Meat)*, 1968, six pages, one typescript page, eight photographs and text mounted on black paper, each page 9.5" × 11.5" (24.1 cm × 29.2 cm) or 11.5" × 9.5" (29.2 cm × 24.1 cm). (Collection of Paul and Karen McCarthy; © Adrian Piper Research Archive (APRA) Foundation Berlin)

round hamburger patties on a white plate on the same pale countertop; exactly twenty-four hours and thirteen minutes later, at 11:48 a.m., four hamburger patties are frying in a small silver frying pan, on a white gas stovetop (figure. 4.10). The next frame gives us four sequential photos, in

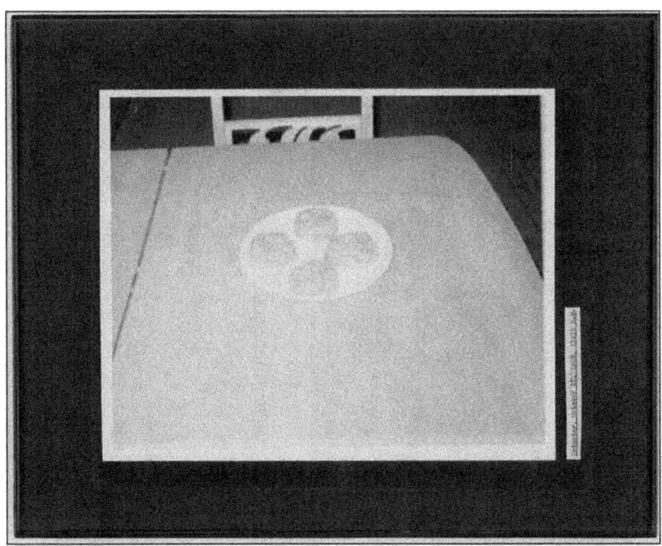

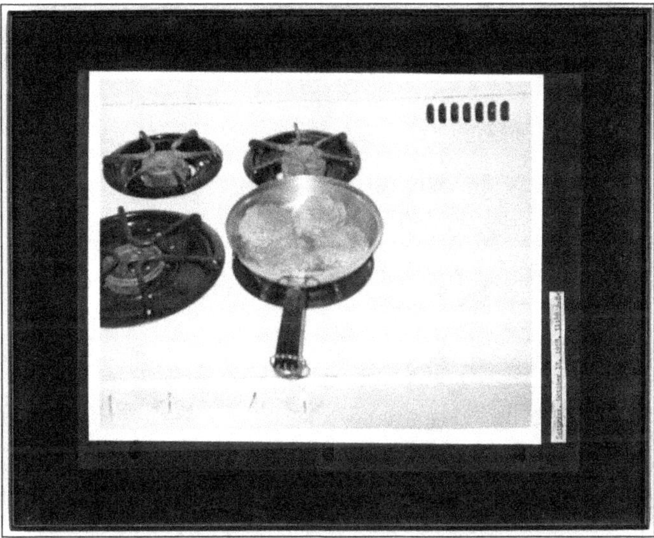

Figure 4.10. Adrian Piper, *Five Unrelated Time Pieces (Meat into Meat)*, 1968, six pages, one typescript page, eight photographs and text mounted on black paper, each page 9.5" × 11.5" (24.1 cm × 29.2 cm) or 11.5" × 9.5" (29.2 cm × 24.1 cm). (Collection of Paul and Karen McCarthy © Adrian Piper Research Archive (APRA) Foundation Berlin)

a square, of a white man eating four burger patties, presumably the same ones cooked the day before; the times—10:50 a.m., 10:52 a.m., 10:54 a.m., and 10:56 a.m. on Sunday, October 13—appear in type on the right side (figure 4.11). Four minutes later, the final photograph shows an empty plate, some crumbs of meat perhaps, an abandoned fork (figure 4.12).

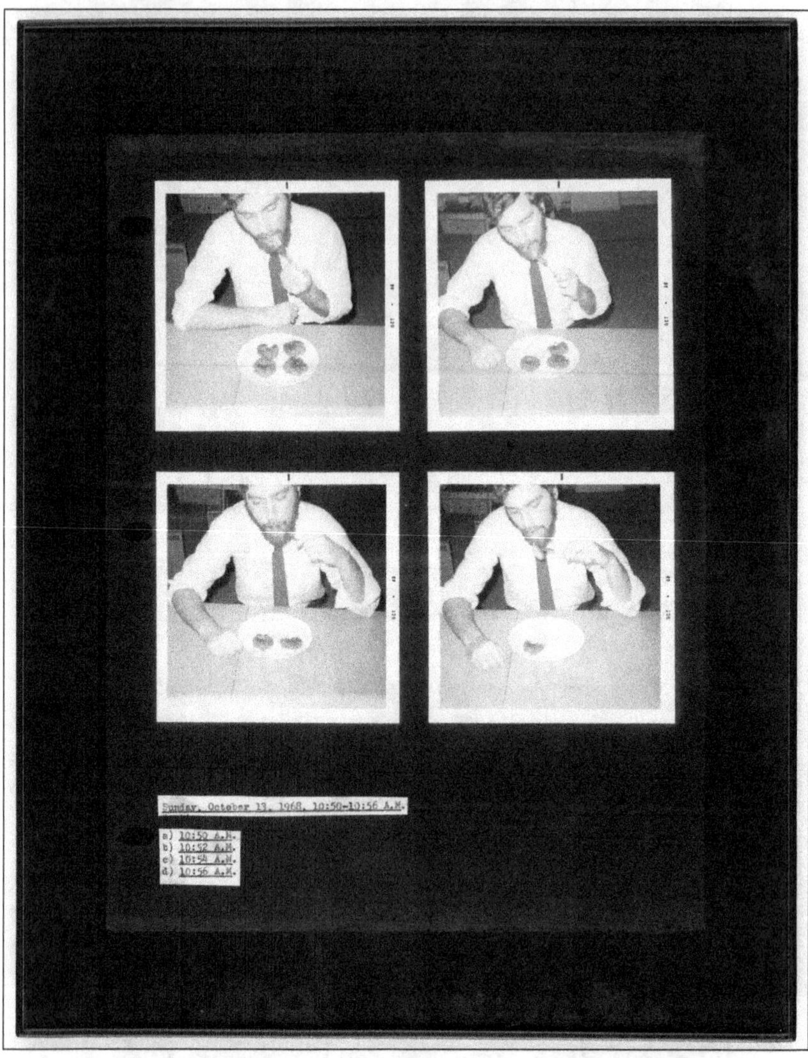

Figure 4.11. Adrian Piper, *Five Unrelated Time Pieces (Meat into Meat)*, 1968, six pages, one typescript page, eight photographs and text mounted on black paper, each page 9.5" × 11.5" (24.1 cm × 29.2 cm) or 11.5" × 9.5" (29.2 cm × 24.1 cm). (Collection of Paul and Karen McCarthy; © Adrian Piper Research Archive (APRA) Foundation Berlin)

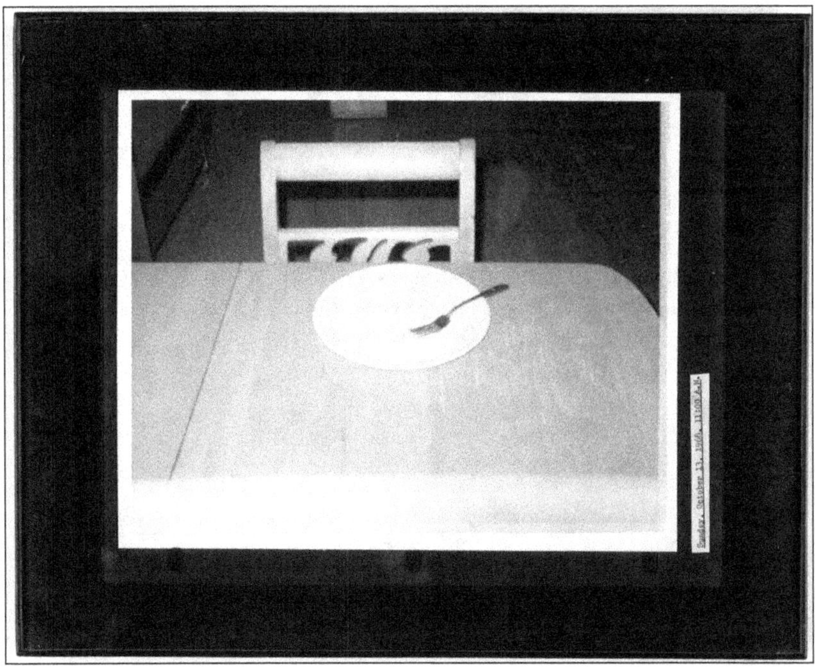

Figure 4.12. Adrian Piper, *Five Unrelated Time Pieces (Meat into Meat)*, 1968, six pages, one typescript page, eight photographs and text mounted on black paper, each page 9.5" × 11.5" (24.1 cm × 29.2 cm) or 11.5" × 9.5" (29.2 cm × 24.1 cm). (Collection of Paul and Karen McCarthy; © Adrian Piper Research Archive (APRA) Foundation Berlin)

At the 2018 MOMA retrospective of Piper's work, *Five Unrelated Time Pieces (Meat into Meat)* was posed on the other side of a doorway from another piece equally engaged with decomposition, a piece that Piper's typed notes indicate she began to plan two days later, after completing *Five Unrelated Time Pieces* on Tuesday, October 15, 1968. Titled *A Conceptual Seriation Arrested at Four Points in Time*, this second piece shows four plastic trays of ferric chloride, a substance commonly used as etching fluid (figure 4.13). As the photographs and typed documentation indicate, after several starts, Piper set up the performance so that four sheets of zinc would be submerged, thirty minutes apart, in ferric chloride. Across a period of seven days, during which she photographed the decomposing zinc for five days, October 22–29, Piper directs the viewer's attention to the effects of the acidic liquid on the metal, playing with the tension between increase

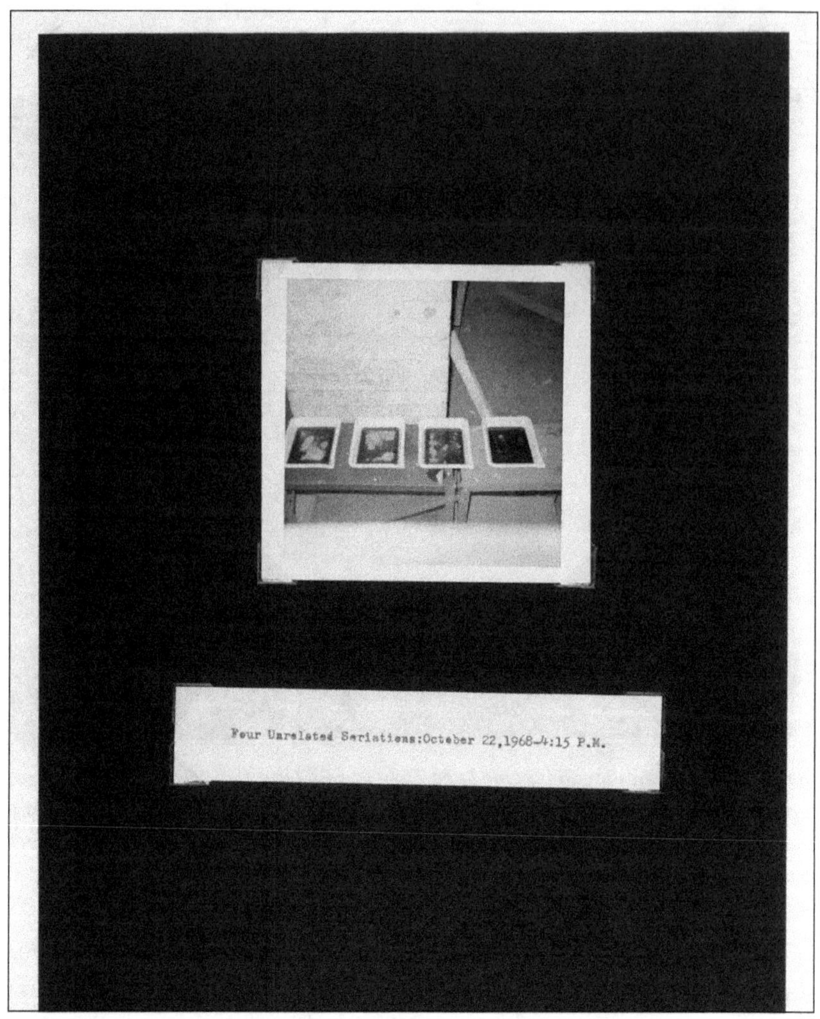

Figure 4.13. Adrian Piper, *A Conceptual Seriation Arrested at Four Points in Time*, 1968, notebook with thirty-five pages: six typescript pages; twenty-five photographs and text mounted on colored paper; and cut-and-pasted text on four sheets of colored paper, each page: 11" × 8.5" (27.9 cm × 21.6 cm). Detail: page 6. (Collection of the Adrian Piper Research Archive (APRA) Foundation Berlin; © APRA Foundation Berlin)

(as the time that the zinc is submerged in the ferric chloride increases) with the amount of change that she can visually track (the decompositional change decreases in rate as time passes), and then, finally, the minimizing difference between all four pans is tracked, as the thirty-minute delay between each sheet's initial submersion gradually effects less difference between them (figure 4.14).

Conceptualism—and this series is from Piper's high conceptualist moment—famously distances itself from the materiality of the art object. Graphing and documenting two sets of matter in opposing processes—the compositional process of making the male body (via disappearing and decomposing animal flesh) as against the decompositional process of dissolving zinc plates in ferrous chloride—the curators take up

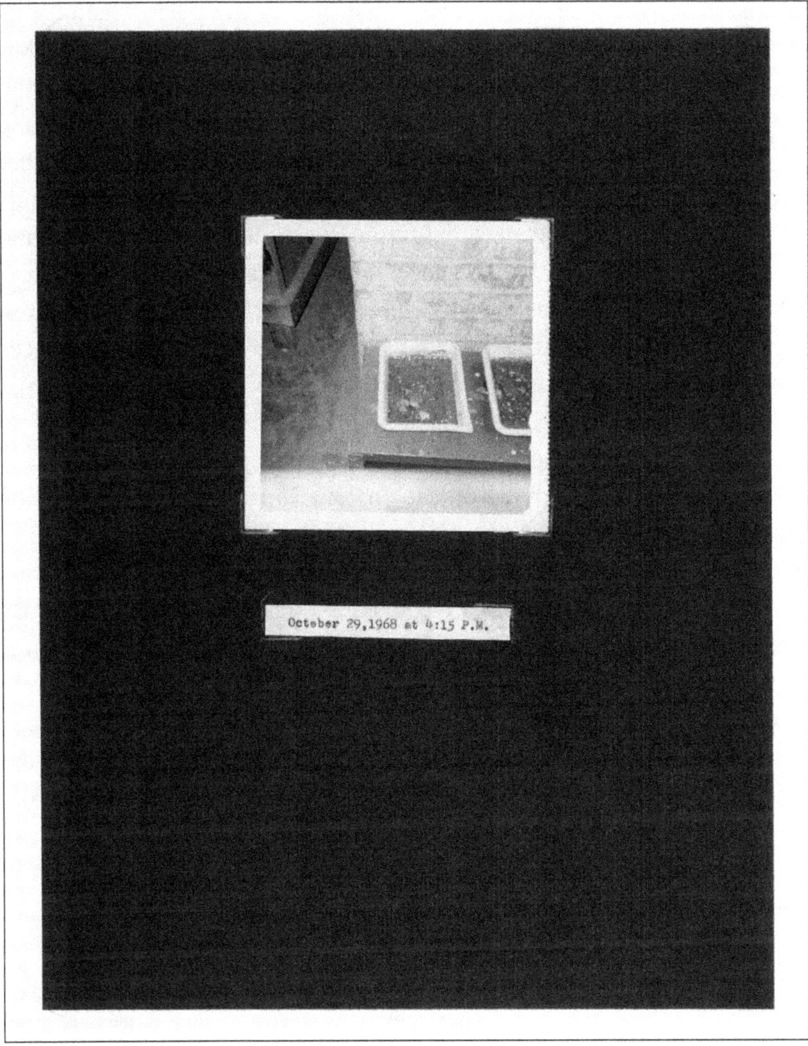

Figure 4.14. Adrian Piper, *A Conceptual Seriation Arrested at Four Points in Time*, 1968, notebook with thirty-five pages: six typescript pages; twenty-five photographs and text mounted on colored paper; and cut-and-pasted text on four sheets of colored paper, each page: 11" × 8.5" (27.9 cm × 21.6 cm). Detail: page 16. (Collection of the Adrian Piper Research Archive (APRA) Foundation Berlin; © APRA Foundation Berlin)

conceptualism's focus on dematerialization. Famously, Piper sees *Five Unrelated Time Pieces* as her very first performance piece. Through the conflict with her white partner at the time, and while photographing the project, she came to realize that disembodied performance was not possible or, more precisely, that it would be impossible for her not to be present in her work. As Uri McMillan argues, Piper's work in this period seems to absent Piper herself from the art she is producing: she hesitated to name herself a Black artist during the period leading up to the work, and she also seemed to absent herself from the many art movements that she found herself caught between (minimalism and conceptualism, among others).[50] I am fully convinced by McMillan and want to build on his argument that objecthood is a primary framework through which Piper examines and also distances herself from the various representational schemas that frame the failures of the US racial and gendered imagination. What is fascinating is that in Piper's two pieces, which predate her more famous *Mythic Being* performances, her interest in the ephemerality of the object aligns with her interest in the processual nature of time as she documents the objects' decomposition across time. As such, she rejects the object as art's necessary end product.

In the other work, however, her work opens up questions of making and unmaking the body-as-object. In *Five Unrelated Time Pieces*, the cow flesh initially sits on the table, a packaged and unopened blob of processed raw flesh; the next day, it is remade into four circular patties; the following day, the patties are cooked and change color; the next day, they are eaten and absorbed into Posner's body, which then metabolizes and repackages them as energy and body. The aesthetic capacity of (female) art (explicitly understood as labor) becomes (male) caloric capacity. Clearly Piper's interest in time also opens onto a concern with the invisibility of immaterial and feminized labor: her occlusion from the visual frame but also the eater's flat affect, making the repetitive everydayness of the work, its concertedly nonmonumental aesthetic, part of the entire piece's argumentative force. Each day, every day, the labor continues; each day, the eater does not register the photographer or the cook. Again and again; again and again: for four days. During the four-day process of producing four hamburger patties, the meat is photographed unrefrigerated outside refrigeration, lying out on the open table; thus, I think that Piper is also playing with hygiene—and therefore disgust—as a way of rendering abject the classically feminine labor of serving men, in particular white men. The rotted—but not necessarily spoiled—meat will disappear into Piper's soon-to-be-ex lover's body, raising the question of how long the dead cow flesh can actually last before becoming unfit for human consumption. Read within this critical frame, this is a deeply aggressive performance as Posner's extractive consumption of both Piper's labor and the decaying hamburger is staged by her, as a performance and serial piece, for her camera and ultimately as a piece that will enter her own oeuvre and repertoire. This even before we consider that given the title, Piper is calling Posner a piece of meat.

What might it mean to map these two performances—*A Conceptual Seriation* and *Five Unrelated Time Pieces*—onto each other in the context of Piper's admission that *Five Unrelated Time Pieces* is the moment in which she realized that she was not able to erase herself from the scene of performance, a realization that led to her later and more famous explorations of race, gender, and embodiment? Read against each other, we can see Piper using performance—the doing of a thing in time—to push at the imperviousness and permanence of the art object, rendering it both quotidian and ephemeral, subject to the decay of time and therefore marginal to the meaning of art itself. To return to the overarching interests of this chapter, I am arguing that Piper makes these arguments by engaging rot and decay. Held up against each other, the soft fleshiness of the meat is not unlike the quality of the corroding zinc plates, their metallic imperviousness surprisingly dissolving into muck and goo, with strange floating bits in it. As in Lin's work, which lets organic processes work in creative collaboration with the artist, there is an undoing here of the idea of the artist as craftsperson, as totalized agential subject: the plates are subjected to biochemical processes beyond Piper's creative engagement, outside her presence, the time lapse and her repeated absence from the pans rendering her agency flickering although still present alongside the biochemical work of decomposition.

But if we consider the dialectic between these two performances within the trajectory of Piper's lifelong exploration of the line between subject and object, we can also understand these works as an attack on that differentiation in much the same way that her later bodily performances enact. In Fred Moten's terms, Piper's interest in becoming an object raising objections to objectification, her critique of the modernist understanding of the object, gives way to a biochemical mediation, something along the lines of a science experiment, an art-science melding that undermines taste as a socially verticalizing discourse keyed to the project of class distinction. It reduces white flesh to the material meatiness that it has always disavowed within the symbolic order, leaving matter and consequent nonmattering to the thick space of necrobiopolitical living.[51] At the very moment that Piper began to engage performance and to meditate on the presence of race and gender as constitutive elements of her work, rot and decay emerged as technologies through which to refigure objecthood and its relation to the subject position of the artist and author.

Let me return to where I started here and close here with some propositions about rot and then some meta and methodological comments about thinking with matter as against disciplinarity. I began this chapter thinking about the Anthropocene, but my work in the end concerns the possibility of following in the pioneering wake of Black feminist criticism and performance to think with the life and death of matter against the murderous logics of the present. My answer to the question of how to think the end of human exceptionalism is contingent, performative, interdisciplinary, and still being worked out: what it does, as Ferreira da Silva says, is what it does. I seek to learn from and emulate Ferreira da Silva, Spillers, Wynter, Cathy Cohen, Kimberlé Crenshaw, and the august matrilineage of Black feminists and other women of color whose intersectional thinking has already laid the foundation for answering that very question: we must rethink human exceptionalism, starting from the wisdom of those who have already and are already surviving it. If it is true that, as Monique Allawaert so beautifully writes in her precise historicization of vital materialism, race, and natural history, *Ariel's Ecology*, that "deviant materialisms could lead to an anarchy of form," then the how of it is not separate from the what of it.[52] Let us be the rot that that decomposes disciplinarity; let us be critics sitting in the decay of history. Let us be the rot that survives.

5

JELLY

Early in the 2013 film *Snowpiercer*, we watch a small mass of people—dirty, shabby, and imprisoned in a train car—waiting to be fed, being counted by armed guards.[1] Part of the survivors of a failed global attempt to remedy global warming, the prisoners inhabit the rear carriage of a train that perpetually circles a frozen planet, waiting, it is implied, for the ice to thaw. There is much to be said about the apocalyptic imagery of the film—imagery that is no longer merely symbolic but that sits rather close to the real of the current planetary crisis. But what I would like to pay attention to here is one of the tiniest and most evocative details of this whole, ravishing film: the food of the prisoners of the last train carriage. These prisoners, designated as the lowest rung of the hierarchy that has emerged on the train, eat blocks of gelatin.

Dark brown and gold, uniform in size and shape, the gelatin blocks shake and catch the light as the prisoners of the back carriage hold and eat them, while they walk in circles, carceral imagery that is in loose imitation of an exercise walk around a prison yard. The blocks are equally repulsive and mesmerizing. But it is not until slightly later in the film, when the prisoners finally break through to a forward carriage, that the fully abject implications of the gelatin blocks become apparent: for seventeen years, the members of the rear car have been eating pulverized and gelatinized cockroaches. The scene in which the cockroaches are revealed makes that fact haptically felt by having the protagonist, Curtis (Chris Evans), and the character called Painter (Clark Middleton) open up and look into the large vats in which the cockroaches are ground up (figure 5.1). Painter first cries out in shock; when Curtis follows Painter up some stairs to look inside the vat, he grasps the edges, bends toward the insects, and peers into the vat. Recoiling almost immediately and turning away, he exhales and inhales quickly, covering his mouth with his hand and then with his fist, seeming to almost gag, to fight to hold back his vomit, to force himself not to exhibit his physiological response (figure 5.2).

Figure 5.1. Bong Joon-ho, dir., *Snowpiercer* (Seoul: Moho Films and Opus Pictures, 2013).

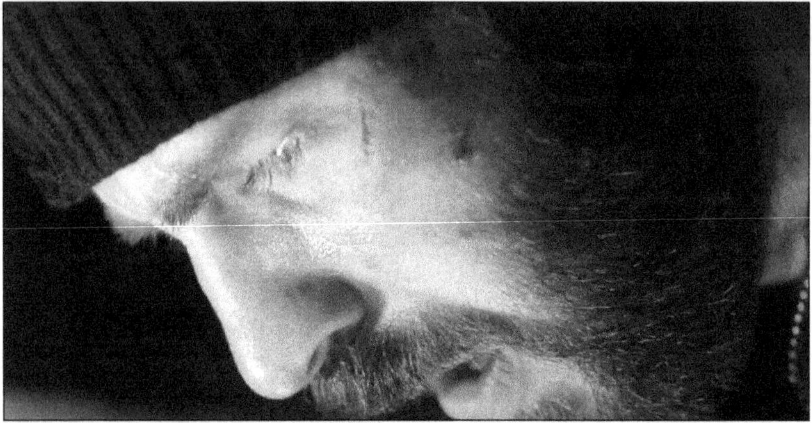

Figure 5.2. Bong Joon-ho, dir., *Snowpiercer* (Seoul: Moho Films and Opus Pictures, 2013).

The sensory effect of Curtis's view of the thousands of cockroaches roiling about in the vat is emphasized by a swell in the rock music that accompanies the scene plus the unexpected color pop—that particular mix of cockroachy brown and warm gold—in a film that up until that point has been dominated by gray and blue tones as well as by the total absence of anything that resembles nature. The cockroaches are circulated and mashed by the rolling corkscrew gears; they are fervid, active, hot in color and film tone, technically quite an amazing display of CGI virtuosity. They flutter their wings and fly around and up out of the vat. What is inside the vat, I want to posit, is life: vital life, energized and roiling and active, the energy of a disposable species—available to be converted into pure sustenance for humans whose social value so clearly equals their own. In a world in which eating is devoid of aesthetic pleasure (indeed, one character upon receiving his protein bar wonders longingly about what steak must have smelled like while it was being cooked), we are beyond or below—or perhaps, in the terms of the train, at the rear—of the hierarchical relations that make possible a notion of taste as aesthetic discernment; instead, the cockroach bars fully anatomize the rear-car inhabitants' status as human refuse. As in the plantation, the border camp, the prison, we are in the realm of survival, of *zoe*, or bare life itself.[2]

Within the first few minutes of the film, the narrative places us at a violent uprising that is driven not only by pure caloric scarcity but also by political and aesthetic rage, a political rage and uprising that ultimately turns out to have been already anticipated by the train's ruling class. But the link I want to return to here is that between food, hunger, and mass political deployment, links made visible not only within the images of the rebellious lower orders of the train but in the sequence that the director and his editor put forward between the organized uprising, the mass of disorganized cockroach bodies, and the food bars. Parsing the relation between the passage from Foucault that I discussed in the introduction and this clip from *Snowpiercer* returns us to the paradoxical relationship between caloric capacity and affective capacity. The roiling bodies of the cockroaches, the raw life of these energetic, protein-intensive insects, *might* be understood to indicate that caloric capacity, the fuel needed to move the body, is inextricably but at the same time somehow inversely linked to political potential, even as the bodies of the cockroaches are analogical to the crowd itself: the action of the populace is the revolutionary capacity that counters or exceeds or defies the managed caloric energy of the population as it appears, extracted, abstracted, and aestheticized, in a block of golden-brown gelatin.

Snowpiercer forces us to think about how the rendering of animal waste is a cultural practice within which the politics of trash—and capitalism's genius move to repurpose trash into more efficient and vertically integrated profit models—joins the question of the animal to the ordering of the species. This joining includes, as Foucault wrote, vis-à-vis sexual deviance, the "sub-species" of humans so ordered.[3] My argument here is that *Snowpiercer*'s use of gelatin as poor people's food is not casual by any means, either historically or, as I will now discuss, aesthetically. While the nineteenth century saw the application of theories of thermodynamics to consumable materials in order to develop the notion of the calorie (which, as I detailed in chapter 1, in the US happened via Atwater's experiments at Wesleyan), early nineteenth-century scientists, including Claude Bernard and Liebig, experimented on themselves, on living animals, and on patients to try to understand how the human machine worked. In particular, they wanted to quantify the "nitrogenic," or nourishing, qualities of food; they sought, among other things, to determine how much gelatin could be mechanically extracted from underused animal flesh and bones with the specific aim of discovering whether gelatin could be used to feed the poor and the ill. The scientific history of both of these technologies can be traced further backward to the period after the Napoleonic Wars, when the French Academie Scientifique convened a Committee on the Status of Gelatin to study emergent food technologies—newly separated as "science" from their traditional social location as "craft"—such as the extraction of gelatin and bouillon from meat and bones.[4] For over three decades, from 1803 to 1841, several incarnations of the committee studied various methods for extracting all possible nutritive value from meat and bones, ultimately concluding that gelatin could not sustain life as a cheap meat alternative.[5] This work received a great deal of French state support, and the news of the gelatin commission's work reached the United States through newspaper bulletins and scientific lectures.

Gelatin thus has a complex history tied both to waste management and to the management of the poor. Keeping this in mind, I now want to turn to the question of the gelatinous as a materiality that might also bring its correspondence with the material conditions of the poor, the enslaved, and the working class into sharper relief. More precisely, how might we think through political affect, particularly minoritarian political affect, in relation to the gelatinous? In the sections that follow, I examine a set of texts that bring forward some of the political aesthetics and social history of the gelatinous, beginning with a pair of short stories by Herman Melville and a scene from Martin Delany's

Blake. Alongside this nineteenth-century literature, I explore gelatin's early nineteenth-century scientific history; I then examine gelatin as a material in Karl Marx. I will also gesture briefly to a few contemporary examples of jellies and gelatinous materials in art: a short film featuring jellies made by the jelly artists Bompas and Parr and, finally, a pornographic computer screen saver called "Generous Gesture" by the queer Afro-Canadian artist dirtysurface.

To be clear, my focus here extends beyond the technical definition of the gelatinous as referring only to something made of gelatin. Rather, my interest here is in the larger class of substances examined by the science of rheology, including complex liquids, hydrocolloids, foams, gels, microemulsions, muds, sludges, and suspensions, all of which demonstrate particular and unusual laws of physics. I am particularly interested in these artists' sensual descriptions or deployments of gelatinous materials and body parts, in their divergent representations of kinetic movement. What I will argue is that for both Herman Melville and Martin Delany—and then too for other political thinkers such as Karl Marx, Audre Lorde, Julia Kristeva, and Gilles Deleuze and Félix Guattari—the aesthetic power of gelatinousness is the potential that these materials hold for forms of movement and shifts in sensory organization that undo the animacy hierarchies that traditionally prioritize agentic, individualized, human selfhood and rather imagine relational forms of inhuman and human collectivity.

The first thing we all know about the gelatinous is that it *moves*. Every one of us can probably visualize that bizarre wiggling that jelly does when you take it out of the fridge or, alternately, the slow rebounding of form that a soft pudding undergoes after it has been poked at. In order to really understand what the gelatinous means, we need to understand how it moves, and the physics of jelly helps us to think about what is uncanny and unusual about these substances.

Rheology is a subset of physics that examines how matter moves and how it is reshaped or deformed. In particular, rheology focuses on classes of liquids that behave as though they were solids and solids that behave as though they were liquids. The science of rheological substances is thus an attempt to understand those substances whose movement cannot be calculated by the usual work of Newtonian mechanics. When stress or pressure is applied to most materials on Earth, they simply give way: a small puddle of water, for instance, breaks apart when a hand comes down on it. Rheological substances, by contrast, are viscous, elastic, sticky, and gelatinous; they harden, as whipped cream consolidates from a liquid to a seeming solid when whipped or as corn starch does when mixed with water, or alternately they liquefy when stress is applied to them, as ketchup does when shaken out of a bottle or punctured by a knife. As a video produced by Nathan Myhrvold's Modernist Cuisine group shows, rheological substances deform when pressured—stretching, bending, giving—and sometimes, when pushed to the point of what is called "yield stress," they break (figures 5.3–5.5).

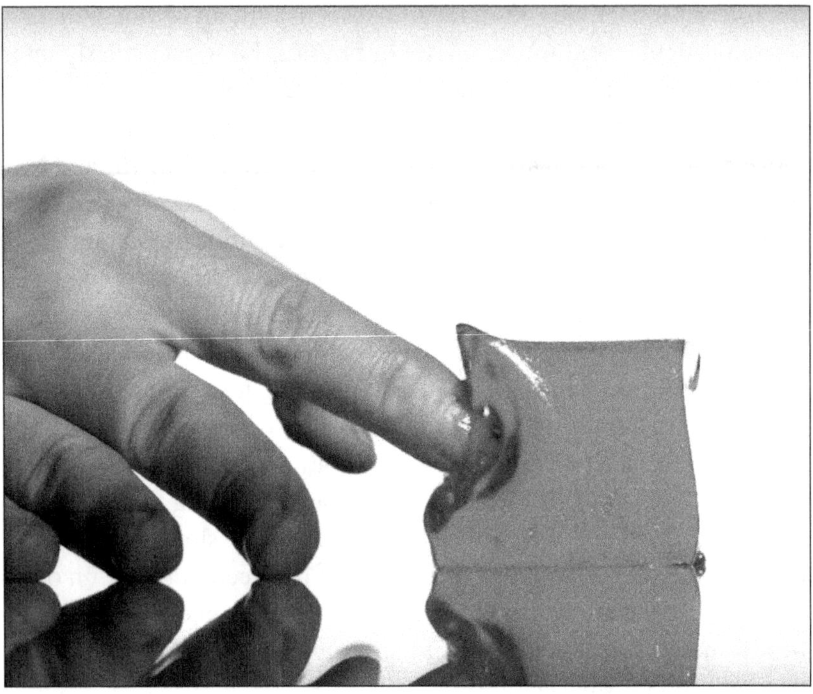

Figure 5.3. Still from ModernistCuisine, "Gelatin Cubes Dropped onto Solid Surface High Speed Video 6200 fps." YouTube, April 19, 2011, www.youtube.com/watch?v=4n5AfHYST6E.

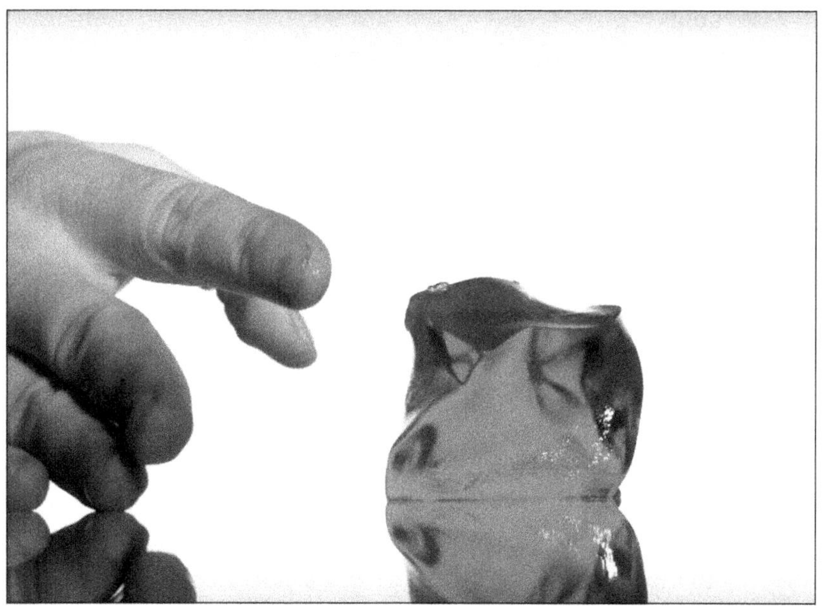

Figure 5.4. Still from ModernistCuisine, "Gelatin Cubes Dropped onto Solid Surface High Speed Video 6200 fps." YouTube, April 19, 2011, www.youtube.com/watch?v=4n5AfHYST6E.

Figure 5.5. Still from ModernistCuisine, "Gelatin Cubes Dropped onto Solid Surface High Speed Video 6200 fps." YouTube, April 19, 2011, www.youtube.com/watch?v=4n5AfHYST6E.

Grouping substances by their unconventional forms of movement or flow and because of their unusual relationship to both stress and energy conservation, rheology classes together a wide group of seemingly very different substances. Industrial and food sciences describe the nature of gelatinous movement as "shear" or "stress": pressure (stress) is applied to the material from one direction, and the rate of the material's give is its shear rate; the slower the give, the higher the material's viscosity. While gelatinous materials, like everything else, will eventually break under enough stress, they are often able to bend and stretch without losing the continuity or integrity of the material: this is what constitutes their particular materiality. Most interestingly, some of these materials can actually retain energy when stressed: when opposing forms of stress are applied to them (when in essence they twist) or when they are compressed (squished, as in between teeth or between tongue and palate), the atomic physical bonds within the material can retain enough energy in order to move back toward their original shape. In other words, rheological materials bounce back.

Rheological materials thus react to external stimuli in surprising ways: they move because they internalize the energy that is directed at them. However, at the level of physics and biochemistry, there is a fundamental accord in the way that human beings and these strange substances move through the world. The science of rheology tells us something about how certain materials respond to stress and, in fact, use stress to capture and retain the capacity for response, for self-direction, and for recovery shaped and dictated by their own internal logics. Two of the main substances in human and animal bodies are rheological: blood and fat. Blood, for instance, demonstrates variable viscosity under different conditions, and in human biomechanics, rheology (or rather biorheology) measures and understands the overall mechanical behavior of skin as it is supported and affected by subcutaneous adipose tissue (otherwise known as fat).[6] Rheology, in other words, is far more relevant than we might think. When we think about the congruencies between human and nonhuman animals and what we might consider not-living but relatively animate rheological materials, we are not simply speaking in metaphor or analogy (this not to disrespect either metaphor or analogy). We are speaking literally: these materials express energy in unexpected ways, reexpressing that energy at times as dance, as in the case of

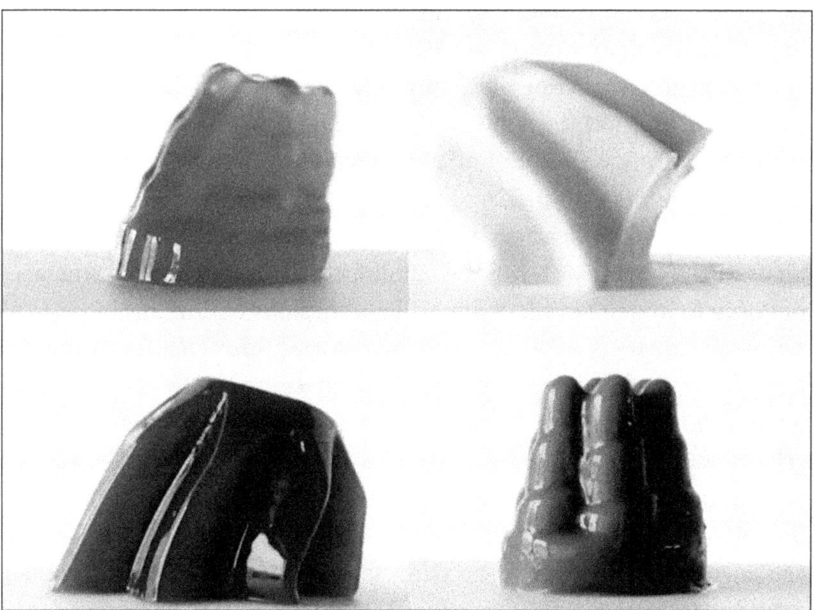

Figure 5.6. Still from "Jenny van Sommers: Jelly Roles: The Poetry of Puddings in Motion, with a Little Help from Bompas & Parr." Nowness, March 21, 2015, www.nowness.com/story/jelly-roles-jenny-van-sommers-bompas-and-parr?utm_source=YOUT&utm_medium=SM&utm_campaign=YT1001.

a video collaboration between the British "jelly artists" Sam Bompas and Harry Parr and the photographer, Jenny Sommers.

In this video collaboration, four different-colored jellies, made from two different mold shapes, appear in a four-paned video screen (figure 5.6). As music by the group Social Skills runs in the background, the four jellies—each in its own separate window—gyrate and move, jiggling and responding to the music in unique ways. One jelly sways from side to side, lifting one prong of its molded shape as though lifting and stamping a foot. Another bounces on itself, its top almost meditatively pointed downward until the music escalates and it begins to sway wildly from side to side. Another continues to sway slowly and dolorously, bouncing up and down in small bops. Each jelly, in a sense, presents its own material character. What the four dancing jellies show us is a kind of relational and yet agential movement: sound made visible. Here, the waves of the music collide with each of the four jellies; the movement of each jelly is a record of how sound moves through space, a record of the impact of sound on matter.

By engaging this ephemeral film, my goal is to quickly characterize what it is that gelatinous objects theorize, that no other kinds of matter can do: they render both sound and touch visible. This exercise is something different from thinking about agential or animate materiality in the sense that Jane Bennett means when she characterizes vibrant matter as a "the capacity of things—edibles, commodities, storms, metals—not only to impede or block the will and designs of humans but also to act as quasi agents or forces with trajectories, propensities or tendencies of their own."[7] The science of rheology brings us to something different from a vitalist or hylomorphic relation to material because the gelatinous—this broad category of colloids, gels, suspensions, emulsions, and so forth—is in fact quite exquisitely relational in its materiality: gelatinous materials manifest and materialize forms of touch that are otherwise not visible to the eye, and they manifest the nature of that contact in and as movement. Thus, what is at stake here in my discussion of the gelatinous is an engagement with sensory organization, as it relates to both the human encounter with nonhuman objects and nonhuman beings and also the human as it encounters its own nonhumanness. That is, my discussion tracks both nonhuman matter and the human body as they exceed or operate outside of sovereign will.

Thinking with the materiality of the gelatinous in terms of Deleuze and Guattari's idea of hapticity "as a tactile space, . . . a sonorous much more than a visual space," gelatinousness is marked by a collapse of the visual into the tactile, the tactile into the sonic, and back again. It is a reorganization—or perhaps disorganization—of the sensory, and it is here that we begin to get at what is at stake for the authors and artists I am about to discuss: Melville, Delany, Lorde, Marx, and much later on, dirtysurface. Their disruption of sensory orders is particularly apparent when we set them against the taxonomic organization of affect and sensation that, I have argued, was part of the larger reorganization of administrative governmentality during the Progressive era. Thinking with their rheological hapticities opens up, perhaps, these artists' investment in invoking—and I do mean "invocation" here in the sense of an incantatory raising—alternative organizations of the sensory itself, reworking the terms of what Rancière called the "distribution of sensibility" toward a reorganization of politicity itself.

POOR MAN'S PUDDING

The three pairs of short stories that have come to be called Melville's diptychs, the "Paradise of Bachelors / Tartarus of Maids," "The Two Temples," and "Poor Man's Pudding / Rich Man's Crumbs," draw from their visual predecessor—the diptych painting—in being meditations on comparison and difference. Each half of Melville's diptych short stories is located on either side of the Atlantic, and each represents a meditation on what we might loosely call the patterns and organization of social differentiation and inequity. Jay Leyda applied the term "diptych" to these three sets of stories after the fact, in his anthology of Melville's short fiction in the 1940s, but "Poor Man's Pudding" and "Rich Man's Crumbs," respectively subtitled "Picture One" and "Picture Two," play on the traditionally allegorical and comparative mode of representation that is inherent to diptych paintings, tempting the reader to draw a moral from the stories.[8] The stories also prefigure naturalism's interest in the details of poverty and class difference and bare survival, while drawing on what would become realism's interest in visual detail.

Nowhere is this meditation on the visual so apparent as in the two short stories "Poor Man's Pudding / Picture First" and "Rich Man's Crumbs / Picture Second." Despite their framing reference to the visual, the Pudding and Crumbs diptych insists on attention to other senses—sound, taste, and touch in particular. These senses, in various ways, all question the political limitations of visuality. Centered on a shared meal in a poor New England cottage and a frenzied banquet in London, food plays a role in each half of the diptych in elaborating what critics like Sianne Ngai have seen as Melville's critique of charitability as both an affect and as a set of actions that does little (to nothing) to undo the problematic distance between classes.[9] As Beryl Rowland claims, the Malthusian aspect of Pudding and Crumbs—and indeed we know that Melville was reading Malthus and writing about him in his notebooks in 1846 and 1849—finds expression in Melville's exploration of a necropolitics of food and hunger.[10] Through the depiction of two meals—one shared by a narrator who imposes himself on a poor family, the other shared (rather brutally) between London beggars and observed by the narrator—Melville develops the narrators' empathetic identification with the sensory degradations of poverty, what Gavin Jones has called the stories' "demarcation of class difference at the visceral level of taste."[11]

Jones uses the word "taste" to gesture to viscerality, signaling feeling at the level of the "gut," and across the story, "taste" is Melville's word as well. But the term "Taste," as Denise Gigante's and Timothy Morton's work has shown us, has a dual but intertwined meaning across the history of aesthetics.[12] In Gigante's work, for instance, "Taste"—big *T*—emerges in the eighteenth century to refer to gradations of aesthetic accomplishment and pleasure; it is both linked to the emergence of gastronomy as an art and science of culinary appreciation and separated from appetites like hunger and base senses such as touch, smell, and—small *t*—taste. I want to propose that Melville's story is an elaboration on the relationship between *t*aste and *T*aste, that the role of eating and of sensation in Pudding and Crumbs is part of Melville's critique of the discourse of Taste as a system of distinction that constructs vertical relations between the classes via the privileged sensation of sight. Via a complex representation of taste, Melville argues that we not neglect *flavor* and, more specifically, mouthfeel, as a means by which to access empathy for the other. A horizontal mode of sensory experience, *mouthfeel* dissolves the distinction between tactility, taste, and sound and thereby suggests otherwise modes through which the work of aesthetics might be re-created.[13] More specifically, Melville's focus on flavor and mouthfeel allows him to occupy disgust as a productive political space wherein he can critique sentimental fictions of poverty and, in doing so, theorize a tactile economy that both structures the experience of material deprivation and offers a sensual language within which to represent the everyday conditions of white working-class life. Melville's favored sensory medium for that body in these two stories is what I call the gelatinous.

"Poor Man's Pudding" and "Rich Man's Crumbs," written in 1854, are not Melville's first meaningful encounter with gelatinous objects: one would be hard-pressed to find a more emblematic scene of an encounter with gelatinousness than the chapter "A Squeeze of the Hand," in *Moby-Dick*. In that scene, Ishmael massages the coagulations out of barrels of spermaceti harvested from a sperm whale. Famously, as he does so, he experiences an ecstatic melting of his ego boundaries into his compatriots, a communion with others that he sees as superseding the bounds of sociality and the masculine body—and indeed of domesticity in all of its heterosocial and national formations:

> I squeezed that sperm till a strange sort of insanity came over me; and I found myself unwittingly squeezing my co-laborers' hands in it, mistaking their hands for the gentle globules. Such an abounding, affectionate, friendly, loving feeling did this avocation beget; that at last I was continually squeezing their hands, and looking up into their eyes sentimentally; as much as to say,—Oh! my dear fellow beings, why should we longer cherish any social acerbities, or know the slightest ill-humor or envy! Come; let us squeeze hands all round; nay, let us all squeeze ourselves into each other; let us squeeze ourselves universally into the very milk and sperm of human kindness.[14]

As Hester Blum comments on Melville's place in oceanic studies, it is important to take account of "the epistemological process by which forms of human or extra-human relation are dissolved and reconstituted in the fluid medium."[15] Melville seems to have had a happy relationship with gelatinous sensations, one often associated with pleasure. Four years later, in the short story "Paradise of Bachelors," published in *Harper's Magazine*, he discusses a fish dish approvingly because it is "gelatinous enough."[16] As Blum has taught us, all of *Moby-Dick* can be read as a meditation on work and labor in the nineteenth century, but "Poor Man's Pudding" and "Rich Man's Crumb"—written two years after *Moby-Dick* was published and first appearing in *Harper's Magazine*—have other work to do in their comparative transnational exploration of class, including a deployment of gelatinous and rheological textures against the easy aesthetic judgments associated with inequality.

"Poor Man's Pudding" opens with the narrator, who will remain unnamed throughout the story, and his friend, the wealthy poet Blandmour, taking a walk on a wet March day. Blandmour, Melville's representative of the unfeeling bourgeois, argues that nature provides for the poor what they are unable to materially provide for themselves. Snow, Blandmour says, provides fertilizer for the poor husbandman's land; he calls it "Poor Man's Manure"; melted snow provides a tonic for his eyes, called "Poor Man's Eyewater." Rainwater, or "Poor Man's Egg," provides leavening for his bread. He continues,

"Did you never hear of the 'Poor Man's Eye-water?'"

"Never."

"Take this soft March snow, melt it, and bottle it. It keeps pure as alcohol. The very best thing in the world for weak eyes, I have a whole demijohn of it myself. But the poorest man, afflicted in his eyes, can freely help himself to this same all-bountiful remedy. Now, what a kind provision is that!"

"Then 'Poor Man's Manure' is 'Poor Man's Eye-water' too?"

"Exactly. And what could be more economically contrived? One thing answering two ends—ends so very distinct."

"Very distinct, indeed."[17]

The first line of the story invokes Kant's most elevated aesthetic media: poetry and the visual arts. Blandmour encourages the narrator to visit a poor family's cottage in an attempt to experience their pastoral poverty. Crossing the Coulters' threshold to meet the family, the narrator samples for himself the eponymous pudding. And it is there, where he crosses the threshold to meet the family, where he samples for himself the eponymous pudding.

There are too many moments in the story during which Melville provokes a visceral sense of the Coulters' life as a series of sticky and viscous sensations—often half wet, half dry—to document exhaustively. We begin with Blandmour's repetitive association of moistness to the experience of poverty: the "damp" snow is meant to "fertilizingly moisten" the land; snow stands in as a binder for bread in the same way as an egg, a glutinous compound; snow also functions as plaster, an emollient substance.[18] Dame Coulter, just leaving her washtub to greet the narrator, stands on a soaked, half-rotten board, above the penetrating damp of the ground; the fire sputters ineffectually, fueled by mossy and toad-stooled sticks that have been lying under rotted leaves for many autumns. The house is constitutionally damp; the windows are damp. Even Dame Coulter's eyes barely seem to stay solid, consistently described as soft, wet, and weeping. The word "damp" actually appears almost a dozen times in the story—three times in the first page of the *Harper's* printing as separate descriptors—and culminating in the narrator's description of the world outside the cottage as "cheerless as it [the cottage] was, and damp damp damp—the heavy atmosphere charged with all sorts of heavy incipiencies."[19] The repetitive incantation of the term across the story builds the word's onomatopoeic power, a point Melville emphasizes. The triple enunciation of "damp" emphasizes the explosive exhale of the *p* at the end, which then echoes in the *p* in "heavy incipiencies" (a second use of "heavy," following "heavy atmosphere"). These consonances purposely evoke what they describe: the dropping *p* loads down the weather of the scene, which seems in its heaviness to be full of promise, to be incipient. (Like much of Melville's work, particularly his short stories, it seems written to be read aloud.)

This emphasis on texture continues throughout the narrator's description of the horrible lunch to which the narrator has been invited. Offered a taste of meat, he sees that the salted pork is old, crusty, and "rankish," and he cannot eat any.[20] Similarly, the pudding piled onto his plate is made of "damaged" rice, milk, and salt boiled together—that is, a mushy mass—flavored with salt left over from last year's brined pork. Nonetheless, on being encouraged, he eats a bite. Says the narrator, "I summoned up all my self-control, and smilingly assented to the proposition of the pudding, without by my looks casting any reflections upon the pork. But to tell the truth, it was quite impossible for me (not being ravenous but only a little hungry at the time) to eat of the latter. It had a yellowish cast all round it, and was rather rankish, I thought, to the taste."[21] Each of these descriptions draws from what William Ian Miller calls the "lexicon of disgust," which includes "the oppositions squishy vs. firm, sticky vs. non-adhering, scabby vs. smooth, viscous vs. free flowing, wriggling and slithering vs. still. . . . For every disgusting scabby or crusty thing there are tens of disgusting oozy, mucky, gooey, slimy, clammy, sticky, tacky, dank, squishy or filmy things. And even the scabby and crusty borrow their disgustingness from the fact that they are formed from the coagulation of viscous substances."[22] And indeed the Poor Man's Pudding—a sticky mass that is actively molding—is a forebear of what we would today think of as simply pudding, as Jell-O Pudding introduced it to us in the 1970s and 1980s: soft, smooth, and starchy. Most nineteenth-century recipes describe what we might today call boiled rice or bread pudding. In that period, it carried the name "Poor Man's Pudding" because it lacked the eggs, meat, or suet that traditionally give pudding nutritional heft.

The lot of the materially deprived, then, is a damp, sticky, and disgusting one, a state of viscous discomfort at the gate of the rich man's castle. It is important to note that we access these feelings via the narrator's observations, his willingness to enter into and inhabit those spaces that Blandmour imagines only from a distance. (In fact, Blandmour's inability to identify with others is analogous to his refusal to taste and touch, hence his name: bland.) The narrator, however, does taste and touch: as Dame Coulter recounts the deaths of her children, he plunges his spoon into his pudding and forces some into his mouth: "The mouthful of pudding now touched my palate, and touched it with a mouldy, briny taste. The rice, I knew, was of that damaged sort sold cheap; and the salt from the last year's pork barrel. 'Bitter and mouldy is the Poor Man's Pudding,' groaned I to myself, half choked with but one little mouthful of it, which would hardly go down."[23] "Not ravenous, only a little hungry": the narrator is able to "taste" in the sense that both Kant and the gastronome Jean Anthelme Brillat-Savarin, author of *Le physiognomie du goût*, wrote of most approvingly. He is able to sample without being driven to gorge by hunger, and he is therefore able to discern aesthetically. The narrator's response to the pudding commingles touch and taste, and despite his disgust, he traverses the physical distance between himself and the Coulters. Though he is choking, almost gagging, on the pudding, the narrator, crucially, experiences empathy for the physical and psychic suffering that their situation entails, traversing the distance that characterizes Blandmour's visual and abstracted charitability.

In "Economimesis," Derrida's commentary on Kant's *Critique of Pure Judgement*, Derrida points out that for Kant, art is opposed by the desire to eat:

> In order to characterize those who are deprived of any "feeling for beautiful nature," Kant . . . has recourse to an oral example. . . . We judge to be coarse and ignoble the "mental attitude" of those who have no feeling for beautiful nature and who "confine themselves to eating and drinking—to the mere enjoyments of sense." . . . What is already announced here is a certain allergy in the mouth, between pure taste and actual tasting [*dégustation*]. We still have before us the question of where to inscribe disgust [*le dégoût*]. Would not disgust, by turning itself against actual tasting, also be the origin of pure taste, in the wake of a sort of catastrophe?[24]

Disgust for Kant marks the limits of aesthetic representation; for Derrida, it is the starting point for the production for the discourse of Taste because it is the rejection of actual tasting. He writes, "The negative [of taste] is its business and its work. What it excludes . . . is what does not allow itself to be digested, or represented, or stated. . . . It is an irreducible heterogeneity which cannot be eaten either sensibly or ideally and which . . . by never letting itself be swallowed must therefore *cause itself to be vomited*."[25] Where the narrative of the "Poor Man's Pudding" engages Derrida is in Derrida's reading of disgust as the birth of capital-*T* Taste, in the Bourdieuvian sense of "distinction" as a *turning away* from actual tasting: I am that which I judge (and therefore claim to know) but do not touch or absorb.[26] In "Poor Man's Pudding," the actual tasting of the thing (*dégustation*) is an act that turns itself against the vertical distinction that is taste (*goût*) and toward the disgusting material conditions (*le dégoût*) enabled by the Coulters' poverty. However, the narrator is able neither to vomit his morsel of pudding nor to assimilate it easily; in this between, the narrator inhabits nausea, the retch or the gag—the Kantian *eckel*. (Note the onomatopoeic work of that word, which retains the physicality of the gag or the gullet.)

This nausea insists on being experienced and thus abolishes the hierarchical distance that is poetic representation, which enabled the untasting poet Blandmour's aesthetic sentimentality toward the poor. That encounter is unutterable in the space of the bourgeois home—around Blandmour's fire—because in that space, it can only be understood as abjection. As the story finishes, the narrator tells Blandmour, "if ever a rich man speaks prosperously to me of a Poor Man, I shall set it down as—I won't mention the word."[27] But perhaps too, the poet's prosperous speech—the unmentionable word that describes his unfeeling aesthetic appreciation of the poor man's material experience—might be understood as vomit or excrement, in other words, the substance whose unassimilability, whose unspeakability, defines the very outside of the discourse of aesthetics.

"Rich Man's Crumbs (Picture Two)" offers a somewhat different encounter with the gelatinous. In this second story, the same unnamed narrator travels to London, where he is taken on a tour of the city and its charities by a "civic subordinate."[28] Led into a Guildhall, he is shown the remains of a royal feast that, after lying in the open air for a day, will be given over to beggars. Different from the quiet despair of the American cottage, he experiences a flood of abject sensations as he and his host push through the crowd to witness the charitable spectacle. At a given sign, the beggars flood into the hall as "a mob of cannibals on some pagan beach." "The beings around me," he writes, "roared with famine."[29] Significantly, as he watches the "meagre, murderous pack," he thinks "of the blue eye of the gentle wife of poor Coulter." Much of the story is given over to describing the wildness of the hungry crowd: "The howls of the mass reverberated. I seemed seething in the Pit with the Lost. . . . Diffusing, the pestiferous mob poured in bright day."[30] There in the Guildhall, the beggars fight over broken meats and leftover pastry crusts in a room in which the floor is "as foul as a kennel," and, as Melville writes, "jelly-eyed and shirtless men gulp golden-hued and half-sucked jellies, disemboweled pasties and plundered pheasants."[31] Says the tour guide, "'But see—now I'd wager a guinea the lord Mayor's lady dipped her golden spoon into yonder golden-hued jelly. See, the jelly-eyed old body has slipped it, in one broad gulp, down his throat.' 'Peace to that jelly!' breathed I. 'What a generous, noble, magnanimous, charity this is! Unheard of in any country but England, which feeds her very beggars with golden-hued jellies.' 'But not three times every day, my friend,' [says the narrator]. 'And do you really think that jellies are the best sort of relief you can furnish to beggars?'"[32] By the time the food is gone, the beggars swarm the tables as though, Melville writes, "to spew up the Rich Man's Crumbs in repentant scorn," and the air is filled with the yells of the beggars, which smell like reek from the sewers.[33] Although the narrator never eats any of the leftover feast, he becomes, in many ways, vomited, picked up, and thrown out into the street on the wave of beggar anger: not only a spectator, he is spewed forth on an excremental and vomitous wave of political disgust that leaves him battered and bruised. The narrator is rushed home to his bed, where he says, "Heaven in its kind mercies save me from the noble charities of London, . . . and Heaven save me equally from the 'Poor Man's Pudding' and the 'Rich Man's Crumbs.'"[34]

The gelatinous, squishy, and sticky have a particular history connected to abjection and, I want to argue, the politicization of minoritarian bodies. Julia Kristeva famously used the example of the coagulated skin of boiled milk—a phenomenon recognizable to an entire generation of French children—to epitomize the expulsion of abject materials from the body and thus the formation of selfhood: "When the eyes see or the lips touch that skin on the surface of the milk, . . . I experience a gagging sensation and, still farther down, spasms in the stomach, the belly; and all the organs shrivel up the body, provoke tears and bile, increase heartbeat, cause forehead and hands to perspire. . . . *Nausea* makes me balk at that milk cream, separates me from the mother and father who proffer it. . . . I give birth to myself amid the violence of sobs, of vomit."[35] Like so much of Kristeva's work, this is a structuralist and psychoanalytic reading of how we create ourselves, and the expulsion of the milk-skin is essential for self-formation. We must expel abjection in order to form the mythology of selfhood.

Perhaps, however, abjection is not only a technology of self-formation. Perhaps abjection can be extraindividual, too: a textural feeling that transmits between subjects, that circulates as the affective condition for the formation of a mass of bodies. Here I want to argue that what I am calling the gelatinous is also related to what the anthropologist Arun Saldanha calls "viscosity," which he sees as a "concept of space in which fixity can emerge from flux under certain conditions."[36] Unlike the structuralist readings of disgust put forward by Julia Kristeva or Peter Stallybrass and Allon White, for that matter, which focus on the reification of boundaries between classes of space, persons, and things, Saldanha's adaptation of Spinozan and Deleuzian materialism in the context of the intoxicating and racialized energies of the Goa rave-dance scene posits viscosity as a quality that is not expelled in order to create *difference as a form of separation*.[37] Rather, viscosity defines the spaces between bodies—human and inhuman—as *connection-in-difference*, thickening and slowing the movements between bodies such that they adhere to each other, open up to each other, and loosen their boundedness. Viscosity lies in social forms experienced via uncanny forms of movement and also via the reordering of the senses, specifically the association of touch with sound that Deleuze and Guattari refer to as "hacceities" or sets of relations.[38] The gelatinous, caught between fixity and flux, marks the sensual condition of the bodies of the poor, of their milieu, but it also defines the movement left to them, as, in Melville's description of the beggars escaping the ravages of the banquet in "Rich Man's Crumbs," "the yet unglutted mob surged against the tables, broke through all the barriers, and billowed over the hall": "It seemed to me as if a sudden impotent fury of fell envy possessed them. . . . That one half-hour's peep at the mere remnants of the glories of the Banquets of Kings, . . . the half-sacked jellies, served to remind them of the intrinsic contempt of the alms, [and] . . . these Lazaruses seemed ready to spew up in repentant scorn the contumelious crumbs of Dives."[39] In the reading I am offering here, gelatinous sensation is not atomic or individual but rather social, experienced in the movements that take place within and between material and human actants in complex nature-culture assemblages that, in brief moments of sensory encounter, imagine something other than expected orderings of the sensible. Revulsion is linked here to sensory materiality—the crowd, like the narrator, seems ready to spew its food but does not—but it is an opening up to the other, instead of a retreat into selfhood.

Of course, what Melville tells us and what we want to retain from Kristeva's interest in abjection is that in the West, the gelatinous has a particular history connected to both culinary objects and culinary aesthetics. Certainly Melville seems to have read or to have known about the European experiments with gelatin as a food for the poor. But moving here from the object to its material life, and thinking with both Saldanha's *and* Deleuze and Guattari's invocation of viscosity as a politically productive sensation perhaps, elides that quality's own social history, one embedded in thinking with and about poverty, class, and crowd energy. The poet Keston Sutherland, in a 2011 essay on the literary and satiric qualities of Marx's *Kapital*, points out that previous German-to-English translations of *Kapital* mistranslate a key phrase ("abstrakt menschliche Arbeit blobe gallerte unterschiedsloser menschlicher Arbeit") as "Human labor is abstract when it is frozen; it is lifeless, cold, immobilized."[40] Sutherland argues that the term "gallerte" is not actually a process but, rather, the name of a specific product that would have been known to German consumers at the time. "Gallerte," that is, is not a lifeless, immobilized mass but rather a semisolid jiggly mass made up of the "'meat, bone [and] connective tissue' of the various animals used to produce it."[41] Human labor, when abstracted from its conditions and value, is gelatinous: it is dead, but it moves; it is solid but soft. The human brains, muscles, nerves, hands, and so on are a productive expenditure within capitalism, mere animal substances boiled into a mass consumed at the feast of the capitalist. Marx's satiric goal, Sutherland argues, is to disgust his German readers by invoking a substance that they might well have consumed themselves.

I want to extend Sutherland's rereading of Marx and then return to Melville's story by pointing out two parallels between them. The first parallel is that both Marx and Melville sought to deploy disgust against social injustice: for Marx, as Sutherland notes, disgust was an indictment of bourgeois indifference. Rejecting the pastoralization of poverty, as it is often defined by visuality (and thus we might argue, by economies of representation), both Marx and Melville believe that the experience of disgust can be an opening toward the other. This sense that disgust is not a closing off but an opening up to otherness is why they use the aesthetics of disgust argumentatively: in invoking these movemential foods, they allow readers and audiences to picture what it means to eat or to have already eaten such materials and then to imagine that these materials are full of an aliveness that will not be contained, even in the mouth. That aliveness is, in the end, a refusal to not live.

The gelatinous or the viscous, in this sense, spans Marx's, Kristeva's, and Spinoza's theorizations, functioning as a keyword for a form of social connection, as a description of a granular quality of the affective everyday that retains its association with abjection, that does not simply adhere to abjected bodies but can enter into others, penetrating them and catching them between adhesion and separation, at the moment of the gag reflex or what Kant termed the *eckel*. In their recitation of unpredictable and liminal tactile sensations and semisolid substances, of objects half expelled from the gullet, the substances in Melville's story and Marx's as well—and the entire material ecology of poverty itself, which both is affiliated with the rheological matter of the pudding and in fact echoes it, dissolving the subject into their environment, making of them one with their milieu—ask the reader to give up the project of distancing themselves from the poor. Instead, these materialities ask the reader to confront the abject status and material conditions of the underclass in both Europe and the United States, to consider what it might mean to be unable to reject them, not only to live beside them but to experience a visceral and viscous accord with them. Here I expand on Sianne Ngai's formulation of desire as the affect that says *yes* and disgust as the affect that says *no* (and, rather beautifully, contempt as the affect that says *whatever*); in thinking from within the hierarchy of animate materialities that affixes itself to levels of social and political abjection, disgust might be the affect that says *no* to this world in the name of imagining the next, an extension of Ngai's postulation that disgustingness undoes liberal tolerance by refusing absorption.[42]

However, these writers' deployment of rheological substances in the service of that project is also telling: they are not simply invoking the historical meaning attached to these substances but rather their particular ways of moving in terms of what rheologists call flow, elasticity, stress, energy, and recovery. We can extend Sutherland's reading—building on his minor gesture toward the question of movement—to consider whether Marx was also using gelatin to describe the quality of political movement or energy that he saw as imminent to working-class populations themselves. Melville's narrator experiences this quality as a moment of political transformation, originating when this lively food, this sticky mass of a pudding, consumed in a colloidal and damp mess of a cottage, refuses to be absorbed or ejected. Thus, pudding and gelatin exemplify the ability of a property to flow, to give in to the stress of deformation without breaking and then recover that energy when the stress is released, deploying that energy to their own internally directed ends. To be proximate to this material, to put it in your mouth, to try to swallow it, to ultimately think with it, is to theorize a form of animatedness that is both giving and resistant, that flows and deforms but pushes back, whose uncanny responsiveness to its sensory surroundings undoes both individual agentic forms of personhood and rehearses forms of human and nonhuman intra-activeness. All of this begs a political and ethical question: What dreams of politics might such movements bring us? Perhaps, we might theorize, a movement truly cannot be a revolution if it cannot dance?

Let me just note here that I do not want to accede too fully to a neoliberal logic of resilience: my argument here is not simply about suppressing the evidence and material effects of harm under the social, and I want to acknowledge that in thinking with rheological movement, without fully working through the damage that accrues to bodies under social pressure, I am flirting with that possibility. Marx's own use of gelatinousness as a metaphor shows us—and here I draw from Nicole Shukin's thinking through of the zoopolitical logic of rendering—that what seems to present itself as metaphor or representation assumes a relationship with the brute profitable rendering or boiling down of animal body parts that animates biopower, even those animal body parts designated as waste.[43] And waste or what seems to be waste—what Marx tells us is the brute logic of capital—forms the raw material that subtends the making of gelatinous form.

The gelatinous adheres to those bodies that are most easily understood as waste, as wasteful, as wasted—to those subjects that will waste away under regimes of slow death, as their usefulness to biopolitical capital wanes. Here, we can begin to texture and complicate these materials: what we hear about in Marx's formulation are quite bouncy and resilient gelatins; but in Melville's stories, that ability to retain energy has quite degraded, and these colloids (the mud, the puddings), while still behaving unusually and against the logic of Newtonian mechanics, are not quite so perfect in their ability to recover. Biopolitically, materially, and representationally aligning subaltern life with animal and vegetable life as it is rendered into profit makes visible not simply a dominant representational schema organized around a sensation and texture but also the material—the nonmetaphoric—logic of capitalism as it uses up the energies of disposable populations and leaves them to die precisely by denying them access to full humanity. The particularly dynamic qualities of gelatinous rheology can point to the subtle and devastating work of survival under the deformative pressures of the everyday: its movemential possibilities reveal perhaps that phobic responses to gelatinousness and viscosity might also seek to suppress the collectivizing and inhuman virtual energies of those peoples aligned with its materiality, and material history, but the conditions of its production attest to something far less utopic, something far more damaging that we must hold alongside its other promise.

PUDDING

We see both of these materialities in a scene in Martin Delany's unfinished novel, *Blake*. Initially published serially in the *Anglo-African Magazine* from January to July 1859, the novel, which tells the story of an escaped enslaved man who seeks to foment an enslaved people's revolution, has never been completed. The scene that interests me takes place in a chapter following Blake's escape from the Frankses' plantation in pursuit of his wife, Maggie, who has escaped with her child rather than be sold away from him. After the escape, the enslaved people of the plantation gather in Mammy Judy's hut for a dinner of cornmeal mush, or "hasty pudding":

> The hut of Mammy Judy served as a sort of headquarters on Saturday and Sunday evenings for the slaves from the plantation, and those in town belonging to the "estate," who this evening enjoyed a hearty laugh at the expense of Daddy Joe. Slaves are not generally supplied with light in their huts; consequently, except from the fat of their meat and that gathered about the kitchen with which they make a "lamp," and the use of pinewood tapers, they eat and do everything about their dwellings in the dark. Hasty pudding for the evening being the bill of fare, all sat patiently awaiting the summon of Mammy Judy, some on blocks, some on logs of wood, some on slab benches, some on inverted buckets and half-barrel wash tubs, and whatever was convenient, while many of the girls and other young people were seated on the floor around against the wall.[44]

Delany here makes a point of saying that enslaved people rarely have light in their cabins: "they eat and do everything about their dwellings in the dark." Shortly after, in the next section, both Mammy Judy and Daddy Joe also try to enforce silence amid the darkness:

> "Hush, chilen!" admonished Mammy Judy, after carefully seeing that each one down to Tony had been served with a quota from the kettle.
>
> "Laud, make us truly tankful fah wat we 'bout to 'ceive!" petitioned Daddy Joe with uplifted hands. "Top dah wid yo' nause an' nonsense ole people cah heah deh yeahs to eat!" admonished the old man as he took the pewter dish between his knees and commenced an earnest discussion of its contents. "Do'n yeh heah me say hush dah? Do'n yeh heah!"[45]

After leading the room in prayer and after telling the children in the room to be quiet, Daddy Joe grabs a bowl of cornmeal pudding and milk, but he is called out to get a horse saddled for Master Franks, who is going in search of the missing woman. Leaving, he warns the children in the room not to touch his mush, but on returning from the stable, the old man notices that something is different about his pudding: "Wat dat yeh all been doin' heah? Some on yeh young folks been prankin' long wid dis mush an' milk!" continues the old man, chomping and chewing in a manner that indicates something more solid than mush and milk.[46] The children deny having touched his food, but the old man insists: "'Hi what dis in heah! Sumpen mighty crisp!' said Daddy Joe, still eating heartily and now and again blowing something from his mouth like coarse meal husks. 'Sumpen heah mighty crisp, ah tells yeh! Ole umin, light dat pine knot dah: so dahk yeh cah'n see to talk. Git light dah quick ole umin! Sumpen heah mighty crisp in dis mush an' milk!—Mighty crisp!'"[47] The bowl, when illuminated, is found "to be partially filled with large black house roaches": Joe has been chewing on them and spitting out the bodies thinking that they are corn husks. The scene ends with Mammy Judy lighting the bowl and an irreligious joke from the children: "'Good Laud! see dah now! Ah tole yeh so!' exclaimed Mammy Judy when, on producing a light, the bowl was found to be partially filled with large black house roaches. 'Reckon Daddy Joe do'n tank'im fah dat!' said little Tony, referring to the blessing of the old man; amidst an outburst of tittering and snickering among the young people. Daddy Joe lost his supper, when the slaves retired for the evening."[48] Chapter 10, "The Discovery," takes place immediately following the chapter in which Henry Blake, later renamed Blackus, escapes, first stopping to foment his plan for an armed rebellion of slaves, which he says will "spread like smallpox."[49] If the narrative condition of the hasty-pudding chapter is both Maggie's escape with her child and Blake's inauguration of his plan to foment slave rebellion, it seems surprising that Delany would return in the next chapter to the contracted confines of the darkened slave cabin.

But I want to pay attention to the sensory work in which Delany is engaged: not unlike Melville's short stories, this scene turns away from the visual and returns to other senses: namely, touch, taste, and sound. Setting the scene in the dark—in obvious and conscious counterpoint to the pastoral setting of the eponymous chapter of Harriet Beecher Stowe's *Uncle Tom's Cabin*—Delany works the children's prank for all of its sensory power: Joe consumes the pudding mouthful after mouthful in the dark of the hut, spitting out carcass after carcass but swallowing the gooey internal parts of the insect with the mush. Following upon the softness of mush and milk, the onomatopoeic "crisp" and "husk" rehearse the sound of the insect's exoskeleton breaking down inside Joe's mouth; the "now and again" of "blowing" makes it obvious that the cockroaches spend some time in there before their crunchy bits, at least, are expelled. Fully utilizing the dense sonic materiality of antebellum dialect literature, Delany wants us to pay attention to what Joe will and will not digest: presumably the cockroach innards will spill out and follow the pudding and milk down Joe's throat. Further dispensing with the bourgeois norms of eating and of bodily boundaries, Joe lets food go in his mouth and come out again. Delany also makes a point of marking the quality of Joe's expectoration: he does not spit but "blow[s]" the skeletons out, the "blow" sounds making a drier business of it. Ultimately, Delany gives us the line, "Daddy Joe lost his supper, when the slaves retired for the evening." In doing so, he makes a point about the visceral and psychic abjection of slavery: the line "Daddy Joe lost his supper" not only indicates that Joe vomits the pudding and cockroaches but means, in nineteenth-century terms, that he loses his appetite. He goes hungry without feeling hungry. And immediately, on the following page, the work of provoking revolution begins.

How does this staging of repulsion work politically? More specifically, how does it work given Delany's interest in sparking a movement? Here I want to bring together Kristeva's sticky story of expulsion with the physics of jelly and then, finally, the material qualities and the sonic resonances that collide in Daddy Joe's mouth. Cornmeal pudding is a hydrocolloid and a rheological substance, a substance that forms a gel in the presence of water. It is this soft-solid that merges with the biorheological solids of cockroach innards to slide down Daddy Joe's throat, while he expels the dry exoskeletons, which he thinks are corn husks. What is expelled, in short, are the dry elements of each material, while the viscera of each merge with Daddy Joe's own mouth and viscera. We are, in short, up until the moment when Daddy Joe stops eating, in an inverse relation to the gelatinous that Kristeva stages in her story about the formation of selfhood: Daddy Joe rejects the dry exoskeletal structure and takes to the sticky matter, perhaps disgorging what is disgusting or perhaps not, but either way swallowing a great deal of it. This expulsion is not without discomfort or unease, and there is a clear sense in the text that the reader is meant to be both entertained and disgusted, a skewering of both minstrel humor and political satire and, of course, a pointed skewering of Stowe. We are in a different but nonetheless related sensory register to Melville's: this sensory calculus allows us to understand the political movement that Delany himself is mapping as always already external to the dry stolidity of the liberal human, allied with the viral, the animal, the abject, the toothsome, the semisolid, the semiwet, the visceral. From this place, Delany's ultimately incomplete revolutionary slave movement emerges: the reorganization of sensibility in the dense cultural field of slave life is itself the birthplace of forms of materiality, affect, and sensory dissensus that produce an understanding of slave insurrection and Blackness itself as always already counter to the limited possibilities of the human as the basic unit upon which liberal freedoms are modeled.

This field, however, is not simply visual but also sonic, a haptic collapsing of the taste/feel texturality of mouthfeel that makes itself felt in the onomatopoeic work of the text. Ashon Crawley, building and extending Fred Moten's work, names this field/textuality as "a vibration, a sonic event," that in its "ongoing movement makes its apprehension both illusory and provisional. Illusory because the thing itself is both given and withheld from view, from earshot. Provisional because it—the vibration, the sonic event, the sound—is not and cannot ever be stilled absolutely. . . . It is the gift, the concept, the inhabitation of and living into otherwise possibilities."[50] Delany's story, in counterpoint to Melville's stories, shows us how the realm of the sensory *also* forms the basis for a counteraesthetic project that takes deviant materiality as the basis from which to think against the murderous imperatives of the everyday. While Melville's stories can only cross the distance with empathy—leaving the poor mired in their gelatinous suffering—Delany, like Melville, collapses both sound and mouthfeel to render suffering acutely present at a sensory level.

As always, I do not seek to pastoralize suffering in this reading: rather the opposite. Disgust is present in these passages to provincialize pastoralism. I am interested in how Delany engages the outer limits of aesthetic ordering in order to get at the conditions that give birth to his vision of a collective slave revolution. Across his career, Delany enacted what Britt Rusert has called "a fugitive science": science deployed in the name of freedom.[51] While Rusert's work on Delany engages his work with astronomy, I am more interested in something closer to the earth: Delany's exploration of the relation between vitality and collective action in his incredibly detailed attention to the sensory orders, or disorders, of plantation life as a condition from which other forms of collective action had to spring.

BUMS

I want to conclude this chapter with one last brief consideration of what it might mean to occupy the gelatinous: a contemporary work by the queer Afro-Canadian photographer and film artist dirtysurface. Here I want to return to a claim that I made at the beginning of this chapter: when we talk about the rheological, we are talking about an accord between the material and human that is not simply analogical or metaphorical. That is, the rheological points us not only to the animated thingness of the material world in the Heideggerian sense of preceding the social but in the sense that the animated thingness of the body exceeds the social. I am thinking directly about the gelatinous qualities of the body, in particular, fat. I am interested in the liveliness of fat, its bounce, its roll, its ability to absorb and echo the world around it and then to snap back into its own shape, much like the gelatin cubes of *Snowpiercer*. The bounce and roll of fat presents something different from the ways that affect theorists discuss affect as the site where the emergent materiality of consciousness precedes or exists anterior to the social—what Brian Massumi talks about as a kind of recursive temporality to affect in its relation to language.[52] In the gelatinous movement of fat, we can theorize instead an afterward to the social: fat's gelatinousness stores life and living in abjected body parts and materials and in abjected political populations. Fat actually encompasses and stores the energy we need to survive the strain and stress visited on us by the world—a way to survive being deformed without breaking, to use the deformations of the world to make our own energy.

Dirtysurface is well known in the arts community in Toronto, Canada, as a filmmaker, activist, and artist. He is also a porn pedagogist: he teaches people to make their own pornography. In a project completed several years ago, dirtysurface made a screen saver that he called "Generous Gesture: Butt-Massage Video Wallpaper." As the video shows in the pretitles, "Generous Gesture" began with one question: What would pornography look like without capitalism? In keeping with this catalyzing question, no one has been paid; instead, what is offered is an exchange of sexual or erotic care. The pretitles also tell us that everyone in the video is above the age of consent; as the artist recounts it, all of the actors appeared in this film after having carefully negotiated the terms and limits of the erotic touch they would accept. Variously lovers, acquaintances, chosen family, and friends, the bodies pictures here form queer community.

The video is just under sixty minutes long, and in it, ten bodies appear on the screen, cut off at the back and below the ass (figures 5.7–5.9). As the video begins, some of them are clothed in underwear; a few are naked already. Lying on what appears to be black velvet cloth, the bodies are splattered or adorned with oil, and as they are massaged, they become increasingly shinier. Bodies are various shades of white and brown and black, as are the hands servicing them. Across the space of the film, some bodies are penetrated, and some are massaged. Some are fucked with toys or fists or fingers. Others are spanked with hands or whipped with clothing and belts. Still others are stroked, prodded, and pulled to reveal the vaginas and anuses beneath. As the erotic intensity of the video climbs, the overhead light shines off buttocks and backs. Bodies slowly open up: legs spread, backs arch, bodies push back into the hands that work into the muscles and explore, with considerable skill, the dif-

Figure 5.7. Still from “Generous Gesture,” directed by dirtysurface. (Property of dirtysurface, copyright 2013)

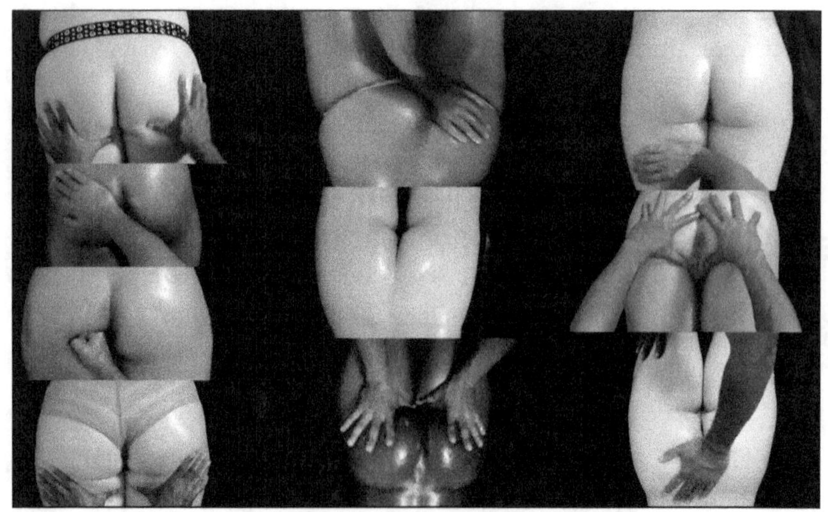

Figure 5.8. Still from "Generous Gesture," directed by dirtysurface. (Property of dirtysurface, copyright 2013)

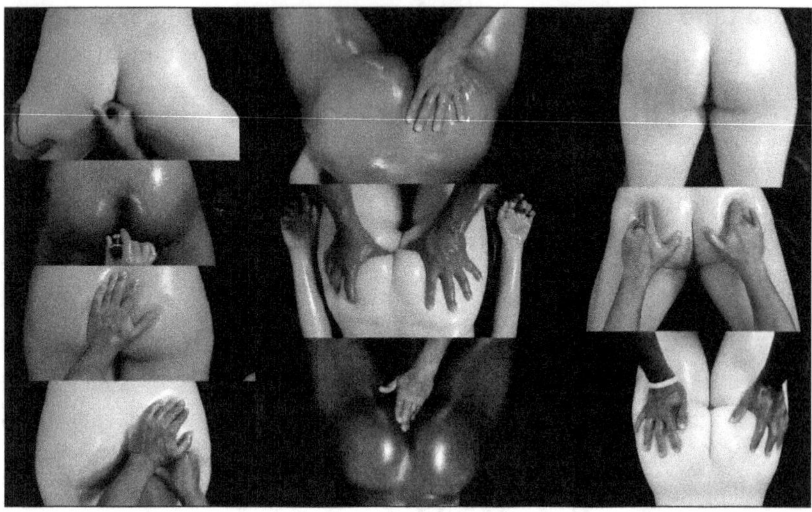

Figure 5.9. Still from "Generous Gesture," directed by dirtysurface. (Property of dirtysurface, copyright 2013)

fuse nerve endings that circulate between back and buttock, around the anus, across the clitoris. Buttocks stretch open; they close. They are pushed up; they drop down. They jiggle when shaken; they dimple and bend when pulled. The video has no sound.

What interests me about "Generous Gesture" is the haptic, touch-intensive quality of the film, the way the greased and oiled bodies and hands are both intimately exposed and anonymous, rendered strange in their dorsal abstraction.[53] This video wallpaper is entirely about touch, the give and take of it, and what touch between bodies reveals to us, particularly the texture of flesh in all of its soft rheological gelatinousness: its squishy, jiggly substantiveness, which both holds shape and is flexible, its ability to return to its original form no matter the pressure it is subjected to. This gelatinousness is somewhat different from the food gelatinousness I talk about elsewhere, but it is not entirely different: the bodies register and demonstrate exactly the same kind of deformative and responsive movement as in, for instance, the Bompas and Parr video. However, here we see a much more detailed visualization of the deformative effects of one body's contact with the other, a deformation in the service of care. In other words, "Generous Gesture" is a screen saver about sex in community: it is about using kink to work out the kinks left in the body after the stress, pressure, and compression of the social have left their deep and invisible marks.

In working from the question "What would pornography look like without capitalism?" I see dirtysurface's work here as a radical extension and reworking of Audre Lorde's thinking on the uses of the erotic, enacting and even expanding what I have always understood as her theorizing of eros as a utopian rethinking of unalienated labor:

> Another important way in which the erotic connection functions is the open and fearless underlining of my capacity for joy. In the way my body stretches to music and opens into response, hearkening to its deepest rhythms, so every level upon which I sense also opens to the erotically satisfying experience, whether it is dancing, building a bookcase, writing a poem, examining an idea. . . . And that deep and irreplaceable knowledge of our capacity for joy comes to demand from all of my life that it be lived within the knowledge that such satisfaction is possible. . . . Our erotic knowledge empowers us, becomes a lens though which we scrutinize all aspects of our existence.[54]

For Lorde in these passages, the erotic proposes a unity of sensation and purpose between body and act, between self and labor, between sensation and idea, the full reward of which is returned to the creator as satisfaction. It is worth recalling here that the thought-image that Lorde proposes to explain the erotic is itself gelatinous—a packet of margarine, as I discuss in detail in the introduction.

"Generous Gesture," then, is a proposal for infusing work, or at least distraction from work, with sex: sex with care, a communitarian and collective ethos that is anonymous, egalitarian in its pleasurable desires but neither pastoral nor sex-phobic. The video is radically nonindividual: it works across gender and against gender; in a few of the shots, it takes a while to be certain who has what kinds of genitalia. Conversely, the video works with race, inhabiting racial difference as part of its central aesthetic work: hands contrast with asses; asses contrast against each other. The visuality of the piece, particularly as the quality of the film blends with the shiny light and the abstracted and anonymous backs, asses, thighs, and genitalia, does not avoid but actually inhabits racial difference. This is not a postracial fantasy but a deeply raced fantasy: it proposes not less race and difference but rather *more* race.

"Generous Gesture" is video wallpaper. It is meant to be atmospheric, textural, a releasing of the aesthetic energy of sex and care into the space into which it is projected or within which it runs, when distraction has taken you away from the work on your computer or smartphone and it pops up on the screen. And in theorizing pornography against capital, it refuses all of the marks of weak narrative absorption that so often hold up the chestnuts of pornographic film: a haphazard story line, two-dimensional characters, sloppy dialogue, but also—importantly—ejaculation, the money shot, any signs of orgasmic completion. It simply runs, escalating into more conventionally "sexual" acts in some parts, like penetration or spanking, and then retreating again into massage. Nobody is paid; there is no profit here—only pleasure, only communality, only flesh. This is the erotic, released from its kernel, flowing through and coloring the everyday.

I have in some ways come full circle in my exploration of this quality I am calling the gelatinous. The gelatinous, I have been arguing, is a textural phenomenon in which we can see that the active materiality of a particular class of substances first of all inspires a long cultural history attached both to the production of political inequality and to ideas about how the energetic qualities of those materials give voice to ways that inequality might be survived or even shifted. What we also see, however, is—and here I am borrowing Eva Hayward's words—a "sensuous rapport" or "energetic cadence" between the biochemically and physically correlated substances of the human body, like fat, and those substances that escape sovereign will, like the gelatins, muds, sludges, suspensions, and hydrocolloids that we have been talking about.[55]

Materials that thicken and give way under stress, that change how they move through space, that reserve the energy that might otherwise flatten them and then use that energy to reform and push back against the world. What might it mean to think with and alongside those materials? To allow them to lead, to understand their movements as a deformative theory that we need to hear?

CONCLUSION

As I conclude this book, I want to return to a conversation that I once had with the late and very much missed performance studies theorist José Muñoz. In writing this book, I have been haunted by a conversation I had with José in 2013. Sitting at the NYU Department of Performance Studies cocktail hour with him during the Performance Studies International conference in Palo Alto (José: "mostly I do these things to make sure the children get fed"), I tried to explain my new project to him. "It's about what it feels like to encounter administrative violence," I told him. "It's about that feeling you get when you apply for welfare or you go into your dean's office, and you encounter that cold, life-sucking wall of chilly bureaucracy, and you know they hate you. It's about how institutions feel institutional." "Yes," he responded sourly, "but why does that violence always feel so aesthetic?"

This book is ultimately an attempt to answer that question—so throwaway to him, so formative to me—that has harassed me ever since. What I see now is what felt like the vague "aboutness" of my explanation ("It's about . . . it's about") was me reaching for a better language to describe how the sensory ecology of institutional or state or racial normativity can feel overwhelmingly environmental or atmospheric, how the air in a room can make you feel that your selfness, simply your way of being, is just *so wrong* in that space, because of that space. This sense of atmosphere as being violently everywhere, of an aesthetic and affective violence that adheres to you as the world you move through or (not so) as a condition of the everyday is something akin to Christina Sharpe's stunning invocation of "the orthography of the wake"—the perpetual circulation of images and environments and events of anti-Black violence and of Black grief—as constructing an affective and representational project on the scale of "the weather."[1] Along the same lines, the geographer Derek P. McCormack describes atmosphere as "envelopment": as "a condition that can be sensed although it is not always. Such sensing is always partial, insofar as an atmosphere is never fully disclosed to something immersed in that atmosphere—hence its allure. Nor is this sensing a distinctively human capacity: it is found in bodies, entities, and agencies of myriad kinds."[2] An atmosphere is something you swim in, something you breathe, and it lives in and as your space, as the impact of an object ideologically acting on you, in the sharp flare in the nostrils of someone who has power over you.

Taking Sharpe's and McCormack's differing but overlapping senses of the everyday as scalar, which is to say as *defined by magnitude*, as my starting point, in this book, I have used the idea of atmosphere to describe my own sense of the deadening force of administrative violence—what I have elsewhere called "civility" or "hygiene"—as an environmental/enveloping project that finds its power in a cluster of affective and aesthetic practices that deploy their particular violence at the affective and aesthetic level precisely because they can pretend to be neither affective nor aesthetic. A more colloquial and contemporary term for such a strategy might be "gaslighting": administrative violence is an affect and an aesthetic that exercises political power by pretending that aesthetics resides elsewhere from itself (in, say, art), in order to uphold its legitimacy and in order to deny political power to those who are deemed unworthy, to guard, in Rancière's terms, the boundaries of *politicity*.[3]

That violence, so often experienced as aesthetic negation, is geared toward the erasure of those people associated with being overly aesthetic or excessive and therefore not entitled to full political citizenship: as being deviant. My word in this book for feeling and being *wrong*, "deviance," derives from Cathy Cohen's foundational work, in which she argues that the term—specifically as it applies to Black life—describes a mode of living against the normative that must be taken seriously, if not precisely as resistance, then nonetheless as a potent and accumulative politic.[4] While maintaining an ethical relation to the way that Cohen grounds the term in an expansive relationship to Black queer studies and to Black life, in particular as regards the political demonization of single Black mothers in the landscape of the neoliberal 1980s, in this book, "deviance" is a central term for me not simply because of how Cohen models its political expansiveness but also because of how "deviance" also signals to altered movement, to scales and strategies for deviating away from impossible normativities, actions that might range from the smallest gesture (a pursed lip) to the minor refusal (being late) to the athwartness of a yes to costly pleasures ("yes, I'll take the purse"). Deviant acts, as Cohen teaches us, gains their power, or at least their significance, from their tendency to accumulate and persist.[5] Deviant acts accumulate into acts of everyday refusal at the level of population.

Itself deviant in method, this book is grounded in what I have elsewhere called "promiscuous method."[6] Focused neither entirely on any one kind of subject or demographic nor even entirely on subjects, in *Deviant Matter*, I also try to listen to objects. Yet even so, in this book, I could not bring myself to rest finally on only one kind of object or even one kind of cultural text but I also sought to move upward and outward to think with the materiality of atmospheres and feelings. *Deviant Matter* is, I hope, as radically interdisciplinary as I have been able to make it because perhaps like other deviants, I am a bad subordinate, mostly to disciplinarity.

What I hope this book has ultimately succeeded in arguing is that just as theorizing the political without thinking with aesthetics is a futile endeavor, so also to theorize art and aesthetics without or beyond a political dimension is fundamentally to leave the aesthetic work of politics untouched and uncritiqued precisely because aesthetic violence is foundational to the modern state's ideological and biopolitical power. My investigation into the history of state aesthetics as it relates to the life of matter fundamentally argues that a defense of aesthetics without politics is a defensive investment in the terms of the political present and its ethically burdened past.

Another goal of this project, however, is to ask how far it is possible to extend the idea of aesthetics into the realm of the everyday, to take aesthetics back from art and return it to a more politically nuanced and deeply historicized idea of the historical shaping of the senses that is less committed to upholding social hierarchy and more open to situating taste within the colonial origins of modern history.[7] Perhaps fittingly, my way into this conversation has deviated from the norm by thinking with the sensory life of matter, by building a link from the history of science at the level of the microbe up to a larger administrative history of the state and then from there to thinking about the state's biopolitical investment in managing the aesthetic and affective dimensions of population energy, or affect, which I join affect theorists in understanding as a form of matter itself. And yet against these regimes ("forms") of state disciplinarity, in *Deviant Matter*, I seek to excavate other figures for energy that escapes the extraction and management schemes devised by biopower: what I here explore under the name of fermentation, intoxication, rot, and jelly.

As I wrap up this book, I wish I could sit down for another meal with José and answer his question: Why *does* that violence always feel so aesthetic? And even more pertinent, Why is it so hard to name that violence, to untangle one's joyful deviance from its civility, its normalcy, its persuasiveness? Here I would answer him: I have learned that state aesthetics pretend not to be aesthetic so that they can protect their access to the realm of politics while preserving for themselves the right to manage the terms of normativity as they are enacted at the sensory and therefore most intimate level. And also, the point of pretending that state violence does not have an aesthetic dimension is to create an alibi for the ways that aesthetics, considered autonomously, are put to violent use.

The difficulty of seeking to describe the workings of this aesthetic violence is ultimately—and it is here that I found the most difficulty in writing this book—a challenge of scale, because the state is nowhere and everywhere, because the state exists but it is also diffuse, multimodal, changing, historical, palimpsestic, located in the most banal of objects, and enacted by the most bland of subjects. One word for state aesthetics in this book is "hygiene" because, as I show, following upon the marriage of microbiology and agricultural chemistry to state projects from the late nineteenth through the early twentieth centuries, citing hygiene as a social project is one major site for the management of the affective effects of various forms of runaway matter and materiality. That hygiene falls within the realm of what legal theorists call "police power" is no coincidence. As I hope I have shown, the historical lines from hygiene to police power to carcerality, particularly at the level of the juridical management and criminalization of particular forms of lively materiality, such as fermentative matter but also including alcohol and unpasteurized foods, as well as narcotics and medicine, is clear. For where else must excess energy go except into machines for extraction like the plantation or the prison, where it can be ascertained that their energy does not become waste?

The imperative answer to that question must be this: excess deviant energy must go to, must be preserved for, joy. This is ultimately what I have learned from *Deviant Matter* by listening to the fizz and pop of effervescent fermentation, to the excesses and deviations of disinhibited intoxication, to the bounce and jiggle of jelly, to the squish and funk of rot. What humans can learn from deviant forms of matter is that we ourselves matter very little except in the ways that we can learn to collate and move with each other and, that in doing so, in putting our bodies together in more and less than human ways, in becoming collective, effervescent, decompositional, in bouncing back and pushing back together against the violent deformations of capital, of racism, and of other painful encounters, we might make a difficult and hurtful world better.

ACKNOWLEDGMENTS

I would like to acknowledge the support of the Warren Center for American History at Harvard University and the American Council for Learned Societies, both of whom funded this project with a year of research leave each. I am grateful to the Pomona College research fund and the endowment of the Department of English at Pomona College for their generous support of this book, as well as the support of the College of Arts and Sciences at the University at Buffalo. I am also grateful to the colleagues and compatriots engaged in institutional change and collaborative friendship, all of whom I hold dear to my heart from my years at Pomona College: Aimee Bahng, fierce feminist warrior, Amaud Johnson, Jordan Kirk, Jonathan Lethem, April Mayes, Claudia Rankine, Prageeta Sharma, Cherene Sherrard-Johnson, Gabrielle Starr, and Valorie Thomas. (Val, we did it! We made change.) To my new colleagues in the Department of Global Gender and Sexuality Studies at the University at Buffalo, I am looking forward to building together. Thank you too to the students at both schools, who made me think harder and better just to live up to their excellence.

I would also like to thank the many departments, programs, and schools that extended their hospitality to me along the way, by either inviting me to be a fellow or visitor or inviting me for a talk or seminar. These include the Departments of English and American Studies at Princeton University (where I was so warmly welcomed into the rebel basement cohort of McCosh), the Department of Gender, Women, and Sexuality Studies at the University of Minnesota, the Department of English and the Program in Gender and Sexuality Studies at the University of Southern California, the Department of American Studies at Brown University, the Department of Performance Studies at New York University, fellows at the Max Planck Institute for the History of Science, and many many other programs and departments where faculty and students gave me feedback that helped strengthen the project.

Along the way, I have had marvelous interlocutors, mentors, sponsors, and readers including Robin Bernstein, Anne Cheng, Sarah Chihaya, Monica Huerta, Zakiyyah Iman Jackson, Nathan Snaza, the members of the Everyday Life seminar at the Warren Center at Harvard, Greta LaFleur, Kyla Schuller, José Muñoz, Tavia Nyong'o, Raul Coronado, Dana Luciano, Ann Pellegrini, Molly McGarry, Heather Lukes, Virginia Jackson, Martin Harries, Karen Tongson, Sarah Kessler, Joshua Chambers-Letson, Sarah Chihaya, and many more. I was honored to deliver part of the chapter on rot at the Futures of American Studies Institute in 2018, but most of all, I was able to deliver it in front of Professor Hortense Spillers, whose work has shaped the thinking of at least three entire generations. Lauren Berlant, I miss knowing that you are in the world but thank you for begrudgingly showing up in my dreams to tell me to finish this book, I'm sure you would have *just loved* knowing you are my interiorized superego. Thank you to Peter Brown for editing and tweaking when I really needed a helping hand. Peter, I can't wait to see what you do. Thank you to Candice Lin and the video artist dirtysurface for your rich interlocution. Thank you to my anonymous readers at NYU Press. Eric Zinner, friend, mensch, hand holder, and editor: thank you for trusting in this deviant project before I could really articulate it while also letting me know that I had not quite articulated it yet. Thank you also to Furqan Sayeed for shepherding the project along more patiently than I had any right to expect.

I count many of the above not simply as interlocutors and colleagues but much more importantly as the dearest of friends and fellow voyagers. I also wanted to take a moment, however, to particularly thank three groups of people whose everyday collectivity, shaped by group texts, private Facebook groups, shared projects, Zoom birthdays and writing sessions, days at the Huntington Library, and a collective ability to wield words as ploughshares and as swords, helped me through a wild five years. First, to my friends of the heart the Ladies of (now no longer early) Middle Age: Sarah Blackwood, Hester Blum, Claire Jarvis, and Sarah Mesle: GR forever. Your presence in my everyday has been more nourishing than I could ever express. Let us always name cockroaches after our enemies. Second, to my sisters and brother in feminist editorial praxis, Aren Aizura, Aimee Bahng, Karma Chavez, Mishuana Goeman, and Amber Musser, thank you for creating something bigger than anything any of us could have done alone and for reminding me of what collective feminist action can be. Finally to my L.A. Book Babes: Evelyn Alsultany, Neetu Khanna, and Natalia Molina, I'm so grateful for your presence during some very fun and also some wild and woolly times. I wish I was still near you. I couldn't have made it without you.

As ever, everything I do in this world is for one Mr. Andualem David Wazana Fisher, Andu to most, Boonie to me. You're the only reason, and you're the best reason, and you always will be.

Some portions of this book previously appeared in *Social Text*, in *American Quarterly*, *Women and Performance*, and in *The Cambridge Companion to Gay and Lesbian Literature*.

NOTES

INTRODUCTION

1 Rai, “Race Racing.”

2 *OED Online*, s.v. “matter, n.1.”

3 *OED Online*, s.v. “-ity, suffix.”

4 *OED Online*, s.v. “nonce, n.1”; l *OED Online*, s.v. “nonce, n.2.”

5 He writes, “If there is someone you do not wish to recognize as a political being, you begin by not seeing him as the bearer of signs of politicity, by not understanding what he says, by not hearing what issues from his mouth as discourse.” Rancière, *Dissensus*, 38.

6 See Durkheim, *Elementary Forms of Religious Life*.

7 Chen, *Animacies*. As my book went into production, I was excited to receive Mel Chen’s luminous new work in their book *Intoxicated: Race, Disability, and Chemical Intimacy across Empire*, but I would just like to acknowledge their work in unpacking the racialization of intoxication in the following work: Chen, “Unpacking Intoxication, Racialising Disability”; and Chen, “Agitation.”

8 Katz, *Fermentation as Metaphor*.

9 Haraway, *Staying with the Trouble*, introduction.

10 Ngai, *Our Aesthetic Categories*; Hartman, *Wayward Lives, Beautiful Experiments*.

11 Foucault, *Security, Territory, Population*, in particular chapter 2 (29–54).

12 Foucault, 41–42 (my emphasis).

13 On the question of hunger and biopolitics, see McNally, “Biopolitics of Food Provisioning.” McNally rightly raises the ongoing problem of Foucault’s elision of food labor, food provisioning, and primary resource extraction from colonial and enslaved-labor economies. For more, see the eternally relevant Mintz, *Sweetness and Power*; and, more recently, Duncan, *In the Shadows of the Tropics*.

14 Gilmore, *Golden Gulag*, 28; Mbembe, “Necropolitics.” I wish also to recall Sharon Holland’s much earlier monograph *Raising the Dead: Readings of Death and (Black) Subjectivity*, which made proleptic and critical connections between Black, queer, and Indigenous relations to death as both biopolitical and a space of radical meaning-making in the time of AIDS. Ian Baucom’s and M. NourbeSe Philip’s work on the Zong massacre, risk, and speculative capitalism provide one example, as do Ann Stoler’s and Sidney Mintz’s works on the centrality of the colonial project to the development of metropolitan biopolitics. See Philips, *Zong!*; Baucom, *Specters of the Atlantic*; Stoler, *Race and the Education of Desire*; and Mintz, *Sweetness and Power*.

15 See Clough et al., "Notes towards a Theory of Affect-Itself."
16 Tompkins, "Introduction," 3–4.
17 Khanna, *Visceral Logics of Decolonization*, 18.
18 Khanna, 20.
19 Wilson, *Psychosomatic*, 42.
20 See LaFleur, *Natural History of Sexuality in Early America*; and Schuller, *Biopolitics of Feeling*.
21 Hendy et al., "Cultures of Fermentation," S201. For the original coining of the term "microbiopolitics" see also Paxson, "Post-Pasteurian Cultures."
22 Hendy et al., "Cultures of Fermentation," S201.
23 Ahuja, "Securitization," 194. See also Ahuja, *Bioinsecurities*.
24 Clough et al., "Notes towards a Theory of Affect-Itself," 64 (citation omitted).
25 Mintz, *Sweetness and Power*, 51.
26 Tsing, "Unruly Edges." Tsing writes, "The huge scale of cane plantations, and their savage labour discipline, are in part a response to fears of fermentation, which inspire on-site, expensive mills—and the desire to keep them running continuously" (149).
27 On the emergence of taste and refinement in and through the political economy of enslavement, see Gikandi, *Slavery and the Culture of Taste*.
28 Bourdieu, *Distinction*.
29 Mintz, *Sweetness and Power*, 174.
30 Wynter, "Rethinking 'Aesthetics,'" 244.
31 Wynter, 247–248.
32 On this, see Hantel, "Plasticity and Fungibility"; as well as Schuller and Gill-Peterson, "Introduction."
33 In *The State as a Work of Art: The Cultural Origins of the Constitution*, Eric Slauter points to how ideas of "beauty" and "harmony" served to facilitate the ratification of the Constitution. I might consider my project in line with scholars who seek to think about representation as both a political and aesthetic project, except inasmuch as working with the overlap between aesthetics and affect takes us further into conversation with what Nigel Thrift has termed "non-representational theory." See Thrift, *Non-Representational Theory*.
34 Sontag, "Fascinating Fascism."
35 See Singh, "Whiteness of Police." I return to the question of police power later in the book. Regarding checkpoints and biopower, see Puar, *Right to Maim*.
36 Spade, *Normal Life*, 23; Dean, *Governmentality*, 26.
37 Spade, *Normal Life*, 143–144.
38 Rancière, *Politics of Aesthetics*, 35.
39 Rancière, *Dissensus*.
40 Marx, *Economic and Philosophic Manuscripts of 1844*, 141.
41 There are too many names here to list, but I would start with Cervenak, *Wandering*; Rai, "Race and Ontologies of Sensation"; Puar, "Spatial Debilities"; Stewart, *Ordinary Affects*; Berlant, *Cruel Optimism*; McCormack, *Atmospheric Things*; and Peterson, *Atmospheric Noise*.

42 Here I am very much grateful to Lauren Berlant, who directed me to the following article to think about "reading with" as a method: Campbell, "Lauren Berlant Discusses 'Reading with' and Her Recent Work." My use of the term "unfurls" is in deep tribute to Martin Manalansan's writing—in particular, his elaboration of "unfurling" in his *Global Divas* as a term that exquisitely describes the tactical feminine and temporal method of being-in-time that is Filipino-trans-femme performance. I very much admire Manalansan's ethnographic engagement with the sensory details of everyday life, and I seek to emulate it in this project. See also Manalansan, "'Stuff' of Archives."

43 Barad, "On Touching," 208–209.

44 Barad, 203.

45 Massumi, *Politics of Affect*.

46 Barad, "On Touching," 214–215.

47 Tompkins, "Crude Matter, Queer Form."

48 Higginbotham, *Righteous Discontent*.

49 Rancière, *Politics of Aesthetics*, 14–15.

50 Lorde, "Uses of the Erotic," 342.

51 See particularly Horton-Stallings, *Funk the Erotic*; and Allen, *¡Venceremos?*

52 Lorde, "Uses of the Erotic," 343.

53 Lorde, 343, 342.

54 Cohen, "Deviance as Resistance," 33. See also Cohen, "Punks, Bulldaggers, and Welfare Queens."

55 See Higginbotham, *Righteous Discontent*. See also Bailey, *Misogynoir Transformed*. Bailey originally coined the term "misogynoir" in 2008.

56 Cohen, "Deviance as Resistance," 37.

57 Cohen, 40.

58 Cohen, 41.

59 This thinking anticipates José Muñoz's intervention into the politics of gesture and ephemerality in performance studies; see his "Ephemera as Evidence."

60 I would be negligent if I did not point to the long tradition of European historians and theorists who have written about the incipient political power of crowds, beginning with Gustave Le Bon's 1896 *The Crowd: A Study of the Popular Mind*, through Wilfred Trotter's idea of "the herd instinct" ("Herd Instinct and Its Bearing on the Psychology of Civilised Man"), and on through Henri Lefebvre, as well as Durkheim's idea of religious experience as "collective effervescence" (*Elementary Forms of Religious Life*). See Lefebvre, "Revolutionary Crowds."

61 Rogers, "Black Friday," 176.

62 See Rudé, Crowd in History. See also Thompson, "Moral Economy of the English Crowd."

63 See Moten, *Stolen Life*. See also B. Anderson, *Imagined Communities*.

64 Assuming or demanding likeness between objects is an assertion of disciplinary boundaries as the only testing ground for evidence-based claims.

65 Barad, "On Touching," 207.

66 Rancière, *Politics of Aesthetics*, in particular chapter 2.

67 Rancière, *Dissensus*. For an elaboration of Rancière in relation to coloniality, see Tolia-Kelly, "Rancière and the Re-distribution of the Sensible."

68 Ngai, *Our Aesthetic Categories*. In particular, see Ngai's discussion of "a more flexible historicity" in the introduction of the book. She writes, "While this book pays close attention to the conditions under which these struggles [over ideological symbols] unfold, and singles out specific contexts in which they become particularly intense, it is not a history of feelings. Its overarching project is rather a theoretical one, calling for a more fluid reading across forms, genres, and periods than is the prevailing norm in academic criticism today. Hence, texts are frequently read in what may seem like jarring juxtapositions" (9).

CHAPTER 1. HYGIENE

1 See here Chen's *Animacies*.

2 I borrow the term "hygiene" from Latour's work, in which he uses the term to describe the larger group of social actors that took up the language of Pasteurian science as a state project in France to facilitate social projects geared toward optimizing, cleansing, and improving the population. Latour, *Pasteurization of France*.

3 Daston and Galison, *Objectivity*, 37.

4 Daston and Galison, 204.

5 Speculatively, the self that Daston and Galison call the "scientific self" could have emerged directly from what Steven Shapin has documented as the "gentlemanly social relations" that underlay economies of trust and believability in seventeenth-century England, which he also defined as "an equation between gentility and truth-telling." See Shapin, *Social History of Truth*, 193, 73.

6 A self-conception that has of course been heavily critiqued by such scholars in the field of science and technology studies as Bruno Latour (Latour and Woolgar, *Laboratory Life*) and Donna Haraway (see, for example, Haraway, "Situated Knowledges").

7 Dean, *Governmentality*, 142.

8 Manalansan, "Messy Mismeasures," 494.

9 On reasonableness as a liberal ideal weaponized against racially minoritized populations, see Pellegrini, "Storm on the Horizon."

10 Joyce and Mukerji, "State of Things," 3 (italics mine).

11 Joyce and Mukerji, 15 (italics mine).

12 Manalansan, "Messy Mismeasures," 495.

13 Joyce and Mukerji, "State of Things," 3.

14 Nyong'o and Tompkins, "Eleven Theses on Civility."

15 Nyong'o and Tompkins.

16 My interest in the conjoining of political aesthetics to political affect is very much shaped by the much-missed Lauren Berlant. In their landmark book *Cruel Optimism*, Berlant wrote,

> Affect's saturation of form can communicate the conditions under which a historical moment appears as a visceral moment, assessing the way a thing

that is happening finds its genre, which is the same as finding its event. So in addition to the unlikely possibility of deriving the state of structural historical relations from patterns of affective response, I am claiming that the aesthetic or formal rendition of affective experience provides evidence of historical processes. How is it possible for affective traces in the aesthetic to provide evidence of anything, and not to amount simply to a record of writerly/readerly cleverness or ideology as such? (16)

17 Foucault, *History of Sexuality*.
18 Ferguson, *Aberrations in Black*, 13.
19 More precisely, sociology vacillated regarding its role: Is it descriptive or prescriptive, analytic or documentary? For a primer on the early debates, see Pettigrew, introduction to *Sociology of Race Relations*, xxiii–xxvi.
20 I am thinking here of Lauren Berlant's prescient statement on her blog *Supervalent Thought* that Donald Trump's incivility, his willingness to say anything, makes his followers feel free. She writes, "You watch him calculating, yet not seeming to care about the consequences of what he says, and you listen to his supporters enjoying the feel of his freedom. See the brilliant interviews on Samantha Bee's *Full Frontal*, where RNC conventioneers say, over and over: We're for Trump because he's not politically correct, PC has harmed America, and you think, *people feel so unfree*." Berlant, "Trump, or Political Emotions."
21 Gaus and Wolcott, *Public Administration and the United States Department of Agriculture*, 3.
22 R. Lee, "Morrill Act of 1862 Indigenous Land Parcels Database."
23 Goldstein, "Ground Not Given," 83–84.
24 See Daston and Galison, *Objectivity*; Lindberg et al., *Cambridge History of Science*; and Schiebinger, *Plants and Empire*.
25 See LaFleur, *Natural History of Sexuality in Early America*.
26 Schiebinger, *Plants and Empire*, 5 (italics added).
27 Schiebinger, 194.
28 US Department of Agriculture, Office of Experiment Stations, *Experiment Station Bulletin No. 2*, 15–16.
29 US Department of Agriculture, *Report of the Commissioner of Agriculture for the Year 1864*, 6.
30 Dodge, "Why and Where Mutton Sheep Are Profitable," 341.
31 US Department of Agriculture, *Report of the Commissioner of Agriculture for the Year 1864*, 6.
32 US Department of Agriculture, 9.
33 Didier, *America by the Numbers*, 340 (italics added).
34 US Department of Agriculture, Office of Experiment Stations, *Experiment Station Bulletin No. 1*, 61.
35 The sheer amount of land and money that the Morrill Act and the bill funding experiment stations raised in the thirteen years is mind-boggling, as is the rate of growth in university infrastructure: "The act appropriating scrip to the amount of

30,000 acres for each Senator and Representative in Congress for the endowment of colleges for the benefit of agriculture and the mechanic arts, which was passed in 1862, has been fruitful. Some of the States endowed single colleges while others divided the gift between two or three. There were 17,430,000 acres of scrip and land granted, and the fund arising from their sales is $7,545,405. This has been increased by gifts from the States and from benevolent individuals of grounds, buildings, and apparatus to the amount of $5,000,000 more. And the last reports show that these colleges employed more than 400 professors and had under instruction more than 4,000 students." US Department of Agriculture, Office of Experiment Stations, 65.

36 Hatch, *Agricultural Experiment Stations.*

37 Hatch, 2.

38 Cullather, "Foreign Policy of the Calorie," 338.

39 Cullather, 339.

40 Daggett, *Birth of Energy*, 13.

41 Atwater, *Methods and Results*, 9, 14–15.

42 Atwater, "New Form of Bomb Calorimeter," 136.

43 Adams, *Great American Fraud*, 12.

44 Latour, *Pasteurization of France*, 19.

45 Fleck, *Genesis and Development of a Scientific Fact*, 92.

CHAPTER 2. FERMENT

1 W. Anderson, *Colonial Pathologies*, 2.

2 Here I engage "feeling" in the sense that Muñoz denotes the organization of racial feeling to be "vast, present and vital. It is an ontopoetic state not just of people who live in the United States under the sign of *latinidad* but of a majority of those who exist, strive, and flourish within the vast trajectory of multiple and intersecting regimes of colonial violence" (Muñoz, *Sense of Brown*, 5). Muñoz's capacious theorization of minoritarian existence as aesthetic, sensual, and sensory aligns, as Joshua Chambers-Letson and Tavia Nyong'o demonstrate in their introduction to *The Sense of Brown*, with Jean Luc Nancy's idea of the senses as the porous boundary between self and world. See Derrida, *On Touching—Jean-Luc Nancy.*

3 W. Anderson, *Colonial Pathologies*, 11.

4 While not entirely focused on race, Nancy Tomes's *The Gospel of Germs* is an essential contribution to the history of Progressive-era and early twentieth-century public health formations following the rise of bacteriology in the nineteenth century.

5 Esposito, *Immunitas.*

6 See Manalansan, "'Stuff' of Archives"; Manalansan, "Messy Mismeasures."

7 See Schuller, *Biopolitics of Feeling*; LaFleur, *Natural History of Sexuality in Early America.*

8 Clough et al., "Notes towards a Theory of Affect-Itself."

9 See Bulloch, *History of Bacteriology*; Maloy and Schaechter, "Era of Microbiology," 1; Pommerville, *Fundamentals of Microbiology*.
10 Discussed in Barnett, "Beginnings of Microbiology and Biochemistry."
11 See García-Carmona and Acevedo-Díaz, "Understanding the Nature of Science." See also Hein, "Liebig-Pasteur Controversy," 614.
12 Latour, *Pasteurization of France*, 54.
13 Latour, 40 (italics added).
14 Malone and Ovenden, "Natureculture," 1.
15 Paxson, "Post-Pasteurian Cultures," 17.
16 Paxson, 17.
17 Here I join with Deleuze and Guattari in agreeing that the molecular and the molar, in their sense of the terms, are overlapping, particularly following the central importance of microbiology to the workings of the state after the 1850s. Some illumination of this comes in their relationship to Gabriel Tarde's wild sociology, which Latour saw as a precursor to actor-network theory in its collapse of the social and the natural, the macro and the micro. See Latour, "Gabriel Tarde and the End of the Social." Deleuze and Guattari, *Thousand Plateaus*.
18 Velmet, *Pasteur's Empire*, 5.
19 Latour, *Pasteurization of France*, 36–37.
20 Gibier, "Microbes and the Social Question," 34 (italics added).
21 Pasteur, *Studies in Fermentation*, 237.
22 Pasteur, 238. See also W. Foster, *History of Medical Bacteriology and Immunology*.
23 See Bulloch, *History of Bacteriology*, 39.
24 Working through an online database of US journals, I found that between 1850 and 1861, the point at which Pasteur initially published his research in France, there were 17 journal articles that mention both Pasteur and fermentation; during the Civil War years between 1861 and 1865, there were 42, for a total of 71 articles in the 1860s entirely. However, by 1880–1889, there were over 200 articles mentioning both Pasteur and fermentation, increasing to around 172 in the last decade of the century alone.
25 Pasteur, "Mémoire sur la fermentation appelée lactique"; Pasteur, *Memoire sur la fermentation alcoolique*; Pasteur, *Studies on Fermentation*.
26 Pasteur, *Studies on Fermentation*, 4.
27 Pasteur, 6.
28 Pasteur, *Études sur la bière*, 7.
29 Translation and italics mine.
30 Pasteur, *Studies on Fermentation*, 7.
31 Tyndall, "On Dust and Disease," 559.
32 *OED Online*, s.v. "foment, v."
33 Haraway, *Companion Species Manifesto*.
34 *OED Online*, s.v. "ferment, v."
35 Milton, "Samson Agonistes," 88.
36 "Joe 'the Wolf,'" 109 (italics mine).

37 "Tough Cases," 145 (italics mine).

38 "History of Slavery in Massachusetts."

39 Quincy, editorial (italics mine). I am guessing at the authorship, as the article is attributed to "E.Q.," who was the Boston correspondent for the *National Standard*.

40 See Daggett, *Birth of Energy*, 8.

41 Famously, in a series of three essays, Norton Wise and Crosbie Smith explored how the marriage of the algebraic principles of balance to the first two laws of thermodynamics came to dominate the moral economy that underlay the guiding principles of liberal capitalism. (The first law, also known as the "Law of Conservation of Energy," states that energy cannot be created or destroyed in an isolated system; the second law of thermodynamics states that the entropy of any isolated system always increases.) See Wise and Smith, "Work and Waste (I)"; Wise and Smith, "Work and Waste (II)"; Wise and Smith, "Work and Waste (III)."

42 Daggett, *Birth of Energy*, 4.

43 I discussed this spread in chapter 1, in relation to the calorie.

44 Mintz shows that, rather than exporting the assembly line and other labor regimes from the metropolis to the plantations, the flow of information was in the other direction, from the Caribbean sugar plantations to the English factories. Further, these new labor orders were energetically fueled by the sugar and caffeine that laborers consumed in greater and greater degrees across the eighteenth centuries (Mintz, *Sweetness and Power*, 101).

45 I have discussed Sylvester Graham at length elsewhere: Tompkins, *Racial Indigestion*, chapter 2.

46 Alcott, *Candy Country*, 4–5.

47 Alcott, 5. A note here on the intersection of text—in particular children's fiction—and performance theory. While performance theory has in the past productively located itself in opposition to textuality, prizing a sense of "liveness" as its particular purview, I do want to argue that the opposition between the two cultural modalities might be enriched by a better historical understanding of the reading technologies and practices through which texts are experienced across different periods. In the nineteenth century, people read out loud to each other far more often than we do now. Literature was often staged in domestic settings, in *tableaux vivants*, for instance, and of course, as is particularly relevant to this chapter, children were even more often read to than adults were, as they are now. The line, in short, between performance and text, certainly in the nineteenth century, is neither firm nor consistent.

48 Alcott, 8.

49 Alcott, 9.

50 Alcott, 9.

51 Alcott, 9.

52 Alcott, 9.

53 Alcott, 10.

54 Of course, as scholars doing work at the intersections of queer theory and settler colonialism have pointed out, the cannibal of colonizing discourse is also often the sodomite or nonbinary-gendered native. Sanborn, *Sign of the Cannibal*.
55 Alcott, *Candy Country*, 10.
56 Alcott, 10.
57 Alcott, 11–12.
58 Alcott, 16.
59 Alcott, 13–14.
60 Alcott, 18.
61 Alcott, 19.
62 Alcott, 11.
63 Alcott, 20.
64 Alcott, 22.
65 Alcott, 23.
66 Alcott, 26.
67 Alcott, 27.
68 Mintz, *Sweetness and Power*, 174.
69 Tompkins, "Sweetness, Capacity, Energy."
70 Alcott, *Candy Country*, 26.
71 Alcott, 23.
72 Alcott, 25.
73 Alcott, 24.
74 Alcott, 24.
75 Thrift, *Non-Representational Theory*, 49.
76 Alcott, *Candy Country*, 19.
77 Alcott, 18–19.

CHAPTER 3. INTOXICATION

1 This chapter first appeared in an issue of *Social Text*. My thanks to the participants of the Everyday Life seminar at the Warren Center for Studies in American History at Harvard University for their judicious and generous reading of the earlier drafts of this chapter. Thanks are due as well to my anonymous readers.
2 Alexander, *New Jim Crow*, 197.
3 Many scholars have made the argument about the racialization of particular drugs. See, for instance Márez, *Drug Wars*; Breen, *Age of Intoxication*; Netherland and Hansen, "White Opioids"; and Bobo and Thompson, "Unfair by Design."
4 Since 2001, I have studied the printing history and representational politics of chromolithographic advertising, in particular the trade card. Across that time, I have examined perhaps thousands of chromolithographic cards and pamphlets, visited multiple advertising archives, and read through over fifty years of documentation on the SSS Company in the historical archives of the American Medical Association. Finally, I have examined hundreds of SSS advertisements in southern newspapers leading up to 1906. See Tompkins, *Racial Indigestion*, chapter 5.

5 See Chen, "Toxic Animacies, Inanimate Affections"; Chen, *Animacies.*

6 Around 1900, a conversation developed in the editorial letter section of the *Journal of American Medical Association* in which regional doctors commented on the prevalence of cocaine addiction, particularly "among the negros" but also, interestingly enough, among medical students. See, for instance, "Cocain Habit" (*JAMA* 34, no. 25); there the editors opine, albeit without any cited evidence,

> The negroes in some parts of the South are reported as being addicted to a new form of vice—that of 'cocain sniffing' or the 'coke habit,' as it appears to have this name also. A negro, it is said, will buy 5 cents' worth of cocain, which is sold in a little paper box for such purposes, and, taking it in the old-fashioned way of snuff-takers, proceed to indulge in a 'coke drunk.' The effects are described as much like those of an ordinary whisky drunk; some cocain 'sniffers' are quarrelsome, some hilarious, some morose, and many are happy and indifferent like the opium smokers, while the intoxication lasts. It appears even that the habit is going to succeed to the recognized legal rights of whisky.

See also F. Jones, "Cocain Habit among the Negroes"; "Cocain Habit" (*JAMA* 36, no. 5).

7 Bouchard, *Lectures on Auto-intoxication in Disease*, 9.

8 Bouchard, 9–10.

9 Marx, *Capital*, vol. 3, 949. Contemporary theorists and environmental scholars have returned to Marx's theory of metabolism to discuss Marx's prediction of coming ecological disaster.

10 See Foster, *Marx's Ecology*, ix; and Foster, "Marx's Theory of Metabolic Rift." For Liebig's discussion of metabolism, see Liebig, *Natural Laws of Husbandry.*

11 Atwater, the nineteenth-century scientist I discussed in chapter 1, not only was a follower of Liebig and the head of the USDA's office of experiment stations but also invented the concept of the calorie by putting undergraduates into a locked chamber called a "respiration calorimeter" for days at a time, measuring their excrement, urine, and the production of heat from their bodies in relation to the food they ate.

12 Aronson, "Nutrition as a Social Problem,"478.

13 Cullather, "Foreign Policy of the Calorie," 338; see also Cullather, *Hungry World.*

14 Seikaly, *Men of Capital.* On metabolism, in the context of modern India as a biopolitical category, see Solomon, *Metabolic Living.*

15 Bouchard, *Lectures on Auto-intoxication in Disease*, 287.

16 J. Harris, *Georgia Possum*; Swift's Specific, *Georgia Watermelon. A Georgia Watermelon* can be found online in the Afro-Americana Imprints database of the Library Company of Philadelphia (see www.readex.com, Record Number 154E9B32234455E8); I originally studied the pamphlet in the advertising archives of the Harvard Business School Library and later found another original on Ebay.com. *A Georgia Possum* can be found online in the digital advertising archives at Duke University (https://repository.duke.edu).

17 To be precise, only *A Georgia Possum* names Harris as the author, although its precise wording ("another story by") implies that both of the stories are by him. "Uncle Remus" was also well known at that time as Harris's principal storytelling character.

18 Harris's relationship with patent remedy companies has been briefly outlined in a few places but not explored in more depth. See Young, "Three Atlanta Pharmacists"; M. Cohen, "Jim Crow's Drug War."

19 SSS Tonic, now marketed as full of "Liquid High Potency Iron and B Vitamins," can be found on the shelves at Target, Walmart, and other large chain stores. The company is still privately owned, still uses the same colors and font on its box as it did during the nineteenth century, and indeed has the tag line "Trusted since 1826" written at the bottom of the box. Phone calls by the author to the head office in Atlanta were not returned. This chapter makes no claims or inferences about the intentions or allegiances of the company that makes the product today.

20 Based on my search of the *Atlanta Constitution*'s online archives for 1881–1945. Of these, 959 were printed between 1882 and 1899. SSS was mentioned another three hundred times in the paper, in various editorial formats, including an April 18, 1926, article celebrating the one hundredth anniversary of the company's founding in 1826, in which the headline proclaimed that SSS's success was entirely based on newspaper advertising. By comparison, SSS is mentioned only eight times in Black newspapers in the same period, evidence of its lack of interest in the parallel Black consumer base: four were short patient testimonials in the African Methodist Episcopal publication the *Christian Recorder* between January 1 and April 9, 1885; one, in 1899, appeared in a list of available groceries printed in the *Parson's Weekly Blade*, a Black Kansas newspaper; and three appeared in the *Huntsville Gazette*, an Alabama newspaper, between 1883 and 1891. The *Atlanta Constitution* was thus central to SSS's self-promotion and self-image. Given the connections between the paper and Atlanta's business community, it is illuminating that the *Constitution*'s most famous associate editor, Harris, might affiliate with the nostrums company by authoring stories that appeared in its advertising pamphlets. According to James Harvey Young, patent medicine almanacs often printed excerpts from American authors, especially comic authors. In his history of the patent medicine business, Young also notes that Harris stories appear in the St. Jacobs Oil Family Calendar for 1883–1884. Young, *Toadstool Millionaires*, 140.

21 As late as 1927, correspondence at the archives of the AMA shows that the AMA anti-patent-remedy office believed that, while SSS no longer advertised itself as a syphilis cure, it was nonetheless advertising itself as a cure for the symptoms of syphilis and should therefore be subject to prosecution and not allowed to advertise in newspapers because of its false claims. Further, correspondence between AMA agents posing as curious consumers and the SSS "medical department" shows that SSS was happy to claim that it cured the syphilis virus in correspondence with customers.

22 Which is to say, neither is this project an inquiry into the veracity of the claims made by the testimonials, nor does it seek to debunk the likelihood that many people suffered extensively from the medical problems they describe in these pamphlets. I am more interested in the racialized performance and experience of these illness, as well as the narrative forms through which pain is narrated and played out (or not) on these pages.

23 In the 1877 election, Republican Rutherford Hayes won the Electoral College vote by a single vote, but he lost the popular vote, largely due to aggressive voter suppression in the South. Hayes was declared president through a compromise with southern Democrats in which he promised to remove northern occupying forces from the South; to reduce northern "interference," much of which supported Black civic involvement and voting rights; and to support the Democratic candidates for governor in South Carolina and Louisiana. This election is often referred to as the Great Compromise and marks the end of the radical Reconstruction project. See Foner, *Short History of Reconstruction*, especially chapter 12.

24 I am here citing Jackson Lears's foundational work on trade cards and late twentieth-century advertising in *Fables of Abundance*.

25 See Mbembe, *On the Postcolony*, especially chapter 3.

26 Swift's Specific Remedy, *Georgia Watermelon*, 1. The SSS pamphlets' pages are not numbered, so my page numbers are approximate but counted from the first page after the cover. The printer for the 1891 *Georgia Watermelon* pamphlet is copyrighted to Swift's Specific, and the printer is legibly named as Foote and Davies; the 1895 *Georgia Possum* pamphlet is also copyrighted to Swift's Specific, but the name of the printer is not legible.

27 Swift's Specific Remedy, 6.

28 The overlap between gustatory and erotic pleasure is discussed in Tompkins, *Racial Indigestion*, and in detail in Probyn, *Carnal Appetites*; and Woodard, *Delectable Negro*.

29 Swift's Specific Remedy, *Georgia Watermelon*, 12.

30 Swift's Specific Remedy, 10.

31 Swift's Specific Remedy, 12.

32 Harris, *Georgia Possum*, 6–7 (italics mine). For all iterations of the n-word in the context of Chandler's dialect representation, I have substituted "n——r."

33 Harris, 12.

34 Harris, 18.

35 Harris, 2. There is another book to be written about these pamphlets, one that seeks to contribute to the corpus of scholarship on Harris. One direction might be a discussion of the dialect speech in the stories, alongside the history of dialect's pathologization; see G. Jones, *Strange Talk*.

36 Johnson, "'Quare' Studies," 20. I am also methodologically inspired by Ashon Crawley when he writes, riffing off Denise Ferreira da Silva, "Black Study is the force of belief that blackness is but one critical and urgently necessary disruption to the epistemology, the theology-philosophy, that produces a world, a set of protocols,

wherein black flesh cannot easily breathe. . . . Black Study is a wholly unbounded, holy, collective intellectual project that is fundamentally otherwise than an (inter) discipline. This refusal of disciplinary boundaries is important because disciplinary knowledges attempt resolution, attempt to 'resolve' knowledge 'into objectivity . . . that ha[s] characterized modern knowledge . . . with certainty.'" Crawley, *Blackpentecostal Breath*, 3, quoting Ferreira da Silva. In other words, Black Study is a project loosened from the disciplinary imperative of Black Studies, even as it remains ethically bound. See also Eve Kosofsky Sedgwick's parsing of the term "queer" in *Tendencies*, xii.

37 Swift's Specific Remedy, *Georgia Watermelon*, 12.

38 Harris, *Georgia Possum*, 3.

39 Harris, 5, 11.

40 Swift's Specific Remedy, *Georgia Watermelon*, 18.

41 The entertainment, of course, was upheld by a rich world of highly racialized public spectacles, such as Indian medicine shows and freak shows, supported by and in turn supporting a growing body of patent remedies and their attendant advertising sales. See McNamara, *Step Right Up*; Anderson, *Snake Oil, Hustlers, and Hambones*; and Wu, *Chang and Eng Reconnected*.

42 Pendergrast, *For God, Country, and Coca-Cola*. While the SSS company continued to claim, in court cases and patent hearings across the early twentieth century, that the middle *S* did not reference syphilis, Pendergrast's claim in *For God* is upheld by the correspondence of the AMA's Fraud Division, led by Arthur Cramp. Its internal communications and correspondence with the public referred to SSS as "Swift's Syphilitic Specific." In a 1927 letter to Cramp dated July 18, 1927, the author cites an article in *JAMA* that demonstrated that, while the company no longer mentioned syphilis in the name, there was extensive documentation of advertising campaigns in which SSS claimed that it cured syphilis, as well as many direct letters to consumers in which it claimed to cure syphilis. The letter's author also notes that SSS claims to treat the symptoms of syphilis and wishes to be known as such because it had not changed its name, nor did it offer any explanation of the middle S. In later correspondence, Cramp argued that while SSS Tonic could no longer claim to heal syphilis, it now advertised through appeals to "pure blood." See *JAMA* 73, no. 9 (August 30, 1919): 707–709. See also head of the Fraud Division to Arthur Cramp, July 18, 1927, folders 1 and 3, box 827, AMA Historical Archives. The AMA's Historical Health Fraud and Alternative Medicine Collection (in Chicago) includes investigative files on SSS from the 1890s to the 1960s, looking into its finances, its in-house doctor, and its advertising claims and practices, including the *Georgia Possum* pamphlet discussed here.

43 Swift's Specific Remedy, *Georgia Watermelon*, 1.

44 Morgensen, "Settler Homonationalism; Rifkin, *When Did Indians Become Straight?*; A. Smith, "Queer Theory and Native Studies."

45 See M. Cohen, "Jim Crow's Drug War."

46 In "Jim Crow's Drug War," Cohen's discussion of the intertwined history of Coca-Cola, addiction, and US racism, he writes that the South, Atlanta in particular, was the major US center for the creation and distribution of patent remedies.
47 Bederman, *Manliness and Civilization*; Lutz, *American Nervousness.*
48 Berlant, *Cruel Optimism*, 95.
49 Swift's Specific Remedy, *Georgia Watermelon*, 12.
50 Bernstein, "Dances with Things," 69.
51 Berlant, *Cruel Optimism*, 93.
52 Deleuze, *Fold.*
53 Caroline Oates, in "Cheese Gives You Nightmares," documents the folklore surrounding "hag" nightmares and cheese consumption all the way back to Apuleius's North African folktales. Additionally and amusingly, I found one more recent article that accounts for the relation between food and nightmares: Nielsen and Powell, "Dream of the Rarebit Fiend." This excellent article found evidence of the cheese-nightmare correlation/causality trope as recently as 2005, when the British Cheese Board argued that different cheeses do indeed cause more intense dreams; see "Sweet Dreams Are Made of Cheese."
54 Cummins, *Welsh Rarebit Tales*, vi.
55 On the intersection of racism, nineteenth-century "freak" culture, and disability, see Wu, *Chang and Eng Reconnected.*
56 See Canemaker, *Winsor McCay*; Roeder, *Wide Awake in Slumberland*; Bukatman, *Poetics of Slumberland*. Says Canemaker of the Rarebit strip, "The ideology of the comics related to their primary purpose—to sell newspapers. No startling intellectual or social theories were embedded in the strips, no suggestions for change from the status quo. The common man, woman, and child could look at or read the comic page with confidence that their world, values, mores, and prejudices would be exactly reflected there. The comic strips validated and celebrated the average American's existence" (*Winsor McCay*, 81).
57 See, for instance, Cotton, *Chafing Dish Recipes*; Rich, *One Hundred Recipes for the Chafing Dish*.
58 Lewis, "Rarebit Symbolism," x.
59 Lewis, x.
60 Winsor McCay, *Dream of the Rarebit Fiend*, *New York Evening Telegram*, September 10, 1904.
61 Winsor McCay, *Dream of the Rarebit Fiend*, *New York Evening Telegram*, October 3, 1904.
62 Winsor McCay, *Dream of the Rarebit Fiend*, *New York Evening Telegram*, October 21, 1904.
63 Winsor McCay, *Dream of the Rarebit Fiend*, *New York Evening Telegram*, October 29, 1904.
64 Winsor McCay, *Dream of the Rarebit Fiend*, *New York Evening Telegram*, December 2, 1904.
65 Winsor McCay, *Dream of the Rarebit Fiend*, *New York Evening Telegram*, June 3, 1905.

66 Winsor McCay, *Dream of the Rarebit Fiend*, *New York Evening Telegram*, January 7, 1905.
67 See Peruna ad, *New York Telegram*, January 4, 1907.
68 Bukatman, *Poetics of Slumberland*, especially chapter 1, "Drawn and Disordered."
69 Gunning, "Cinema of Attractions," 39.
70 Stramer and Dunn, "Cells on Film." See also Landecker, "Cellular Features."
71 Landecker, "New Times for Biology," 670.
72 Hannah Landecker's work details much of these developments: Landecker, "Cellular Features"; Landecker, "Microcinematography and the History of Science and Film"; Landecker, "Life of Movement."
73 Gal, "Pasteur and the Art of Chirality," 604; Brink, "Ordering the Invisible"; "Wonders under Microscopes," 7.
74 Landecker, "Cellular Features," 904.
75 Gardner, *Projections*, 2. Elsewhere he writes, "The comic form, like film, is intimately rooted in the sequential images of Zoetrope wheels, magic lantern slides, and praxinoscope ribbons, and thus it is not surprising that they shared many concerns and formal properties" (7).
76 Bukatman, *Poetics of Slumberland*, 215.
77 Bukatman, "Comics and the Critique of Chronophotography," 89.
78 See Gaycken, *Devices of Curiosity*; Curtis, *Shape of Spectatorship*.
79 "Recreation with the Microscope: New York Society of Those Devoted to Microscopy a Pioneer Organization in This Country," *New York Times*, March 22, 1903, 33.
80 See Toulmin, *Electric Edwardians*.
81 Winsor McCay, *Dream of the Rarebit Fiend*, *New York Evening Telegram*, April 15, 1905.
82 See Landecker, "Microcinematography and the History of Science and Film." See also Landecker, "Cellular Features."
83 Winsor McCay, *Dream of the Rarebit Fiend*, *New York Evening Telegram*, September 16, 1909.
84 Winsor McCay, *Dream of the Rarebit Fiend*, *New York Evening Telegram*, July 16, 1908.
85 Winsor McCay, *Dream of the Rarebit Fiend*, *New York Evening Telegram*, August 19, 1909.
86 Kracauer, *Theory of Film*, 50. Also quoted in Landecker, "Microcinematography and the History of Science and Film," where Landecker incisively writes, "Cinema in early twentieth-century biology consisted of experiments on film in a doubled sense of the phrase. . . . Time-lapse microcinematography, through magnification and acceleration, was generative simultaneously of theories of life and theories of film" (905–906).
87 See Landecker, "Cellular Features."
88 Bouchard, *Lectures on Auto-intoxication in Disease*, 316.
89 Bukatman, "Comics and the Critique of Chronophotography," 95.
90 Daggett, *Birth of Energy*, 24.

CHAPTER 4. ROT

1 Haraway, *Staying with the Trouble*, 4.

2 See Vizenor, *Survivance*; and Derrida, *Beast and the Sovereign*, 130–132.

3 Robinson, *Black Marxism*; Wynter, "Unsettling the Coloniality of Being/Power/Truth/Freedom"; and Ahuja, *Bioinsecurities*. E. Williams, *Capitalism and Slavery*; Hong, "Capital."

4 Wynter, "Novel and History, Plot and Plantation"; McKittrick, *Sylvia Wynter*.

5 C. Cohen, "Deviance as Resistance," 43.

6 Alvarado, *Abject Performances*; Rodríguez, *Sexual Futures, Queer Gestures*. See also Hancock, *Politics of Disgust*; M. Smith, "Affect and Respectability Politics."

7 Foucault, *Order of Things*.

8 Alexander, *New Jim Crow*; Hartman, *Scenes of Subjection*.

9 Here let me locate myself within hemispheric, racial, and class privilege: that is what has already happened to Indigenous peoples, to the Global South, to working-class people of color, and to poor whites in poor neighborhoods.

10 Gilmore, *Golden Gulag*.

11 In thinking through ferment and its overlaps with decomposition, I am deeply grateful to conversations with Dr. Zita Worley, whose brilliant dissertation rethinking temperance from the point of view of enclosure laws I read soon after she completed it. Worley, "In the Valley of the Moon."

12 I'm thinking here of Douglas's episteme-shifting statement that dirt is matter out of place (Douglas, *Purity and Danger*).

13 Haraway, "The Camille Stories: Children of Compost," in *Staying with the Trouble*, 134–168. See also Armiero, "Case for the Wasteocene." Armiero writes, "I would say that, in my interpretation of wasting, the key issue is not that waste is 'matter out of place' but, rather, that places (including humans and nonhumans) are produced through the power of classifying who and what is disposable and who and what is not" (425). He is of course referencing, as I just did, Douglas.

14 See Wynter, "Unsettling the Coloniality of Being/Power/Truth/Freedom"; and Mintz, *Sweetness and Power*.

15 As a meditation on the "multisensory and multidimensional philosophy" that is funk, see Horton-Stallings, *Funk the Erotic*.

16 Chen, "Unpacking Intoxication, Racialising Disability."

17 Tsing, "Unruly Edges."

18 Lee, "My Mushroom Burial Suit."

19 Barnard Center for Research on Women, "Denise Ferreira da Silva."

20 Moten, *In the Break*, 14.

21 Butler, introduction to *Bodies That Matter*, 1–23.

22 Ferreira da Silva, "1 (life) ÷ 0 (blackness) = ∞−∞ or ∞/∞."

23 See Baker, *Modernism and the Harlem Renaissance*; Goldsby, "Closer to Something Unnameable."

24 Wynter, "Rethinking 'Aesthetics,'" 243.

25 Spillers, "Formalism Comes to Harlem," 63.

26 Spillers, 63.

27 Spillers, 63.

28 Aliyyah I. Abdur-Rahman beautifully addresses this seeming absence in her essay "As Though a Metaphor Were Tangible."

29 Baldwin, *Giovanni's Room*, 74.

30 Baldwin, 74.

31 Baldwin, 86–87.

32 Halberstam, *Queer Art of Failure*.

33 Ferguson, *Reorder of Things*.

34 As I mentioned earlier, Jackie Goldsby terms this incompleteness "formlessness" in her essay ("Closer to Something Unnameable").

35 Kelman, in "Boundary Issues: Clarifying New Orleans's Murky Edges," writes,

> If New Orleans's situation is remarkably good, its site may be equally bad. The city was built on sediment, the long ramp of the Mississippi's levee. The highest ground is found along the river frontage. From there the land slopes down—roughly fifteen feet over a distance of about one and a half miles—until it craters at the city's rear, where much of the ground is below sea level. Through the start of the twentieth century, a cypress wetland, known locally as the backswamp, stretched from there to the shore of Lake Pontchartrain, several soggy miles away, where the terrain climbs to the peak of the lake's levee. New Orleans, then, is a bowl ringed by bodies of water, which stare down into town like voyeurs. And because the city is surrounded by levees and sits on a high water table, there is no natural drainage, a hazard in a place that averages nearly sixty inches of rain annually. (696)

36 "Public Butcheries," *New Orleans Commercial Bulletin*, August 20, 1868. Available at https://lasc.libguides.com.

37 B. Butler, "Some Experience with Yellow Fever and Its Prevention."

38 Ross, "Justice Miller's Reconstruction," 667.

39 Mitchell, "Identifying White Mediocrity."

40 *Black's Law Dictionary*, s.v. "police."

41 Blackstone, *Commentaries on the Laws of England*, book 4, chapter 13, 163.

42 Bentham, *Works of J. Bentham*, 169.

43 Quinn, "Bentham on Preventive Police."

44 Marinković and Ristić, "Foucault and the Birth of the Police."

45 Rancière writes,

> There is thus an "aesthetics" at the core of politics that has nothing to do with Benjamin's discussion of the "aestheticization of politics" specific to the "age of the masses." This aesthetics should not be understood as the perverse commandeering of politics by a will to art, by a consideration of the people qua work of art. If the reader is fond of analogy, aesthetics can be understood in a Kantian sense—re-examined perhaps by Foucault—as the system of a priori forms determining what presents itself to sense experience.

It is a delimitation of spaces and times, of the visible and the invisible, of speech and noise, that simultaneously determines the place and the stakes of politics as a form of experience. Politics revolves around what is seen and what can be said about it, around who has the ability to see and the talent to speak, around the properties of spaces and the possibilities of time. (*Politics of Aesthetics*, 14–15).

46 Lin, "Hard White Body," 9. The naming of R. Kelly of course now takes on allusions to sexual violence given the confirmation of his history of abusing young Black women. It is not my intention to obscure that history of harm here by containing it within an overarching idea of deviance. Rather, it should fully signify here as pointing to the imminence of the possibility of harm in this narrated sexual encounter between two young people.

47 Lin, "Hard White Body," 10.

48 Lin, 11.

49 See Shotwell, *Against Purity*.

50 McMillan, *Embodied Avatars*.

51 Moten, "Resistance of the Object: Adrian Piper's Theatricality," in *In the Break*, 233–254.

52 Allawaert, *Ariel's Ecology*, 179.

CHAPTER 5. JELLY

1 Joon-ho, *Snowpiercer*.

2 Agamben, *Homo Sacer*.

3 Foucault, *History of Sexuality*, 43.

4 Semba, *Vitamin A Story*, especially chapter 2, "Paris in the Time of Magendie."

5 Viel and Fournier, "Histoire des procédés d'extraction de la gélatine."

6 The gun and criminology industries use rheology to measure the impact of bullets on the human body, following the course of bullets through mixtures of ballistic gelatin—which is extracted from pig cartilage to replicate human tissue.

7 Bennett, *Vibrant Matter*, viii.

8 For Leyda's naming of these stories see Melville, *Complete Stories of Herman Melville*.

9 Ngai, *Ugly Feelings*, 66.

10 Rowland, "Sitting Up with a Corpse."

11 G. Jones, *American Hungers*, 49.

12 See Gigante, *Taste*; Morton, *Cultures of Taste / Theories of Appetite*.

13 A small note about the senses, and in particular here about the sensory encounter I am calling "mouthfeel." Mouthfeel is the physiological experience of a substance in the mouth. More than taste, which limits oral experience to flavor, mouthfeel collapses the difference between two senses previously considered separate: taste (meaning the experience of flavor) and touch (and sometimes sound as well). "Mouthfeel" literally rounds out the mouth as a multisensory space. Though the *Oxford English Dictionary* dates the term "mouthfeel" to 1973, my point, even

ahistorically, is to think about what Melville is doing with sensory disorder in these stories. By thinking through the encounter between subjects and via objects, Melville allows these disorderly encounters to theorize otherwise to a sensual ordering that prizes hierarchy—such as a pure sense of vision. Mouthfeel, then, is what the narrator consents to, which produces his critique of Blandmour's visual ordering.

14 Melville, *Moby-Dick*, 388.
15 Blum, "Introduction," 153.
16 Melville, "Paradise of Bachelors and the Tartarus of Maids," 672.
17 Melville, "Poor Man's Pudding and Rich Man's Crumbs," 96.
18 Melville, 96.
19 Melville, 98.
20 Melville, 97.
21 Melville, 97.
22 Miller, *Anatomy of Disgust*, 60.
23 Melville, "Poor Man's Pudding and Rich Man's Crumbs," 98.
24 Derrida, "Economimesis," 16.
25 Derrida, 21.
26 Bourdieu, *Distinction.*
27 Melville, "Poor Man's Pudding and Rich Man's Crumbs," 98.
28 Melville, 99.
29 Melville, 99.
30 Melville, 99.
31 Melville, 100.
32 Melville, 100.
33 Melville, 100.
34 Melville, 101.
35 Kristeva, *Powers of Horror*, 3.
36 Saldanha, "Reontologising Race," 18.
37 Stallybrass and White, *Politics and Poetics of Transgression.*
38 They write,

> A body is not defined by the form that determines it nor as a determinate substance or subject nor by the organs it possesses or the functions it fulfills. On the plane of consistency, a body is defined only by a longitude and a latitude: in other words the sum total of the material elements belonging to it under given relations of movement and rest, speed and slowness (longitude); the sum total of the intensive affects it is capable of at a given power or degree of potential (latitude). Nothing but affects and local movements, differential speeds. The credit goes to Spinoza for calling attention to these two dimensions of the Body, and for having defined the plane of Nature as pure longitude and latitude. Latitude and longitude are the two elements of a cartography. (Deleuze and Guattari, *Thousand Plateaus*, 260; see also the discussion of music on pages 296–297)

39 Melville, "Poor Man's Pudding and Rich Man's Crumbs," 100.
40 Sutherland, "Marx in Jargon."
41 Sutherland.
42 Ngai, *Ugly Feelings*, 332.
43 Shukin, *Animal Capital.*
44 Delany, *Blake*, 50–51.
45 Delany, 50–51.
46 Delany, 52.
47 Delany, 52.
48 Delany, 52.
49 Delany, 42.
50 Crawley, *Blackpentecostal Breath*, 2.
51 Rusert, *Fugitive Science.*
52 See Massumi, *Politics of Affect.*
53 "Haptic visuality" is Juana María Rodríguez's term for the video in her brief discussion of it in her book *Sexual Futures, Queer Gestures, and Other Latina Longings.* She sees the film as exploring the erotic possibilities of friendship as a way of life.
54 Lorde, "The Uses of the Erotic," in *Sister Outsider*, 57.
55 See Hayward, "Sensational Jellyfish," 165.

CONCLUSION

1 Sharpe writes, "at stake is not recognizing antiblackness as total climate" (*In the Wake*, 21).
2 McCormack, *Atmospheric Things*, 4.
3 Rancière, *Politics of Aesthetics*, 13.
4 C. Cohen, "Deviance as Resistance."
5 Thank you to Nathan Snaza for suggesting accumulation as a key term for this project.
6 See Tompkins, "You Make Me Feel Right Quare."
7 As another example of this work, see Gikandi, *Slavery and the Culture of Taste.* Then too, as I discuss in detail in the introduction, see Sylvia Wynters's work, especially "Unsettling the Coloniality of Being/Power/Truth/ Freedom" and "Rethinking 'Aesthetics.'"

BIBLIOGRAPHY

Abdur-Rahman, Aliyyah I. "'As Though a Metaphor Were Tangible': Baldwin's Identities." In *The Cambridge Companion to James Baldwin*, edited by Michele Elam, 164–179. New York: Cambridge University Press, 2015.

Adams, Samuel Hopkins. *The Great American Fraud: Articles on the Nostrum Evil and Quacks, Reprinted from Collier's Weekly*. Chicago: American Medical Association, 1907.

Agamben, Giorgio. *Homo Sacer: Sovereign Power and Bare Life*. Translated by Daniel Heller-Roazen. Stanford, CA: Stanford University Press, 1998.

Ahuja, Neel. *Bioinsecurities: Disease Interventions, Empire, and the Government of Species*. Durham, NC: Duke University Press, 2016.

———. "Securitization." In *Keywords for Gender and Sexuality Studies*, ed. Keywords Feminist Editorial Collective, 194–195. New York: New York University Press, 2021.

Alcott, Louisa May. *The Candy Country*. Boston: Little, Brown, 1900.

Alexander, Michelle. *The New Jim Crow: Mass Incarceration in the Age of Colorblindness*. New York: New Press, 2010.

Allawaert, Monique. *Ariel's Ecology: Plantations, Personhood, and Colonialism in the American Tropics*. Minneapolis: University of Minnesota, 2013.

Allen, Jafari S. *¡Venceremos? The Erotics of Black Self-Making in Cuba*. Durham, NC: Duke University Press, 2011.

Alvarado, Leticia. *Abject Performances*. Durham, NC: Duke University Press, 2018.

Anderson, Ann. *Snake Oil, Hustlers, and Hambones: The American Medicine Show*. Jefferson, NC: McFarland, 2000.

Anderson, Benedict. *Imagined Communities: Reflections on the Origins and Spread of Nationalism*. London: Verso Books. 2016.

Anderson, Warwick. *Colonial Pathologies*. Durham, NC: Duke University Press, 2006.

Armiero, Marco. "The Case for the Wasteocene." *Environmental History* 26, no. 3 (2021): 425–430.

Aronson, Naomi. "Nutrition as a Social Problem: A Case Study of Entrepreneurial Strategy in Science." *Social Problems* 29, no. 5 (1982): 474–487.

Atwater, Wilbur Olin. *Methods and Results of Investigations on the Chemistry and Economy of Food*. No. 21. Washington, DC: US Government Printing Office, 1895.

———. "A New Form of Bomb Calorimeter and Determinations of Heats of Combustion." In *Seventh Annual Report of the Storrs Agricultural Experiment Station*, 135–157. Middletown, CT: Pelton and King, 1895.

Bailey, Moya. *Misogynoir Transformed: Black Women's Digital Resistance*. New York: New York University Press, 2021.

Baker, Houston A., Jr. *Modernism and the Harlem Renaissance*. Chicago: University of Chicago Press, 1987.

Bakhtin, Mikhail. *Rabelais and His World*. Translated by Helene Iswolsky. Bloomington: Indiana University Press, 1984.

Baldwin, James. *Giovanni's Room*. 1956. Reprint, New York: Vintage, 2013.

Barad, Karen. "On Touching—The Inhuman That Therefore I Am." *Differences: A Journal of Feminist Cultural Studies* 23, no. 3 (2012): 206–223.

Barnard Center for Research on Women. "Denise Ferreira da Silva—Hacking the Subject: Black Feminism, Refusal, and the Limits of Critique." Video. 1:07:02. Recorded October 22, 2015, posted November 24, 2015. Transcribed from video. http://amara.org.

Barnett, James A. "Beginnings of Microbiology and Biochemistry: The Contribution of Yeast Research." *Microbiology* 149, no. 3 (2003): 557–567.

Baucom, Ian. *Specters of the Atlantic: Finance Capital, Slavery, and the Philosophy of History*. Durham, NC: Duke University Press, 2015.

Bederman, Gail. *Manliness and Civilization: A Cultural History of Gender and Race in the United States, 1880–1917*. Chicago: University of Chicago Press, 1995.

Bennett, Jane. *Vibrant Matter: A Political Ecology of Things*. Durham, NC: Duke University Press, 2010.

Bentham, Jeremy. *Works of J. Bentham, Published under the Superintendence of His Executor John Bowring*. Vol. 11. Edinburgh: William Tait, 1843.

Berlant, Lauren. *The Anatomy of National Fantasy: Hawthorne, Utopia, and Everyday Life*. Chicago: University of Chicago Press, 1991.

———. *Cruel Optimism*. Durham, NC: Duke University Press, 2012.

———. *The Female Complaint: The Unfinished Business of Sentimentality in American Culture*. Durham, NC: Duke University Press, 2008.

———. *The Queen of America Goes to Washington City: Essays on Sex and Citizenship*. Durham, NC: Duke University Press, 1997.

———. "Trump, or Political Emotions." *Supervalent Thought*, August 4, 2016. https://supervalentthought.wordpress.com.

Bernstein, Robin. "Dances with Things: Material Culture and the Performance of Race." *Social Text* 27, no. 4 (2009): 67–94.

Black's Law Dictionary. 2nd ed. Eagan, MN: West, 1995. https://thelawdictionary.org.

Blackstone, William. *Commentaries on the Laws of England*. Oxford: Oxford University Press, 2016.

Blum, Hester. "Introduction: Oceanic Studies." *Atlantic Studies* 10, no. 2 (2013): 151–155.

Bobo, Lawrence D., and Victor Thompson. "Unfair by Design: The War on Drugs, Race, and the Legitimacy of the Criminal Justice System." *Social Research: An International Quarterly* 73, no. 2 (2006): 445–472.

Bouchard, Charles. *Lectures on Auto-Intoxication in Disease; or, Self-Poisoning of the Individual*. Translated by Thomas Oliver. Philadelphia: F. A. Davis, 1906.

Bourdieu, Pierre. *Distinction: A Social Critique of the Judgement of Taste*. Translated by Richard Nice. New York: Routledge, 2010.

Breen, Benjamin. *The Age of Intoxication: Origins of the Global Drug Trade*. Philadelphia: University of Pennsylvania Press, 2019.

Brillat-Savarin, Jean Anthelme. *Physiologie du goût, ou, Méditations de gastronomie transcendante: ouvrage théorique, historique et à l'ordre du jour*. Paris: A. Sautelet et Cie libraires, 1826.

Brink, Emily. "Ordering the Invisible: Silk, Contagion, and the Visual Practices of Louis Pasteur." *Antennae: The Journal of Nature in Visual Culture* 49 (2019): 129–147.

Bukatman, Scott. "Comics and the Critique of Chronophotography, or 'He Never Knew When It Was Coming!'" *Animation: An Interdisciplinary Journal* 1, no. 1 (2006): 83–103.

———. *The Poetics of Slumberland: Animated Spirits and the Animating Spirit*. Berkeley: University of California Press, 2012.

Bulloch, William. *The History of Bacteriology*. New York: Oxford University Press, 1938.

Butler, Benjamin F. "Some Experience with Yellow Fever and Its Prevention." *North American Review*, November 1888, 527–543.

Butler, Judith. *Bodies That Matter: On the Discursive Limits of "Sex."* New York: Routledge, 1993.

Campbell, Andy. "Lauren Berlant Discusses 'Reading with' and Her Recent Work." *Art Forum*, January 30, 2014. www.artforum.com.

Canemaker, John. *Winsor McCay: His Life and Art*. Rev. and expanded ed. Boca Raton, FL: CRC, 2018.

Cervenak, Sarah Jane. *Wandering: Philosophical Performances of Racial and Sexual Freedom*. Durham, NC: Duke University Press, 2014.

Chambers-Letson, Joshua, and Tavia Nyong'o. Introduction to *The Sense of Brown*, by José Esteban Muñoz, ix–xxxiii. Durham, NC: Duke University Press, 2020.

Chen, Mel Y. "Agitation." *South Atlantic Quarterly* 117, no. 3 (2018): 551–566.

———. *Animacies: Biopolitics, Racial Mattering, and Queer Affect*. Durham, NC: Duke University Press, 2012.

———. *Intoxicated: Race, Disability, and Chemical Intimacy across Empire*. Durham, NC: Duke University Press, 2023.

———. "Toxic Animacies, Inanimate Affections." *GLQ: A Journal of Lesbian and Gay Studies* 17, nos. 2–3 (2011): 265–286.

———. "Unpacking Intoxication, Racialising Disability." *Medical Humanities* 41, no. 1 (2015): 25–29.

Clough, Patricia Ticineto, Greg Goldberg, Rachel Schiff, Aaron Weeks, and Craig Willse. "Notes towards a Theory of Affect-Itself." *Ephemera: Theory & Politics in Organization* 7, no. 1 (2007): 60–77.

"Cocain Habit, The." *JAMA* 34, no. 25 (1900): 1637. https://doi.org/10.1001/jama.1900.02460250049013.

"Cocain Habit, The." *JAMA* 36, no. 5 (1900): 330. https://doi.org/10.1001/jama.1901.02470050034011.

Cohen, Cathy J. "Deviance as Resistance: A New Research Agenda for the Study of Black Politics." *Du Bois Review: Social Science Research on Race* 1, no. 1 (2004): 27–45.

———. "Punks, Bulldaggers, and Welfare Queens: The Radical Potential of Queer Politics?" *GLQ: A Journal of Lesbian and Gay Studies* 3, no. 4 (1997): 437–465.

Cohen, Michael M. "Jim Crow's Drug War: Race, Coca Cola, and the Southern Origins of Drug Prohibition." *Southern Cultures* 12, no. 3 (2006): 55–79.

Cotton, Olive A. *Chafing Dish Recipes: Soups, Sauces, Oysters, Clams, Meats, Fish, Menus, Etc.* Chicago: R. R. Donnelly and Sons, 1898.

Coviello, Peter. Introduction to *Billy Budd, Bartleby, and Other Stories*, by Herman Melville, vii–xxv. New York: Penguin, 2016.

Crawley, Ashon T. *Blackpentecostal Breath: The Aesthetics of Possibility*. New York: Fordham University Press, 2017.

Cullather, Nick. "The Foreign Policy of the Calorie." *American Historical Review* 112, no. 2 (2007): 337–364.

———. *The Hungry World: America's Cold War Battle against Poverty in Asia*. Cambridge, MA: Harvard University Press, 2010.

Cummins, Harle Oren. *Welsh Rarebit Tales*. Illustrated by R. Emmett Owen. Boston: Mutual Book Company, 1902.

Curtis, Scott. *The Shape of Spectatorship: Art, Science, and Early Cinema in Germany*. New York: Columbia University Press, 2015.

Daggett, Cara New. *The Birth of Energy: Fossil Fuels, Thermodynamics, and the Politics of Work*. Durham, NC: Duke University Press, 2019.

Daston, Lorraine, and Peter Galison. *Objectivity*. New York: Zone Books, 2007.

Dean, Mitchell. *Governmentality: Power and Rule in Modern Society*. Los Angeles: Sage, 2010.

Delany, Martin R. *Blake; or, The Huts of America*. 1859. Edited by Floyd J. Miller. Boston: Beacon, 1971.

Deleuze, Gilles. *The Fold: Leibniz and the Baroque*. Translated by Tom Conley. Minneapolis: University of Minnesota Press, 1992.

Deleuze, Gilles, and Félix Guattari. *A Thousand Plateaus: Capitalism and Schizophrenia*. Minneapolis: University of Minnesota Press, 1987.

Derrida, Jacques. *The Beast and the Sovereign*. Vol. 2. Edited by Michel Lisse, Marie-Louise Mallet, and Ginette Michaud. Translated by Geoffrey Bennington. Chicago: University of Chicago Press, 2011.

———. "Economimesis." Translated by R. Klein. *Diacritics* 11, no. 2 (1981): 2–25.

———. *On Touching—Jean-Luc Nancy*. Stanford, CA: Stanford University Press, 2005.

Didier, Emmanuel. *America by the Numbers: Quantification, Democracy, and the Birth of National Statistics*. Translated by Priya Vari Sen. Cambridge, MA: MIT Press, 2020.

Dodge, J. R. "Why and Where Mutton Sheep Are Profitable." In *Report of the Commissioner of Agriculture for the Year 1866*, 341–354. Washington, DC: Government Printing Office, 1867.

Douglas, Mary. *Purity and Danger: An Analysis of the Concepts of Pollution and Taboo.* New York: Routledge, 2002.

Duncan, James S. *In the Shadows of the Tropics: Climate, Race and Biopower in Nineteenth Century Ceylon.* Burlington, VT: Ashgate, 2007.

Durkheim, Émile. *The Elementary Forms of Religious Life.* Translated by Karen E. Fields. New York: Free Press, 1995.

Esposito, Roberto. *Immunitas: The Protection and Negation of Life.* Translated by Zakiya Hanafi. Malden, MA: Polity, 2011.

Ferguson, Roderick A. *Aberrations in Black: Toward a Queer of Color Critique.* Minneapolis: University of Minnesota Press, 2004.

———. *The Reorder of Things: The University and Its Pedagogies of Minority Difference.* Minneapolis: University of Minnesota Press, 2012.

Ferreira da Silva, Denise. "In the Raw." *e-flux Journal* 93 (2018). https://bit.ly/3kgbf7R.

———. "1 (life) ÷ 0 (blackness) = ∞ − ∞ or ∞ / ∞: On Matter beyond the Equation of Value." *e-flux Journal* 79 (2017). https://bit.ly/3Ck6wZa.

Fleck, Ludwig. *Genesis and Development of a Scientific Fact.* Translated by Frederick Bradley and Thaddeus J. Trenn. 1935. Reprint, Chicago: University of Chicago Press, 1979.

Foner, Eric. *A Short History of Reconstruction.* Updated ed. New York: Harper Perennial Modern Classics, 2015.

Foster, John Bellamy. *Marx's Ecology: Materialism and Nature.* New York: Monthly Review Press, 2000.

———. "Marx's Theory of Metabolic Rift: Classical Foundations for Environmental Sociology." *American Journal of Sociology* 105, no. 2 (1999): 366–405.

Foster, William Derek. *A History of Medical Bacteriology and Immunology.* Oxford, UK: Butterworth-Heinemann, 2014.

Foucault, Michel. *The History of Sexuality.* New York: Pantheon Books, 1978.

———. *The Order of Things: An Archaeology of the Human Sciences.* New York: Vintage, 1994.

———. *Security, Territory, Population: Lectures at the Collège de France, 1977–1978.* Edited by Michel Senellart and translated by Graham Burchell. New York: Palgrave Macmillan, 2009.

Gabriel, Joseph M. *Medical Monopoly: Intellectual Property Rights and the Origins of the Modern Pharmaceutical Industry.* Chicago: University of Chicago Press, 2014.

Gal, Joseph. "Pasteur and the Art of Chirality." *Nature Chemistry* 9, no. 7 (2017): 604–605.

García-Carmona, Antonio, and José Antonio Acevedo-Díaz. "Understanding the Nature of Science through a Critical and Reflective Analysis of the Controversy between Pasteur and Liebig on Fermentation." *Science & Education* 26 (2017): 65–91.

Gardner, Jared. *Projections: Comics and the History of Twenty-First-Century Storytelling.* Stanford, CA: Stanford University Press, 2012.

Gaus, John M., and Leon Wolcott. *Public Administration and the United States Department of Agriculture.* Chicago: Public Administration Service (published for the Committee on Public Administration of the Social Science Research Council), 1940.

Gaycken, Oliver. *Devices of Curiosity: Early Cinema and Popular Science*. New York: Oxford University Press, 2015.

Gibier, Paul. "Microbes and the Social Question." *Dietetic and Hygienic Gazette: A Monthly Journal of Physiological Medicine* 10, no. 1 (1894): 33–35.

Gigante, Denise. *Taste: A Literary History*. New Haven, CT: Yale University Press, 2005.

Gikandi, Simon. *Slavery and the Culture of Taste*. Princeton, NJ: Princeton University Press, 2011.

Gilmore, Ruth Wilson. *Golden Gulag: Prisons, Surplus, Crisis, and Opposition in Globalizing California*. Berkeley: University of California Press, 2007.

Goldsby, Jacqueline. "'Closer to Something Unnameable': Baldwin's Noel Form." In *The Cambridge Companion to James Baldwin*, edited by Michele Elam, 25–40. New York: Cambridge University Press, 2015.

Goldstein, Alyosha. "The Ground Not Given: Colonial Dispositions of Land, Race, and Hunger." *Social Text* 36, no. 2 (2018): 83–106.

Gunning, Tom. "The Cinema of Attractions: Early Film, Its Spectator, and the Avant-Garde." In *Theater and Film: A Comparative Anthology*, edited by Robert Knopf, 37–45. New Haven, CT: Yale University Press, 1986.

Halberstam, Jack. *The Queer Art of Failure*. Durham, NC: Duke University Press, 2011.

Hancock, Ange-Marie. *The Politics of Disgust: The Public Identity of the Welfare Queen*. New York: New York University Press, 2004.

Hantel, Max. "Plasticity and Fungibility: On Sylvia Wynter's Pieza Framework." *Social Text* 38, no. 2 (2020): 97–119.

Haraway, Donna J. *The Companion Species Manifesto: Dogs, People, and Significant Otherness*. Chicago: Prickly Paradigm, 2003.

———. "Situated Knowledges: The Science Question in Feminism and the Privilege of Partial Perspective." *Feminist Studies* 14, no. 3 (1988): 575–599.

———. *Staying with the Trouble: Making Kin in the Chthulucene*. Durham, NC: Duke University Press, 2016.

Harris, Cheryl I. "Whiteness as Property." *Harvard Law Review* 106, no. 8 (1993): 1707–1791.

Harris, Joel Chandler. *A Georgia Possum*. Swift's Specific, 1895. Item AO430. Emergence of Advertising in America. Duke University Advertising Archives, Durham, NC.

Hartman, Saidiya. *Scenes of Subjection: Terror, Slavery, and Self-Making in Nineteenth-Century America*. New York: Oxford University Press, 1997.

———. *Wayward Lives, Beautiful Experiments: Intimate Histories of Riotous Black Girls, Troublesome Women, and Queer Radicals*. New York: Norton, 2019.

Hatch, William. *Agricultural Experiment Stations*. Report No. 848, to accompany H.R. 2933. Committee on Agriculture, US House of Representatives, 49th Cong., 1st sess. (March 3, 1886).

Hayward, Eva. "Sensational Jellyfish: Aquarium Affects and the Matter of Immersion." *Differences: A Journal of Feminist Cultural Studies* 23, no. 3 (2012): 161–196.

Hein, George E. "The Liebig-Pasteur Controversy: Vitality without Vitalism." *Journal of Chemical Education* 38, no. 12 (1961): 614–619.

Hendy, Jessica, Matthäus Rest, Mark Aldenderfer, and Christina Warinner. "Cultures of Fermentation: Living with Microbes: An Introduction to Supplement 24." *Current Anthropology* 62, no. S24 (2021): S197–S206.

Higginbotham, Evelyn Brooks. *Righteous Discontent: The Women's Movement in the Black Baptist Church, 1880–1920*. Cambridge, MA: Harvard University Press, 1994.

"History of Slavery in Massachusetts: Judge Tucker's Queries Respecting Slavery, with Dr. Belknap's Answers." *The Liberator* (Boston) 1, no. 10 (March 4, 1831).

Holland, Sharon Patricia. *Raising the Dead: Readings of Death and (Black) Subjectivity*. Durham, NC: Duke University Press, 2000.

Hong, Grace Kyungwon. "Capital." In *Keywords for Gender and Sexuality Studies*, edited by the Keywords Feminist Editorial Collective, 34–39. New York: New York University Press, 2021.

Horton-Stallings, LaMonda. *Funk the Erotic: Transaesthetics and Black Sexual Cultures*. Urbana: University of Illinois Press, 2015.

"Joe 'the Wolf.'" *National Police Gazette* 35 (October 25, 1879): 109.

Johnson, E. Patrick. "'Quare' Studies, or (Almost) Everything I Know about Queer Studies I Learned from My Grandmother." *Text and Performance Quarterly* 21, no. 1 (2001): 1–25. https://doi.org/10.1080/10462930128119.

Jones, F. A. "Cocain Habit among the Negroes." *JAMA* 35, no. 3 (1900): 175. https://doi.org/10.1001/jama.1900.02460290045024.

Jones, Gavin. *American Hungers: The Problem of Poverty in U.S. Literature, 1840–1945*. Princeton, NJ: Princeton University Press, 2007.

———. *Strange Talk: The Politics of Dialect Literature in Gilded Age America*. Berkeley: University of California Press, 1999.

Joon-ho, Bong, dir. *Snowpiercer*. Seoul: Moho Film and Opus Pictures, 2013.

Joyce, Patrick, and Chandra Mukerji. "The State of Things: State History and Theory Reconfigured." *Theory and Society* 46, no. 1 (2017): 1–19.

Katz, Sandor Ellix. *Fermentation as Metaphor*. White River Junction, VT: Chelsea Green, 2020.

Kelman, Ari. "Boundary Issues: Clarifying New Orleans's Murky Edges." *Journal of American History* 94, no. 3 (2007): 695–703.

Khanna, Neetu. *The Visceral Logics of Decolonization*. Durham, NC: Duke University Press, 2020.

Kracauer, Siegfried. *Theory of Film: The Redemption of Physical Reality*. Princeton, NJ: Princeton University Press, 1960.

Kristeva, Julia. *Powers of Horror: An Essay on Abjection*. Translated by Leon S. Roudiez. New York: Columbia University Press, 1982.

LaFleur, Greta. *The Natural History of Sexuality in Early America*. Baltimore: Johns Hopkins University Press, 2018.

Landecker, Hannah. "Cellular Features: Microcinematography and Film Theory." *Critical Inquiry* 31, no. 4 (2005): 903–927.

———. "The Life of Movement: From Microcinematography to Live-Cell Imaging." In "Science and Documentary," edited by Joshua Malitsky and Oliver Gaycken. Special issue, *Journal of Visual Culture* 11, no. 3 (2012): 378–399.

———. "Microcinematography and the History of Science and Film." *Isis* 97, no. 1 (2006): 121–132.

———. "New Times for Biology: Nerve Cultures and the Advent of Cellular Life in Vitro." *Studies in History and Philosophy of Science Part C: Studies in History and Philosophy of Biological and Biomedical Sciences* 33, no. 4 (2002): 667–694.

Latour, Bruno. "Gabriel Tarde and the End of the Social." In *The Social in Question*, edited by Patrick Joyce, 117–132. London: Routledge, 2012.

———. *The Pasteurization of France*. Translated by Alan Sheridan and John Law. Cambridge, MA: Harvard University Press, 1993.

Latour, Bruno, and Steve Woolgar. *Laboratory Life: The Construction of Scientific Facts*. Princeton, NJ: Princeton University Press, 2013.

Lears, Jackson. *Fables of Abundance: A Cultural History of Advertising in America*. New York: Basic Books, 1994.

Le Bon, Gustave. *The Crowd: A Study of the Popular Mind*. New York: Routledge, 2017.

Lee, Jae Rhim. "My Mushroom Burial Suit." Filmed July 2011 in Edinburgh, Scotland. TED video. https://bit.ly/1Z5SWiP.

Lee, Robert. "Morrill Act of 1862 Indigenous Land Parcels Database." *High Country News*, March 2020.

Lefebvre, Georges. "Revolutionary Crowds." In *New Perspectives on the French Revolution*, edited by Jeffry Kaplow and translated by Orest Ranum and Robert Wagoner, 173–190. New York: John Wiley, 1965.

Lewis, Randolph C. "Rarebit Symbolism." In *Dream of the Rarebit Fiend*, x. New York: New York Evening Telegram (New York Herald Co.), 1905.

Liebig, Justus Freiherr von. *The Natural Laws of Husbandry*. Edited by John Blyth. New York: D. Appleton, 1863.

Lin, Candice. "A Hard White Body / Un Corps Blanc Exquis." BS no. 22. Bétonsalon Centre d'Art et de Recherche, December 23, 2017.

Lindberg, David C., Katharine Park, Lorraine Daston, Roy Porter, Mary Jo Nye, Theodore M. Porter, and Dorothy Ross, eds. *The Cambridge History of Science: Early Modern Science*. Vol. 3. Cambridge: Cambridge University Press, 2003.

Lorde, Audre. *Sister Outsider: Essays and Speeches*. Repr. ed. Berkeley, CA: Crossing, 2007.

———. "The Uses of the Erotic: The Erotic as Power." In *The Lesbian and Gay Studies Reader*, ed. Henry Abelove, Michele Aina Barale, and David M. Halperin, 339–343. New York: Routledge, 1993.

Lutz, Tom. *American Nervousness, 1903: An Anecdotal History*. Ithaca, NY: Cornell University Press, 1991.

Malone, Nicholas, and Kathryn Ovenden. "Natureculture." In *The International Encyclopedia of Primatology*, vol. 2, ed. Augustín Fuentes, 1–2. Hoboken, NJ: Wiley, 2016. https://bit.ly/3tGZ1bA.

Maloy, Stanley, and Moselio Schaechter. "The Era of Microbiology: A Golden Phoenix." *International Microbiology* 9, no. 1 (2006): 1–7.

Manalansan, Martin F., IV. *Global Divas: Filipino Gay Men in the Diaspora*. Durham, NC: Duke University Press, 2003.

———. "Messy Mismeasures: Exploring the Wilderness of Queer Migrant Lives." *South Atlantic Quarterly* 117, no. 3 (2018): 491–506.

———. "The 'Stuff' of Archives: Mess, Migration, and Queer Lives." *Radical History Review* 2014, no. 120 (2014): 94–107.

Márez, Curtis. *Drug Wars: The Political Economy of Narcotics*. Minneapolis: University of Minnesota Press, 2004.

Marinković, Dušan, and Dušan Ristić. "Foucault and the Birth of the Police." *Revija za kriminalistiko in kriminologijo* 70, no. 4 (2019): 352–363.

Marx, Karl. *Capital: A Critique of Political Economy*. Vol. 1. 1867. Translated by Ben Fowkes. London: Penguin, 1990.

———. *Capital: A Critique of Political Economy*. Vol. 3. 1894. Translated by David Fernbach. London: Penguin, 1991.

———. *Economic and Philosophic Manuscripts of 1844*. Translated by Martin Milligan. Moscow: Progress, 1959. https://bit.ly/3nzDv7F.

Massumi, Brian. *Politics of Affect*. Hoboken, NJ: Wiley, 2015.

Mbembe, Achille. "Necropolitics." Translated by Libby Meintjes. *Public Culture* 15, no. 1 (2003): 11–40.

———. *On the Postcolony*. Berkeley: University of California Press, 2001.

McCormack, Derek P. *Atmospheric Things: On the Allure of Elemental Envelopment*. Durham, NC: Duke University Press, 2018.

McKittrick, Katherine, ed. *Sylvia Wynter: On Being Human as Praxis*. Durham, NC: Duke University Press, 2015.

McMillan, Uri. *Embodied Avatars*. New York: New York University Press, 2015.

McNamara, Brooks. *Step Right Up*. Rev. ed. Jackson: University Press of Mississippi, 1995.

Melville, Herman. *The Complete Stories of Herman Melville*. Edited by Jay Leyda. New York: Random House, 1949.

———. *Moby-Dick*. Edited by Hester Blum. New York: Oxford University, 2022.

———. "The Paradise of Bachelors and the Tartarus of Maids." *Harper's New Monthly Magazine* 10, no. 59 (April 1855): 670–678.

———. "Poor Man's Pudding and Rich Man's Crumbs." *Harper's New Monthly Magazine* 9, no. 49 (June 1854): 95–101.

Miller, William Ian. *The Anatomy of Disgust*. Cambridge, MA: Harvard University Press, 1998.

Milton, John. "Samson Agonistes. A Dramatic Poem." In *The Complete Works of John Milton*, vol. 2, *The 1671 Poems: "Paradise Regain'd" and "Samson Agonistes,"* edited by Laura Lunger Knoppers, 65–120. New York: Oxford University Press, 2013.

Mintz, Sidney W. *Sweetness and Power: The Place of Sugar in Modern History*. New York: Penguin, 1986.

Mitchell, Koritha. "Identifying White Mediocrity and Know-Your-Place Aggression: A Form of Self-Care." *African American Review* 51, no. 4 (2018): 253–262.

Molina, Natalia. *How Race Is Made in America*. Berkeley: University of California Press, 2014.

Morgensen, Scott Lauria. "Settler Homonationalism: Theorizing Settler Colonialism within Queer Modernities." *GLQ: A Journal of Lesbian and Gay Studies* 16, nos. 1–2 (2010): 105–131.

Morton, Timothy, ed. *Cultures of Taste / Theories of Appetite: Eating Romanticism*. New York: Palgrave Macmillan, 2004.

Moten, Fred. *In the Break: The Aesthetics of the Black Radical Tradition*. Minneapolis: University of Minnesota Press, 2003.

———. *Stolen Life*. Vol. 2. Durham, NC: Duke University Press, 2018.

Muñoz, José Esteban. "Ephemera as Evidence: Introductory Notes to Queer Acts." *Women & Performance: A Journal of Feminist Theory* 8, no. 2 (1996): 5–16.

———. *The Sense of Brown*. Edited by Joshua Chambers-Letson and Tavia Nyong'o. Durham, NC: Duke University Press, 2020.

Nally, David. "The Biopolitics of Food Provisioning." *Transactions of the Institute of British Geographers* 36, no. 1 (2011): 37–53.

Netherland, Julie, and Helena Hansen. "White Opioids: Pharmaceutical Race and the War on Drugs That Wasn't." *Biosocieties* 12, no. 2 (2017): 217–238.

Ngai, Sianne. *Our Aesthetic Categories: Zany, Cute, Interesting*. Cambridge, MA: Harvard University Press, 2012.

———. *Ugly Feelings*. Cambridge, MA: Harvard University Press, 2005.

Nielsen, Tore, and Russell A. Powell. "Dream of the Rarebit Fiend: Food and Diet as Instigators of Bizarre and Disturbing Dreams." *Frontiers in Psychology* 6 (2015): 1–15.

Nyong'o, Tavia, and Kyla Wazana Tompkins. "Eleven Theses on Civility." *Social Text Online* 11 (2018). https://socialtextjournal.org.

Oates, Caroline. "Cheese Gives You Nightmares: Old Hags and Heartburn." *Folklore* 114, no. 2 (2003): 205–225.

OED Online. Oxford: Oxford University Press. Accessed June 19, 2023. www.oed.com.

Pasteur, Louis. *Études sur la bière: Ses maladies, causes qui les provoquent, procédé pour la rendre inaltérable; avec une théorie nouvelle de la fermentation*. Paris: Gauthier-Villars, 1876.

———. *Memoire sur la fermentation alcoolique and examen critique d'un ecrit posthume de Claude Bernard sur la fermentation*. Paris: Mallet-Bachelier, 1860; Paris: Gauthier-Villars, 1879.

———. "Mémoire sur la fermentation appelée lactique." *Mémoires de la Société des Sciences, de l'Agriculture et des Arts de Lille*, 2nd ser., 5 (1858): 13–26.

———. *Studies in Fermentation: The Diseases of Beer, Their Causes, and the Means of Preventing Them*. Translated by Frank Faulkner and D. Constable Robb. London: Macmillan, 1879.

Paxson, Heather. "Post-Pasteurian Cultures: The Microbiopolitics of Raw-Milk Cheese in the United States." *Cultural Anthropology* 23, no. 1 (2008): 15–47.

Pellegrini, Ann. "'A Storm on the Horizon': Discomforting Democracy and the Feeling of Fairness." *Cultural Studies Review* 18, no. 2 (2012): 16–31.

Pendergrast, Mark. *For God, Country, and Coca-Cola: The Definitive History of the Great American Soft Drink and the Company That Makes It*. 2nd ed. New York: Basic Books, 2000.

Peterson, Marina. *Atmospheric Noise: The Indefinite Urbanism of Los Angeles*. Durham, NC: Duke University Press, 2021.

Pettigrew, Thomas. Introduction to *The Sociology of Race Relations: Reflection and Reform*, edited by Thomas Pettigrew, xiii–xxxiii. New York: Free Press, 1980.

Philip, M. NourbeSe. *Zong!* Middletown, CT: Wesleyan University Press, 2008.

Pommerville, Jeffrey C. *Fundamentals of Microbiology*. 3rd ed. Burlington, MA: Jones and Bartlett Learning, 2016.

Probyn, Elspeth. *Carnal Appetites: Foodsexidentities*. London: Routledge, 2000.

Puar, Jasbir K. "Prognosis Time: Towards a Geopolitics of Affect, Debility and Capacity." *Women & Performance: A Journal of Feminist Theory* 19, no. 2 (2009): 161–172.

———. *The Right to Maim: Debility, Capacity, Disability*. Durham, NC: Duke University Press, 2017.

———. "Spatial Debilities: Slow Life and Carceral Capitalism in Palestine." *South Atlantic Quarterly* 120, no. 2 (2021): 393–414.

———. *Terrorist Assemblages: Homonationalism in Queer Times*. Durham, NC: Duke University Press, 2007.

Quincy, Edmond. Editorial. *National Standard*. Reprinted in *North Star* (Rochester, NY), June 29, 1849.

Quinn, Michael. "Bentham on Preventive Police: The Calendar of Delinquency in Evaluation of Policy and the Police Gazette in Manipulation of Opinion." *International Criminal Justice Review* 31, no. 3 (2021): 229–256.

Rai, Amit S. "Race and Ontologies of Sensation." In *Deleuze and Race*, edited by Arun Saldanha and Jason Michael Adams, 269–287. Edinburgh: Edinburgh University Press, 2012.

———. "Race Racing: Four Theses on Race and Intensity." *Women's Studies Quarterly* 40, nos. 1–2 (2012): 64–75.

Rancière, Jacques. *Dissensus: On Politics and Aesthetics*. Edited and translated by Steven Corcoran. New York: Continuum, 2010.

———. *The Politics of Aesthetics: The Distribution of the Sensible*. Edited and translated by Gabriel Rockhill. New York: Bloomsbury, 2013.

Rich, Theodore D. *One Hundred Recipes for the Chafing Dish*. New York: Gorham Manufacturing, 1894.

Rifkin, Mark. *When Did Indians Become Straight? Kinship, the History of Sexuality, and Native Sovereignty*. New York: Oxford University Press, 2011.

Robinson, Cedric J. *Black Marxism: The Making of the Black Radical Tradition*. Chapel Hill: University of North Carolina Press, 1983.

Rodríguez, Juana María. *Sexual Futures, Queer Gestures, and Other Latina Longings*. New York: New York University Press, 2014.

Roeder, Katherine. *Wide Awake in Slumberland: Fantasy, Mass Culture, and Modernism in the Art of Windsor McCay*. Jackson: University Press of Mississippi, 2014.

Rogers, Kenneth. "Black Friday: Crowdsourcing Communities of Risk." *Women's Studies Quarterly* 40, nos. 1–2 (2012): 171–186.

Roosth, Sophia, and Astrid Schrader. "Feminist Theory Out of Science: Introduction." *Differences: A Journal of Feminist Cultural Studies* 23, no. 3 (2012): 1–8.

Ross, Michael A. "Justice Miller's Reconstruction: The Slaughter-House Cases, Health Codes, and Civil Rights in New Orleans, 1861–1873." *Journal of Southern History* 64, no. 4 (1998): 649–676.

Rowland, Beryl. "Sitting Up with a Corpse: Malthus according to Melville in 'Poor Man's Pudding and Rich Man's Crumbs.'" *Journal of American Studies* 6, no. 1 (1972): 69–83.

Rudé, George. *The Crowd in History: A Study of Popular Disturbances in France and England, 1730–1848*. London: John Wiley, 1965.

Rusert, Britt. *Fugitive Science: Empiricism and Freedom in Early African American Culture*. New York: New York University Press, 2017.

Saldanha, Arun. "Reontologising Race: The Machinic Geography of Phenotype." *Environment and Planning D: Society and Space* 24, no. 1 (2006): 9–24.

———. "Vision and Viscosity in Goa's Psychedelic Trance Scene." *ACME: An International Journal for Critical Geographies* 4, no. 2 (2005): 172–193.

Sanborn, Geoffrey. *The Sign of the Cannibal: Melville and the Making of a Postcolonial Reader*. Durham, NC: Duke University Press, 1998.

Schiebinger, Londa. *Plants and Empire: Colonial Bioprospecting in the Atlantic World*. Cambridge, MA: Harvard University Press, 2004.

Schuller, Kyla. *The Biopolitics of Feeling: Race, Sex, and Science in the Nineteenth Century*. Durham, NC: Duke University Press, 2017.

Schuller, Kyla, and Jules Gill-Peterson. "Introduction: Race, the State, and the Malleable Body." *Social Text* 38, no. 2 (2020): 1–17.

Seddon, Toby. "Inventing Drugs: A Genealogy of a Regulatory Concept." *Journal of Law and Society* 43, no. 3 (2016): 393–415.

Sedgwick, Eve Kosofsky. *Tendencies*. Durham, NC: Duke University Press, 1993.

Seikaly, Sherene. *Men of Capital: Scarcity and Economy in Mandate Palestine*. Stanford, CA: Stanford University Press, 2015.

Semba, Richard D. *The Vitamin A Story: Lifting the Shadow of Death*. New York: Karger, 2012.

Shah, Nayan. *Contagious Divides: Epidemics and Race in San Francisco's Chinatown*. Berkeley: University of California Press, 2001.

Shapin, Steven. *A Social History of Truth: Civility and Science in Seventeenth-Century England*. Chicago: University of Chicago Press, 1994.

Sharpe, Christina. *In the Wake: On Blackness and Being*. Durham, NC: Duke University Press, 2016.

Shotwell, Alexis. *Against Purity: Living Ethically in Compromised Times*. Minneapolis: University of Minnesota Press, 2016.

Shukin, Nicole. *Animal Capital: Rendering Life in Biopolitical Times*. Minneapolis: University of Minnesota Press, 2009.

Siebers, Tobin. *Disability Aesthetics*. Ann Arbor: University of Michigan Press, 2010.

Singh, Nikhil Pal. "The Whiteness of Police." *American Quarterly* 66, no. 4 (2014): 1091–1099.

Slauter, Eric. *The State as a Work of Art: The Cultural Origins of the Constitution*. Chicago: University of Chicago Press, 2009.

Smith, Andrea. "Queer Theory and Native Studies: The Heteronormativity of Settler Colonialism." *GLQ: A Journal of Lesbian and Gay Studies* 16, nos. 1–2 (2010): 42–68.

Smith, Michelle. "Affect and Respectability Politics." *Theory & Event* 17, no. 3 (2014). www.muse.jhu.edu.

Solomon, Harris. *Metabolic Living: Food, Fat, and the Absorption of Illness in India*. Durham, NC: Duke University Press, 2016.

Sontag, Susan. "Fascinating Fascism." *New York Review of Books*, February 6, 1975.

Spade, Dean. *Normal Life: Administrative Violence, Critical Trans Politics, and the Limits of Law*. Durham, NC: Duke University Press, 2015.

Spillers, Hortense J. "Formalism Comes to Harlem." *Black American Literature Forum* 16, no. 2 (1982): 58–63.

———. "Mama's Baby, Papa's Maybe: An American Grammar Book." *Diacritics* 17, no. 2 (1987): 65–81.

Stallybrass, Peter, and Allon White. *The Politics and Poetics of Transgression*. Ithaca, NY: Cornell University Press, 1986.

Stewart, Kathleen. *Ordinary Affects*. Durham, NC: Duke University Press, 2007.

Stoler, Ann Laura. *Race and the Education of Desire: Foucault's* History of Sexuality *and the Colonial Order of Things*. Durham, NC: Duke University Press, 1995.

Stramer, Brian M., and Graham A. Dunn. "Cells on Film—The Past and Future of Cinemicroscopy." *Journal of Cell Science* 128, no. 1 (2015): 9–13.

Sundquist, Eric J. "Mark Twain and Homer Plessy." *Representations* 24 (1988): 102–128.

Sutherland, Keston. "Marx in Jargon." *World Picture Journal* 1 (2008). http://worldpicturejournal.com.

"Sweet Dreams Are Made of Cheese." *Daily Mail Online*, September 12, 2005. https://bit.ly/3nGdl34.

Swift's Specific Remedy. *The Georgia Watermelon*. Atlanta: Foote and Davies, 1891. Author's personal collection.

Thompson, E. P. "The Moral Economy of the English Crowd in the Eighteenth Century." *Past and Present* 50, no. 1 (February 1971): 76–136.

Thrift, Nigel. *Non-Representational Theory: Space, Politics, Affect*. New York: Routledge, 2008.

Tolia-Kelly, Divya P. "Rancière and the Re-distribution of the Sensible: The Artist Rosanna Raymond, Dissensus and Postcolonial Sensibilities Within the Spaces of the Museum." *Progress in Human Geography* 43, no. 1 (2019): 123–140.

Tomes, Nancy. *The Gospel of Germs: Men, Women, and the Microbe in American Life*. Cambridge, MA: Harvard University Press, 1998.

Tompkins, Kyla Wazana. "Crude Matter, Queer Form." *ASAP Journal* 2, no. 2 (2017): 264–268.

———. "'Hearty and Happy and with a Lively, Yeasty Soul': Feeling Right in Louisa May Alcott's *The Candy Country*." *Women & Performance: A Journal of Feminist Theory* 24, nos. 2–3 (2014): 153–66.

———. "Introduction: On the Visceral 2." *GLQ: A Journal of Lesbian and Gay Studies* 21, no. 1 (2015): 3–4.

———. *Racial Indigestion: Eating Bodies in the 19th Century*. New York: New York University Press, 2012.

———. "Sweetness, Capacity, Energy." *American Quarterly* 71, no. 3 (2019): 849–856.

———. "'You Make Me Feel Right Quare': Promiscuous Reading, Minoritarian Critique, and White Sovereign Entrepreneurial Terror." *Social Text* 35, no. 4 (2017): 53–86.

"Tough Cases." *National Police Gazette* 36 (July 3, 1880): 145.

Toulmin, Vanessa. *Electric Edwardians: The Films of Mitchell and Kenyon*. London: Bloomsbury, 2019.

Trotter, Wilfred. "Herd Instinct and Its Bearing on the Psychology of Civilised Man." *Sociological Review* 1, no. 3 (1908): 227–248.

Tsing, Anna. "Unruly Edges: Mushrooms as Companion Species: For Donna Haraway." *Environmental Humanities* 1, no. 1 (2012): 141–154.

Tyndall, John. "Dust and Disease." *British Medical Journal*, June 24, 1871, 661–662.

———. "On Dust and Disease." *Eclectic Magazine of Foreign Literature* 11, no. 5 (1870): 556–563.

Urban, Charles, dir. *The Cheese Mites: The Unseen World*. 35mm, 150 feet, black and white, silent. London: Charles Urban Trading Company, 1903.

US Department of Agriculture. *Report of the Commissioner of Agriculture for the Year 1864*. Washington, DC: Government Printing Office, 1865.

US Department of Agriculture, Office of Experiment Stations. *Experiment Station Bulletin No. 1: Organization of the Agricultural Experiment Stations in the United States, February 1889*. Washington, DC: Government Printing Office, 1889.

———. *Experiment Station Bulletin No. 2: Digest of the Annual Reports of the Agricultural Experiment Stations in the United States for 1888*. Washington, DC: Government Printing Office, 1889.

Velmet, Aro. *Pasteur's Empire: Bacteriology and Politics in France, Its Colonies, and the World*. New York: Oxford University Press, 2020.

Viel, Claude, and Josette Fournier. "Histoire des procédés d'extraction de la gélatine et débats des commissions académiques (XIXe siècle)." *Revue d'Histoire de la Pharmacie* 349, no. 1 (2006): 7–28.

Vizenor, Gerald, ed. *Survivance: Narratives of Native Presence*. Lincoln: University of Nebraska Press, 2008.

Wiley, Harvey W. *Harvey W. Wiley: An Autobiography*. Indianapolis: Bobbs-Merrill, 1930.

Williams, Eric. *Capitalism and Slavery*. Chapel Hill: University of North Carolina Press, 2021.

Williams, Raymond. *Marxism and Literature*. Oxford: Oxford University Press, 1977.

Wilson, Elizabeth A. "Gut Feminism." *Differences: A Journal of Feminist Cultural Studies* 15, no. 3 (2004): 66–94.

———. *Psychosomatic: Feminism and the Neurological Body*. Durham, NC: Duke University Press, 2004.

Wise, M. Norton, and Crosbie Smith. "Work and Waste: Political Economy and Natural Philosophy in Nineteenth Century Britain (I)." *History of Science* 27, no. 3 (1989): 263–301.

———. "Work and Waste: Political Economy and Natural Philosophy in Nineteenth Century Britain (II)." *History of Science* 27, no. 4 (1989): 391–449.

———. "Work and Waste: Political Economy and Natural Philosophy in Nineteenth Century Britain (III)." *History of Science* 28, no. 3 (1990): 221–261.

"Wonders under Microscopes; Exhibition Made by the Society Which Studies Minute Objects." *New York Times*, April 15, 1896. https://nyti.ms/3khqU6R.

Woodard, Vincent. *The Delectable Negro: Human Consumption and Homoeroticism within US Slave Culture*. Edited by Dwight McBride and Justin A. Joyce. New York: New York University Press, 2014.

Worley, Zita Marie. "In the Valley of the Moon: Enclosure, Temperance, and the American War on John Barleycorn." PhD diss., University of California Riverside, 2015. https://escholarship.org.

Wu, Cynthia. *Chang and Eng Reconnected: The Original Siamese Twins in American Culture*. Philadelphia: Temple University Press, 2012.

Wynter, Sylvia. "Novel and History, Plot and Plantation." *Savacou* 5 (1971): 95–102.

———. "Rethinking 'Aesthetics': Notes towards a Deciphering Practice." In *Ex-iles: Essays on Caribbean Cinema*, ed. Mbye Cham, 237–279. Trenton, NJ: Africa World, 1992.

———. "Unsettling the Coloniality of Being/Power/Truth/Freedom: Towards the Human, after Man, Its Overrepresentation—an Argument." *CR: The New Centennial Review* 3, no. 3 (2003): 257–337.

Young, James Harvey. "Three Atlanta Pharmacists." *Pharmacy in History* 31, no. 1 (1989): 16–22.

———. *The Toadstool Millionaires: A Social History of Patent Medicines in America before Federal Regulation*. Princeton, NJ: Princeton University Press, 2016.

INDEX

Page numbers in italics indicate Photos

ABOUT THE AUTHOR

Kyla Wazana Tompkins is Professor and Chair of Global Gender and Sexuality Studies at the University at Buffalo. She is the author of *Racial Indigestion: Eating Bodies in the Nineteenth Century*, which won the Lora Romero award for best first book in American Studies and best book from the Association for the Study of Food and Society. She is a recipient of the Frederick Burkhardt Fellowship of the American Council of Learned Societies and the Warren Center Fellowship at Harvard University, as well as support from Mellon Foundation. In 2021, she was the managing editor of *Keywords for Gender and Sexuality Studies*, which was named as Choice Outstanding Title by the Association of College and Research Libraries. In 2023, she won a James Beard Award for her essay "On Boba," published in the *Los Angeles Review of Books*.

www.ingramcontent.com/pod-product-compliance
Lightning Source LLC
Chambersburg PA
CBHW061017120726
47910CB00006B/1990

9781479819225